Sea Kayaking and Stand Up Paddling

Connecticut, Rhode Island, and the Long Island Sound

Sea Kayaking and Stand Up Paddling

Connecticut, Rhode Island, and the Long Island Sound

David Fasulo

GUILFORD, CONNECTICUT

An imprint of Globe Pequot
Falcon and FalconGuides are registered trademarks and Make Adventure Your Story is a trademark of Rowman & Littlefield.

Distributed by NATIONAL BOOK NETWORK

British Library Cataloguing-in-Publication Information available

Library of Congress Cataloging-in-Publication Data available

ISBN 978-1-4930-2445-2 (paperback)
ISBN 978-1-4930-2446-9 (e-book)

∞™ The paper used in this publication meets the minimum requirements of American National Standard for Information Sciences—Permanence of Paper for Printed Library Materials, ANSI/NISO Z39.48-1992.

The author and Rowman & Littlefield assume no liability for accidents happening to, or injuries sustained by, readers who engage in the activities described in this book.

PLEASE NOTE: The charts included with this guide are intended for an overall familiarity with the paddling destinations, and North is set to True North (direction of North Pole). Paddlers should always carry real nautical/NOAA charts to navigate waterways.

This book required the help of many local kayakers and stand up paddleboarders. Special thanks to: Kate Powers, Scott Martin, Claudine Burns, Carl Tjerandsen, Nick Shade, Bob Ten Eyck, Tim Motte, Robert and Roz Weinstein, Brian and Lauren Weinstein, Curt Anderson, and Brenda Rashleigh, as well as the information gleaned from the ConnYak and RICKA websites. Special thanks to Jonathan Alvarez for his assistance with the "Something Fishy" sections and Erik Baumgartner for his photo contributions. As with his help on previous books, a big thanks to Ron Gautreau for the considerable amount of time he spent helping explore new waters throughout Connecticut and Rhode Island.

Contents

Introduction

Welcome to some of the best paddling waters in the country. What makes these areas so special? Most of Connecticut is protected from large ocean swells by Long Island, and much of the Rhode Island waters are protected by Conanicut and Aquidneck Islands. These land masses form two exceptionally large tidal estuaries—Long Island Sound and Narragansett Bay. The estuaries offer protection from the open ocean swell, while still providing moving water for playful waves and plentiful sea life. The Connecticut and Rhode Island coastlines, along with the many small islands, offer a number of diverse coastal tours. Within a short distance you can tour rocky islands and rugged shorelines, coastal mansions, and wide-open beaches. Entertaining surfing waves can found, depending on conditions, throughout Long Island Sound, Block Island Sound, and Narragansett Bay.

For big-wave surfing, select areas in Rhode Island provide world-class surf for those inclined. Fishers Island Sound, much of which is located in New York but accessed from Connecticut, is a very popular touring and fishing area. With their close proximity to the Connecticut shore, the New York islands of North and South Dumpling, as well as Fishers Island, are frequent destinations for sea kayakers. In fact, experienced paddlers commonly link three states in a day by launching from Barn Island, Connecticut, and paddling to Fishers Island, New York, then heading over to Napatree Point, Rhode Island, and back to the Barn Island launch (about 10 miles total).

The key to understanding the format of this book is recognizing that each suggested route depends on *conditions*. Wind, current (tidal and river), waves, and temperature all create the conditions you will encounter. Since this is New England, these conditions change constantly. Wind is typically the biggest factor, since it affects the waves and has a significant impact on your ability to make progress or remain stable. The best time to be on the water is typically early morning or late day, if you are trying to avoid the afternoon winds and waves.

The sea kayak season for Connecticut and Rhode Island is generally long—depending on your skill level and equipment. It is common for sea kayakers to be out all winter long (when the days are above 32 degrees Fahrenheit and the wind is manageable) wearing specialized waterproof dry suits. The general rule is to dress for immersion (temperature of the water). For stand up paddlers, the season is typically shorter due to the difficulties encountered when trying to dress for air temperature as well as immersion (such as in the spring). However, some stand up paddlers use dry suits and paddle early or late season.

In terms of paddling seasons, spring is usually the most dangerous time on the water, because while the air temperature may be 80 degrees, the water may be 50 degrees. Hypothermia can quickly take hold if you are unable to get back into your boat or on

Returning with Ron Gautreau and the Tuesday Night Paddlers to Esker Point in mild conditions.
PHOTO DAVID FASULO

your board. Therefore, spend the extra money for paddle-specific protective clothing and *always* wear a PFD.

Popular Areas and Tours

The three most frequented areas in Connecticut for sea kayakers are the Norwalk Islands (western Connecticut coast), the Thimble Islands (central Connecticut coast), and Fishers Island Sound (eastern Connecticut coast). Stand up paddlers seem to congregate in quieter pockets of water along the shore, in bays, and where group paddles and rental facilities are most common.

Popular tours from western to eastern Connecticut include:

- Norwalk Islands, Norwalk
- Branford Harbor and Farm River, Branford
- Thimble Islands, Branford
- Guilford coast/Faulkners Island, Guilford
- Hammonassett Beach/Clinton Harbor, Madison/Clinton
- Connecticut River, Essex/Deep River
- Rocky Neck, Old Lyme/East Lyme
- Pine Island/Dumpling Islands, Groton/New York
- Mystic/Mason's Island, Groton/Stonington
- Sandy Point Island, Stonington

The Rhode Island shoreline is vast and varied, and the more popular locations are listed below. As with Connecticut, stand up paddlers seem to congregate in quieter pockets of water along the shore, in bays, and where group paddles and rental facilities are most common.

Popular tours from western to eastern Rhode Island include:

- Napatree Point/Watch Hill Cove, Westerly
- Ninigret Pond and Quonochontaug Pond, Charlestown
- Point Judith Pond, South Kingstown
- Point Judith/Narragansett coast/Dutch Island, Narragansett
- Fort Wetherill/Jamestown coast/Jamestown circumnavigation, Jamestown
- Bristol Harbor/Hog Island/Colt State Park, Bristol
- Newport Harbor/Fort Adams/Kings Beach, Newport
- Third Beach/Sakonnet River, Middletown
- Sakonnet Point, Little Compton
- Block Island coast and Great Salt Pond, New Shoreham/Block Island

Choosing the Right Equipment

The Internet provides paddlers an enormous amount of information on choosing a boat or board that best suits their budget and needs. Kayaks generally fall into three categories: recreational, sea, and fishing. Recreational kayaks are typically wide, have a large

A full-on sea kayak, with additional safety gear, exploring the waters near Faulkners Island. These kayaks have waterproof bulkheads for storage and additional seaworthiness and a spray skirt to keep out water, as well as additional length and a narrow beam for speed. **PHOTO ERIK BAUMGARTNER**

Kayaks made of wood (they are fiberglassed as well) are really worth considering. They are lightweight, typically less expensive than newer glass boats, and easily customized. Pictured is the author's hand-built Guillemot Night Heron. **PHOTO DAVID FASULO**

Stand up paddleboards are becoming popular due to their ease of transport, athletic nature, and comfort during the summer months. Val Rahmanl touring Compo Beach. **PHOTO DAVID FASULO**

cockpit, and often do not have bulkheads. Sea kayaks have a smaller cockpit to accommodate a spray skirt, are generally narrower for speed and rough water handling, and have bulkheads to keep the kayak afloat if the cockpit fills with water. The bulkheads also allow for hatches and storage, for touring or camping. Fishing kayaks are not meant to go long distances, but accommodate the equipment and techniques required for fishing. Of course, there are many variations on kayaks depending on materials (do not forget wood) and more specialty uses.

Stand up paddleboards seem to fall into three main categories: all-around use, boards better for surfing, and boards built for speed. There are also hybrids that are used for fishing. As with kayaks, materials and more-specialized uses mean several choices. Stand up paddleboards are gaining in popularity, but remember they are more

Bob Nagy finding fish using a specialized kayak fishing setup. **PHOTO BOB NAGY**

susceptible to changing sea conditions. Do not venture out too far until you are confident in your skills.

Specialized fishing kayaks are becoming increasingly popular. These vessels always start, are inexpensive to maintain and transport, and allow for a stealth approach to fishy areas. Many large bass and blackfish can be found in relatively shallow water, prowling

Purchasing, or renting, a recreational kayak is a good way to get your feet wet. Recreational kayaks are stable in flat water, and a spray skirt is optional. However, for more demanding conditions, a full-on sea kayak is best. **PHOTO DAVID FASULO**

among the rock piles. Large and schoolie bluefish are always a good fight—but beware of removing hooks due to the sharp teeth. You can also troll with wind and tide by setting up on the ebb tide with a west wind for fluke (great eating). In this book, the "Something Fishy" sections describe some of the more commonly known fishing areas accessible by kayaks, without giving away all the locals' secret areas.

Along with your Internet research, your best bet is to rent, or demo, a few times before your first purchase. Then, have that essential chat with the retail establishment about the required accessories for safety, comfort, and to transport your new toy. I recommend taking a lesson from a qualified professional to enhance your experience and level of safety. Otherwise, there are plenty of groups and clubs to join throughout Connecticut and Rhode Island that organize events, and they are always willing to help mentor people new to the sport.

Launch Ramp Etiquette and Public Access

Shoreline access points are often shared with powerboaters. Please make sure to keep the ramp clear; double-park if kayaking with a group and only trailer spaces are available; and be respectful if changing clothes in the parking area (use a large beach towel or cover garment). Carpool whenever possible to ease the burden on the relatively few free shoreline access points.

In Connecticut, Rhode Island, and New York, with the exception of special circumstances described below, it is your right to land waterward of the mean high-water line. However, show proper etiquette by always being courteous, keeping a low profile, and leaving no trace. **PHOTO DAVID FASULO**

In almost every case, you can land on beaches in Connecticut waterward of the mean high-water line. This public trust is often marked by wet sands or a line of debris (seaweed or driftwood) on beaches and tidal islands. The exceptions are areas marked off for bird nesting, swimming, homeland security, or specific safety considerations.

According to the Connecticut Department of Energy & Environmental Protection website, "While much of the Connecticut shore is privately owned, the coastal tidelands actually belong to all the people—not just in terms of our environmental and cultural heritage, but in a specific legal sense as well. Under the common law public trust doctrine, a body of law dating back to Roman times, coastal states (as sovereigns) hold the submerged lands and waters waterward of the mean high water line in trust for the public. The general public may freely use these intertidal and subtidal lands and waters, whether they are beach, rocky shore, or open water, for traditional public trust uses such as fishing, shellfishing, boating, sunbathing, or simply walking along the beach. In Connecticut, a line of state Supreme Court cases dating back to the earliest days of the republic confirms that in virtually every case private property ends at the mean high water line (the line on the shore established by the average of all high tides) and that the state holds title as trustee to the lands waterward of mean high water, subject to the private rights of littoral access, that is, access to navigable waters."

Also of note, in 2001 the Connecticut Supreme Court ruled against the town of Greenwich in *Leydon v. Town of Greenwich*, a landmark case in which the court ruled that Greenwich could not deny nonresidents access to their town-owned beaches. Since the ruling, all Connecticut towns are required to permit nonresident access to town-owned parks and beaches.

With regards to Rhode Island, according to a brochure prepared by the State of Rhode Island Coastal Resource Management Council (2004), "Every state has its own laws on this issue, but by law in Rhode Island, the public has the right to access the beach seaward of the mean high water mark (mean high tide is seaward of the seaweed line and where the beach gets wet on any given day). Confusion exists because the mean high water is not the same as the high tide mark. In actuality, MHW [mean high water], as determined by the Ibbison case, is much further seaward than most think. This is confusing because under the State Constitution, Article 1, Sect. 17, the public has the right to lateral access without mention of this difference."

If paddling in New York waters (Fishers Island Sound), the public trust doctrine is similar to Connecticut and Rhode Island. Essentially, the beach area seaward of the mean high-water mark (debris line) is public land.

With regard to state beaches, in Connecticut many have cartop boat launching areas away from the swimming areas. In Rhode Island, state beaches are managed as protected public swimming areas and not designated launch sites for cartop boats. However, paddlers (kayaks, stand up paddleboards, surfboards) utilize state beaches off-season (after Labor Day and before Memorial Day weekend).

Paddling with Groups and Leadership

There are several groups in Connecticut and Rhode Island that bring paddlers together. For kayakers, Connecticut Sea Kayakers, or ConnYak (www.connyak.org), and the Rhode Island Canoe/Kayak Association, or RICKA (www.ricka.org), have been reliable sources of information and bringing people together for several years. Many Meetup-style groups are also available for all types of cartop boaters.

Accomplished sea kayaker Tim Motte, a BCU 5 Star Sea Kayak Leader, RICKA Member for Life, and SOLO Wilderness First Responder, wrote the following section on sea kayak–specific leadership. His words can be applied to several different group outings:

Although sea kayaking can be enjoyed as a solo pursuit, it is often engaged in as a group activity. This lends itself to the formation of clubs of like-minded individuals.

Group leadership is an important component of being on the water. Brenda Rashleigh leading a group of twenty sea kayakers along the rocky Newport coastline. **PHOTO DAVID FASULO**

These clubs run the gamut of informal groups of a few people to more formally structured organizations with many members. These groupings of individuals can vary greatly. Even the larger, more structured clubs can have very different approaches on the water. Some follow the "Common Adventure" outdoor model with no specific group leader. This results in most people paddling separately, together as "captains of their own ship." No one is responsible for leading the group as if it were a single ship. Many people want to believe that their individual decision making and personal skills will prevail. This approach may lead to a false sense of security on the water, with many different personalities doing their own thing. Bad things are more likely to happen and when they do, the response is often underwhelming.

The alternative approach to the Common Adventure model is a more structured approach with a formal trip leader. The trip leader is responsible for coordinating the trip. This includes looking at routing, weather, tide, current, swell, water temperatures, and any other pertinent factors. Often a level of difficulty rating, or "trip level," is assigned to the trip. On the water the leader must act as a facilitator, keeping the interests and needs of the individual group members in mind. The trip leader must "captain the

Group planning also takes into account safety equipment and the participants—especially on a windy day in early spring. Ron Gautreau came prepared with a life jacket, dry suit, extra paddle, proper boat, partners, and the skills to rescue himself or others if needed. **PHOTO DAVID FASULO**

ship," constantly making adjustments as the group progresses through the trip, allowing it to function as if it were a single vessel on the water. The entire assets of the group can be brought to bear to counter liabilities faced both within and outside of the group. This can provide for a much more productive, as well as a safer, experience on the water for all group members. It is also noteworthy that a well led group can accomplish and experience more on the water, in a much safer fashion, than a leaderless group of individuals.

Various groups, such as the American Canoe Association, provide formal sea kayaking leadership training. One of the premier international training groups is British Canoeing. In North America, Paddlesports North America is the "home nation" for British Canoeing. The organization provides general paddlesport training as well as discipline-specific training in the area of sea kayaking. It also provides "awards" to kayakers that have demonstrated specific abilities to certain standards through personal "assessment." The highest final two of these awards are in discipline-specific leadership for progressively more demanding environmental conditions. For sea kayaking these awards are 4 Star Sea Kayak Leader and 5 Star Sea Kayak Leader, respectively.

British Canoeing has a couple practical tenets for sea kayakers functioning as a group. These tenets apply to all members of the group, not just the trip leader. The first is expressed as the CLAP acronym. *C* is for communication back and forth throughout the entire group. It is absolutely vital if the group is to function as a single team. *L* is for line of sight. This means that usually all members can see each other and therefore be seen themselves. *A* is for assessment and avoidance of situations as they present themselves. *P* is for position of most usefulness, being able to help out in the group as conditions warrant. This is an area where experienced paddlers, whether they are actively leading or not, can really make a difference in a group. It is the gift of being in the right place at the right time.

The next paradigm relates to the "rules of engagement" (incident management) when things go wrong. Sea kayakers should prioritize "Self, Team, Casualty, and then Equipment." This means that foremost, you should not compromise yourself to the point you will not be able to help your team or group. The next priority is maintaining the safety of the group. When you and the group are secure, the casualty can be helped. Finally, the casualty's equipment can be retrieved (if the overall scene is safe). It should be noted that in a group that is functioning well, all of this prioritization happens seamlessly.

Besides the factors mentioned above, a vast number of other factors come into play when leading a sea kayaking group, many of which can be extremely nuanced to individual members of the group. Personal comfort is a good example of one of these factors. It applies to all members of the group, including the trip leader. While this does include physical comfort, the biggest impact on the group is often psychological comfort. People need to have some psychological grounding in more-demanding conditions to feel empowered to succeed.

There is an extremely fine line for trip leaders of keeping individuals within their comfort levels and achieving goals for the group. Sometimes these two demands are mutually exclusive. However, these two goals can often be achieved with the added support of the group. Sometimes skilled leaders can "shepherd" anxious paddlers through more psychologically demanding sections of water, allowing the group to meet its goal. By paddling immediately next to a more compromised paddler, a trip leader can support the anxious paddler with energy and confidence, "psychologically towing" the paddler through the area of concern.

As many people enjoy kayaking and stand up paddling as a group activity, it makes sense to maximize the enjoyment and safety of each group's individuals through solid leadership. Whereas conditions, trips, and groups will vary, the process of effective sea kayaking leadership remains the same. A well-led group of paddlers is safer, more productive, and more enjoyable than a group of leaderless individuals.

Navigation

Navigation is one of the first problems that beginners encounter when they set out. Getting lost or in over your head on the water can be very dangerous. The traditional tool for boating is NOAA (National Oceanic and Atmospheric Administration) navigational charts. These charts require the paddler to understand aids to navigation such as channel markers (avoiding boat traffic as much as possible) and how to utilize a map and compass to find your location and plot a course. Charts can also show features visible

Caroline Zeiss, on a mild winter day, finding her way on Cockenoe Island in the Norwalk Islands chain. **PHOTO DAVID FASULO**

from the water (bridges, breakwaters, spires, towers) which can be used as landmarks, and also identify contractions where water flow is likely altered. In addition, all cartop boaters should review the "rules of the road" and how to apply them to nautical charts.

However, in the author's opinion, for coastal paddling a hybrid option exists. Aside from a nautical chart, some paddlers carry a picture of the area from Google or Bing Maps using the satellite or bird's-eye view (the computer's snipping tool is useful here). Mark magnetic north, south, east, and west (with degrees) on the pictures and use a waterproof chart holder. The combination of a NOAA chart and another visual typically makes coastal navigation easier. Waterproof chart holders, along with a deck-mounted compass, assist with ongoing navigation. Also, for the GPS savvy, having waypoints programmed into a waterproof GPS unit is a great backup.

Sea State/Conditions

Please remember the *conditions* determine the difficulty level each time you are on the water. The sea state, which is actually a rather complex term involving wind waves and ocean swell, is a factor in assessing the current conditions. Before you set out, consider and plan for the dynamic factors that will influence the conditions throughout the day such as: wind, waves, temperature, tidal and river current, structure (reefs or rocks), and the changing of the tides. In the opinion of the author, it is the *wind* and *water temperature* that most new paddlers underestimate.

The ever-changing sea state/conditions need to be continually evaluated. Wind, water and air temperature, and currents need to be planned for to keep everyone safe. **PHOTO DAVID FASULO**

A tragic example of underestimating conditions in Connecticut occurred in June 2016. After launching from Hammonasset State Beach in Madison, a paddling group headed into Long Island Sound. Tragically the group underestimated the force of the

The south side of Fishers Island in December requires specialized equipment, advanced paddling and self-rescue skills, navigation skills, and signaling devices. Nick Shade wearing a dry suit and neoprene mittens (pogies), with Race Rock Lighthouse in the background. **PHOTO DAVID FASULO**

If the conditions are benign, minimal equipment is required. Jack and Logan stand up paddleboarding in the Connecticut River on a warm summer day, wearing life jackets, carrying a whistle, and under adult supervision. **PHOTO DAVID FASULO**

offshore wind and a stand up paddleboarder and kayaker died. Two survivors of the group were located across Long Island Sound (nearly 20 miles from the launch) on Long Island, New York. The effect of wind on paddlers, especially stand up paddlers, can be significant.

Aside from checking, and reevaluating, the forecasted conditions, always dress for the water temperature in case of a capsize (immersion) and *always wear a life jacket.* The Rhode Island Canoe and Kayak Association (RICKA) uses guidelines that take into account some of the conditions when planning for group paddling events for sea kayakers (see "Sea Kayak Level System" in the Sources section).

Respecting the Sea and Coastal Wildlife

The wildlife is rebounding in several coastal areas, and often are observed by cartop boaters. Birds such as snowy egrets, great egrets, glossy ibis, and little blue herons nest on islands that were once popular landing spots, such as Charles Island in Milford and Duck Island in Westbrook, Connecticut. However, many islands now have seasonal closures. For example, Charles Island and Duck Island are closed to the public May 26 through September 9 and landing watercraft on the beaches is prohibited. Most of the islands have signs to prevent disturbing the birds—please respect all closures.

Seals are becoming a common sight in certain waters, ocean sunfish (*Mola mola*) are always a sight to behold, and even whales are returning to the Long Island Sound.

If you paddle backwards, seals tend to pop up relatively close. However, keep your distance as much as possible to prevent disturbing them. **PHOTO DAVID FASULO**

According to "Whales Return to Long Island Sound after Long Hiatus," by Dave Collins for *The Hour* (September 23, 2015), "The highly unexpected sightings began in May, when three belugas were spotted off Fairfield, Connecticut. A minke whale was seen off Norwalk later in May. And there have been several humpback sightings in recent weeks, including as far west as Mamaronek, New York, according to records kept by The Maritime Aquarium in Norwalk. Whales haven't been seen in the western part of the sound since 1993, when a 30-foot finback was spotted in New Haven Harbor, said Joe Schnierlein, research and university liaison for the aquarium."

How close is too close when it comes to wildlife? According to the Connecticut Department of Energy & Environmental Protection (CT DEEP) website, "Generally it's best to stay at least 100 yards away from seabirds and marine mammals. If you can see a nest, you're probably too close. If disturbed, an adult may abandon their nest leaving young birds vulnerable to predators or eggs from being kept warm. When eagles detect humans in their space, they fly away from their nests. Their territorial range can be as much as 3,000 feet from the nest location. Please avoid seabird-nesting areas from April to mid-August."

With regard to seals, the CT DEEP website states, "Long Island Sound is also home to four species of seals including Harbor, Harp, Hooded and Grey Seals. Seals have their pups beginning mid-May through June. If seals are on a ledge and appear restless, or they plunge into the water, leaving their pups behind, it means you are too close. If disturbed, they may leave their young to die. Harassment of a marine mammal is a

A humpback whale breaching in Long Island Sound, near New Rochelle, New York.
PHOTO HANNAH DOYLE

federal offense. It is best to observe them from a distance." Regarding whales, CT DEEP publishes guidelines, provided by NOAA Fisheries, for different zones (head on is a no-approach zone, as well as time limits in other zones). Search NOAA Fisheries Whale Watching Guidelines for detailed information.

Rough Water Paddling

The southeastern Connecticut coast, sections of the Rhode Island coast, and adjacent New York waters have become focal points for rough water sea kayakers throughout the Northeast. Rough water in the scope of this guide comes in three forms: wind waves, tidal races, and surf. In the above-mentioned waterways, these contributing factors are in abundance. In fact, on most days, one or more of these factors is firing off somewhere accessible to shoreline paddlers.

The "grandfather" of rough water paddling in Connecticut is Carl Tjerandsen. Carl was the first to plan, using available data, for the factors creating certain conditions at specific areas. When the contributing factors aligned, Carl and area locals would venture out to the reefs and shorelines to test the waters. After years of exploration, and sharing of information, many of the rough water areas described in this book are considered world-class venues. Stonington, Connecticut, now attracts paddlers from around the country, and even overseas, to challenge themselves in its rough water venues. The following sections, "Wind Waves," "Tidal Races," and "Surf," were written by Carl.

Wind Waves

Wind waves are created by the drag of moving air across the water. Increasing fetch, wind velocity, and opposing current make for larger waves. Typically, waves entering shallower water will steepen. Winds blowing from the WSW up Long Island Sound famously create playable wind waves. When the wind is up from a favorable direction, paddlers set up transport arrangements and do "downwinders" (paddling one-way downwind) of 12 to 15 miles. These can be quite tiring, as the paddlers are frequently "putting the pedal to the metal" to catch and surf the wind waves. An off-season favorite is from Eastern Point Beach in Groton, Connecticut, to Stonington, Connecticut.

Nick Schade during a "downwinder" from Eastern Point Beach in Groton, Connecticut, to Stonington, Connecticut. **PHOTO DAVID FASULO**

Tidal Races

The number and quality of tidal races gives our area of southern New England its most attractive water feature. Our races set up where water accelerates over a shallow area, like a reef, and flows directly into relatively deeper water. This transition zone is where one finds the front wall of the race—often the steepest and largest standing waves. The wave faces the direction from which the current is coming.

The race player typically paddles against the current, attempting to catch the standing waves, gaining velocity, and zooming from one wave wall to the next all the way to the front. On a good day the height of these standing waves can reach 5 to 7 feet. On occasion they can be much higher. Discovering conditions of this magnitude, most of the locals hold up on the periphery to appreciate the aesthetics of the thundering chaos, all the while making certain they are not drawn into the maelstrom by the unrelenting tidal stream.

A couple important points: Opposing wind to the current is a magnifier of the wave height in the races. Conversely, a strong wind in the direction of the current will significantly tamp it down. Spring tides (on days around new and full moons) typically make for more-robust race conditions. Many race paddlers prefer modest to 4-plus-knot currents because it is easier to catch waves and not have to overcome faster currents.

Some races set up as a mirror image during the ebb and flood races on either side of a reef. Examples are reefs at Wicopesset Passage, Ram Reef, and The Race. Others are one-way only (due to bottom terrain) and include Sugar Reef and Catumb Rocks, which are both ebb sites. Furthermore, the texture and pattern of the water surface can be quite variable. Smooth, orderly lines of standing waves are preferred by many paddlers. On occasion, especially in The Race, you might encounter a vertical surging effect some liken to the agitation cycle of a washing machine. In some areas, smooth boils of water may form on the periphery. More often, wind waves will enter the tidal race in a crossing pattern. This, along with frequent boat wakes, can contaminate the purity of the wave lines—keeping the paddler en garde at all times.

Tidal races are dangerous places. When the wind, current, and perhaps ocean swell or large vessel wakes present to maximum effect, it can be highly exhilarating—even for the most experienced paddler. It is also easy, way easy, to get flipped. Failing to right yourself with a roll—this is the ultimate combat roll scenario—the swimmer can be very difficult to sort out or even approach. Some races extend for hundreds of yards in their extreme-energy state. That's a long time to try to hold on to a wildly bucking and tumbling boat, which now weighs a ton and seems determined to beat the stuffing out of the paddler.

Along these lines, in a race that is kicking up, you have about a minute in 3- to 4-knot currents to notice a swimmer. Past that time, the swimmer/boat combo are beyond seeing. It is not a good feeling to hear, "Hey, has anyone seen Stephanie?" Therefore, keep an eye on one another, and scan the field regularly (take regular head counts). Rough water paddlers carry waterproof VHF radios, turned on to an agreed-upon channel, to keep everyone informed at all times. Often the dynamic races have mild-condition days and are suitable for persons learning this venue, but only under the supervision of experienced paddlers who can effect safe rescues.

Surf

Persons liable to become addicted should skip this section. SUPs (stand up paddleboards) and long kayaks are surfing machines. Picture this: bobbing bow-in 50 yards offshore, twisting seaward to glimpse that dancing, irregular, swelling line on the horizon—the Big Wave. There! Wave ho! Rush to position your boat, accelerate, feel your stern briskly lifting skyward, hear the rush of the oncoming swell and water rushing by,

Carl Tjerandsen finding rough water in Rhode Island. PHOTO RON GAUTREAU

as your boat accelerates nose-down into the trough. Don't bury the bow! Don't veer off into a teeth-chattering bongo slide! Don't get trashed, your torso getting rag-dolled in the green room! Don't collide with those defenseless surfers paddling out to the break! OK . . . avoided all that.

You are now flying shoreward, tucked into the face of the wave. Now the break—blinding white chaos explodes around you! Feeling the power of the sea and capturing it to your purpose. When you are in the zone at a surf break, you can feel drained after a couple hours and still find yourself in the line three hours later. There is always another wave on the horizon, promising the best ride ever. Exhilaration? Joy? Oh yeah. Big time.

In Rhode Island, there is ocean swell point break at Napatree Point (beware of rocks and pilings) and secondary small waves that are safe after the pilings. Matunuck and the Narrow River outlet (north end of Narragansett Town Beach) are superb ocean wave surfing sites. Unlike most kayaking venues, many surf breaks are densely populated with boardies, short boats, and SUPs. Where there are crowds doing the same thing, there are rules. Best learn them.

Boater Regulations and Safety Tips

A word to the wise: Always assume that powerboaters, and especially sailboats, cannot see you. Keeping this in mind, stay out of channels as much as possible and take extra care when crossing channels. Also, whether it is the required season (October 1 through

All vessels need to be aware of, and follow, the "rules of the road." Navigation marker in the popular Narrow River, Narragansett, Rhode Island. PHOTO DAVID FASULO

May 31 in Connecticut) to wear a PFD or not, always wear a Coast Guard–approved PFD—it is just plain smart.

The states covered in this guide vary to some degree with regard to safety regulations and requirements, as well as regulations in specific bodies of water (such as Fishers Island Sound). Please refer to the most recent state publications for up-to-date information and to review the rules of the road regarding navigational aids, onboard lights (power and sailboats), and right-of-way.

In accordance with federal regulations, the US Coast Guard has determined that a stand up paddleboard is a vessel when used "beyond the narrow limits of a swimming, surfing, or bathing area." This means that SUPs are required to have a PFD on board when not in surf zones.

Some general regulations, as referenced from the *2016 Connecticut Boater's Guide*, published by CT DEEP, are as follows:

Life jackets must:

- Be US Coast Guard approved.
- Be worn by children under 13 years old on any vessel that is under way unless the child is below deck or in an enclosed cabin.
- Be worn by anyone in a manually propelled vessel from October 1 through May 31 (must be Type I, II, III, IV, or V-hybrid). ***Note:*** They are required to be on the vessel (kayak or SUP) if not being worn year-round.

Note: Persons operating racing shells, racing canoes, racing kayaks, and rowing sculls and involved in competitive racing or the preparation for competitive racing are not required to wear or carry life jackets if accompanied at all time by an escort vessel.

Visual Distress Signals (VDS):

- In the State of Connecticut no VDS are required anywhere except when boating in Long Island Sound and on Fishers Island Sound.
- Recreational vessels under 16 feet, and manually propelled vessels, are required to carry VDS only on Long Island Sound and Fishers Island Sound between sunset and sunrise.
- Boats less than 16 feet must carry approved visual distress signal for nighttime use when operating at night. Boats 16 feet to 26 feet must carry visual distress signals approved for both daytime use and nighttime use.

Sound-Producing Devices:

- Must have some means of making an efficient sound signal.

Navigational Lights (Underway):

- Recreational boats must display their required navigational lights at all times between sunset and sunrise, and during daylight periods of reduced visibility. Sample illustration from the boater's guide displays a canoe with a single white light.
- More specifically per Rule 25 of the Navigational Rules: (ii) A vessel under oars may exhibit the lights prescribed in this Rule for sailing vessels, but if she does not, she shall have ready at hand an electric torch or lighted lantern showing a white light which shall be exhibited in sufficient time to prevent collision.

Safety Tips:

The safety tips below are cross referenced from a variety of sources, and condensed to a top ten list.

1. Wear a life jacket and carry a whistle at all times.
2. Take a course. This is especially helpful for efficient paddle strokes and self-rescues for kayaks.
3. Know how to self-rescue (get back into your kayak or on your SUP).
4. Avoid main channels and high-traffic areas; you are usually invisible, so be on the defensive.
5. Tell someone where you are going—file a float plan. As possible, do not paddle alone.

Wearing a PFD at all times is paddling smart. **PHOTO DAVID FASULO**

6. Carry a device that allows you to communicate if in distress and monitor the weather.
7. Wear a leash (paddle or SUP) as appropriate. Kayakers should carry a spare paddle.
8. Attach an "If Found" decal to your vessel. For kayaks, attach an extra decal inside a hatch so it does not wear out and become unreadable.
9. Bring a chart and compass, and know how to use them, if venturing offshore.
10. Unless you are specifically looking for it, avoid rough water and be mindful of offshore winds.

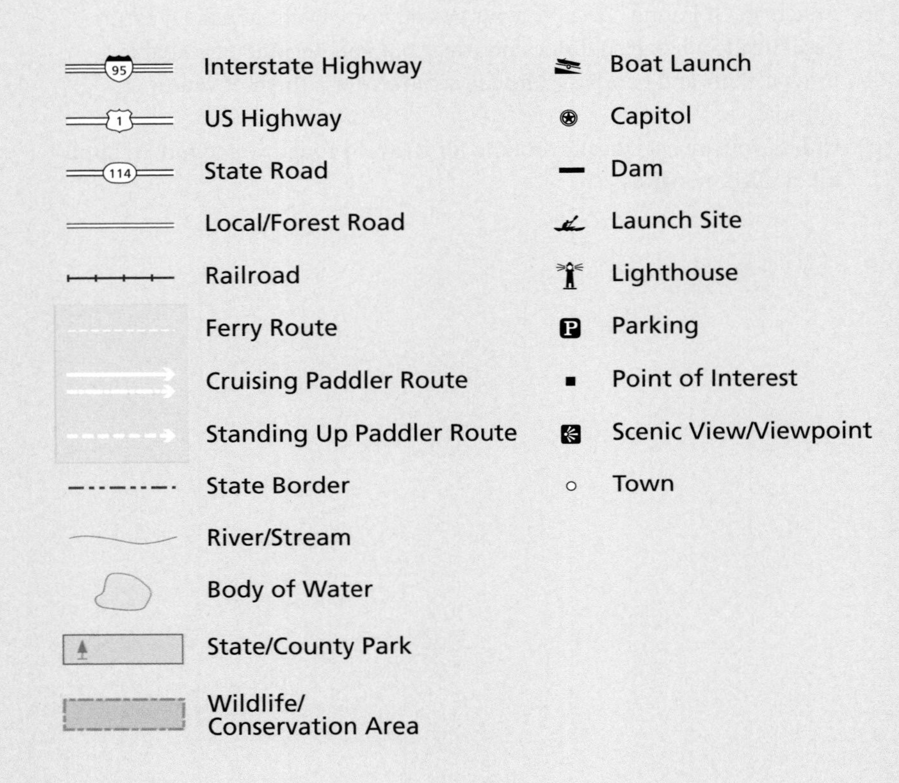

Map Legend
95
Interstate Highway
1
US Highway
114
State Road
Local/Forest Road
Railroad
Ferry Route
Cruising Paddler Route
Standing Up Paddler Route
State Border
River/Stream
Body of Water
State/County Park
Wildlife/
Conservation Area
Boat Launch
Capitol
Dam
Launch Site
Lighthouse
P
Parking
Point of Interest
Scenic View/Viewpoint
Town

Connecticut

In terms of protection from large ocean swells, a comfortable climate for much of the year, and ease of access for cartop boaters, the Connecticut coastal waters are hard to beat. The primary waterway, Long Island Sound, is actually an enormous tidal estuary providing moving water (freshwater and seawater) for abundant sea life and interesting tidal races over rocks and ledges. The shoreline has a notable mix of islands, beaches, and parks, as well as numerous small bays to explore.

The Norwalk Islands are one of Connecticut's finest paddling destinations. **PHOTO ERIK BAUMGARTNER**

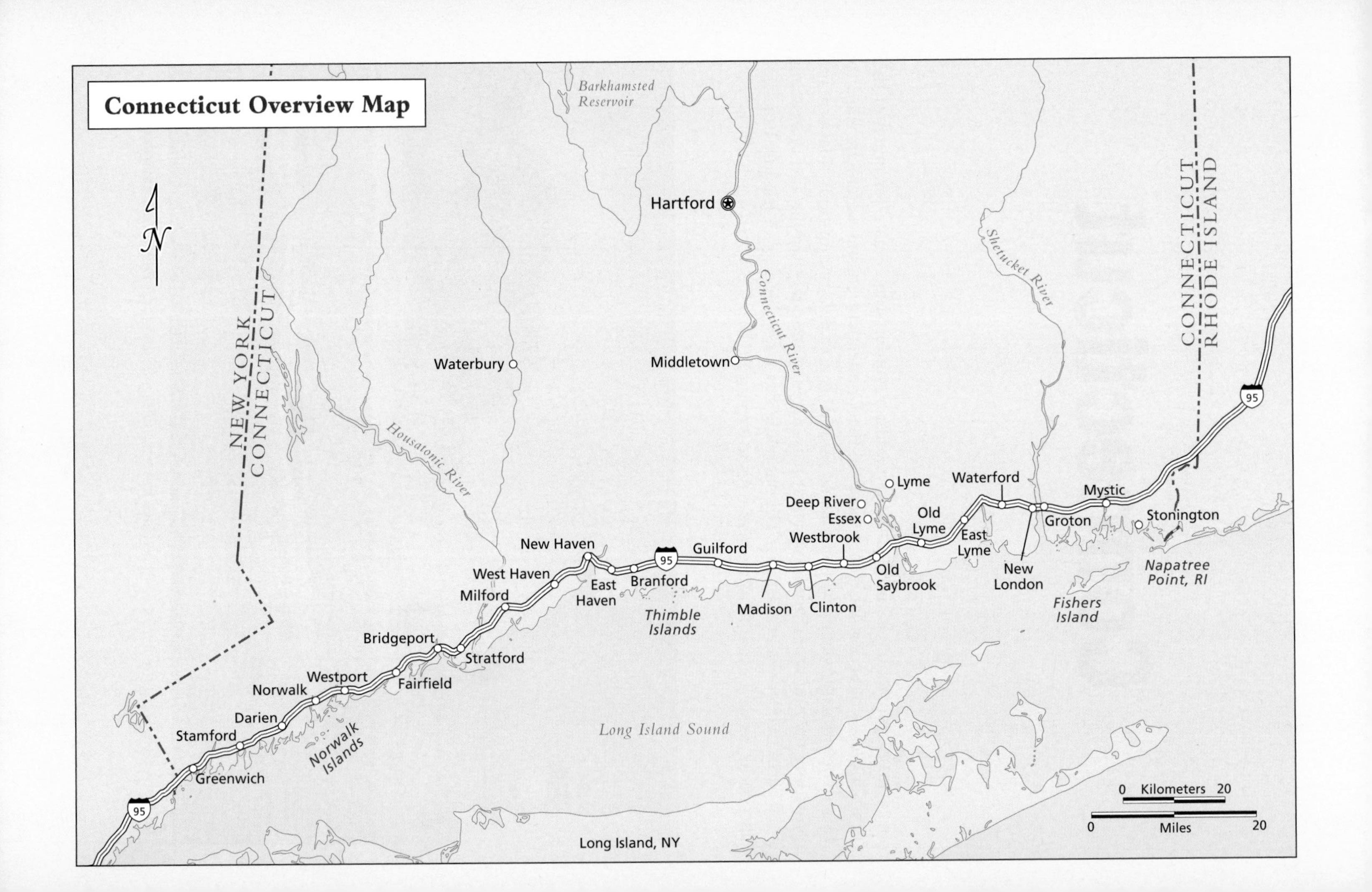

Connecticut Overview Map
N
NEW YORK
CONNECTICUT
CONNECTICUT
RHODE ISLAND
Barkhamsted Reservoir
Hartford
Waterbury
Middletown
Connecticut River
Shetucket River
Housatonic River
Lyme
Deep River
Essex
Waterford
Mystic
Stonington
Groton
Old Lyme
East Lyme
New London
Westbrook
Guilford
Old Saybrook
Madison
Clinton
New Haven
West Haven
East Haven
Branford
Milford
Thimble Islands
Fishers Island
Napatree Point, RI
Bridgeport
Stratford
Fairfield
Westport
Norwalk
Darien
Stamford
Greenwich
Norwalk Islands
Long Island Sound
Long Island, NY
95
0 Kilometers 20
0 Miles 20

Since the entire coastline is protected from large ocean swells, and there are many submerged rock piles resulting from the ice age, the Connecticut coastal waters have several productive locations for kayak anglers. The numerous bays provide additional protection for SUPs, and when the late-day wind is light, the waves in Long Island Sound are manageable for all paddlers.

Tours from western to eastern Connecticut:

Norwalk Islands, Norwalk
Branford Harbor and Farm River, Branford
Thimble Islands, Branford
Guilford coast/Faulkners Island, Guilford
Hammonassett Beach, Madison
Connecticut River, Essex/Deep River
Rocky Neck, East Lyme
Pine Island/Dumpling Islands, Groton/New York
Mystic/Mason's Island, Groton/Stonington
Sandy Point Island, Stonington

In terms of kayak fishing, anglers tend to travel to different areas depending on the season. Connecticut serves as a convenient stopover for migrating striped bass each spring. Leaving their estuaries in the Hudson River and Chesapeake Bay, these fish visit the shallow waters of Connecticut's diversified bottom habitats to forage on a variety of species including lobsters, crabs, small baitfish, Atlantic menhaden, croakers, and scups. The midseason tends to change over to fluke, black sea bass, and scup, with the continued hunt for stripers and bluefish all season long. The bluefish can be thick in the fall (located by spotting birds), with a hunt for albies during this time as well. To close the season, tautog (blackfish) are a favorite of many anglers.

Kayakers who take to the water should be aware of shore fishermen along the jetties and breakwaters and be mindful of the concentrated boat traffic that occurs along these adjacent navigational channels. Fish a moving tide with either bloodworms, clam bellies, menhaden chunks, soft plastics, or plugs reeled very slowly.

Greenwich, CT

When heading west past the outer Greenwich Islands, on a clear day, the Manhattan skyline can be seen in the distance and Long Island dominates the vista to the south. The islands are not too far from the mainland (about 2 miles) and make for interesting destinations and scenery. The islands include: Little Captain Island/Island Beach (same island but formerly known as Little Captain Island, Town of Greenwich), Great Captain's Island (Town of Greenwich), Calf Island (Stewart B. McKinney National Wildlife Refuge), Shell Island (Greenwich Land Trust), and the small Bowers Island. The protected Greenwich Cove provides shelter for paddleboarders and recreational kayakers, while windsurfers and kite surfers are a common sight at Greenwich Point.

Because of the facilities, Great Captain's Island and Little Captain Island/Island Beach are unique destinations for Connecticut coastal waters (keep clear of the swimming areas). To access the islands by kayak or SUP, above the high-water mark May through October, a day pass is required (www.greenwichct.org). A camping permit is required to access Great Captain's Island between 10:30 p.m. and 7 a.m.

According to Greenwich Parks and Recreation, "Great Captain's Island includes an active recreation area, a natural area and a managed conservation area. The recreation area has a beach, boat mooring, shelter and rest rooms. A rockweed cove and saltmarsh lagoon are found on the southern side in the natural area. A path through the natural areas leads to the lighthouse. Green Heron, Black- and Yellow-crowned Night-Heron, Mallards, Flickers, Grackles and Sparrows have been sighted. The eastern and western sections are connected by a tombolo—sand or gravel bar."

Calf Island offers protection and interesting island scenery. According to the Calf Island Conservancy, "At 31.5 acres, Calf Island is the largest offshore island in Greenwich, CT. It is located directly south of Byram Harbor, approximately 3,000 feet from the mainland, and is connected at low tide to the Greenwich Land Trust's Shell Island. Today, Calf Island provides roosting and foraging habitat for the waterbird colony at Great Captain's Island, located one mile from Calf Island. Although colony numbers have fluctuated over the years, Great Captain's is the site of the largest wading bird rookery in Connecticut, with approximately 300 nesting pairs of great egrets, snowy egrets and black-crowned night-herons. Also of significance are the colonies of common terns, double-crested cormorants and gulls on nearby Bowers and Diving Islands."

Exploring the Greenwich coast, viewing mansions and manicured properties, makes for a memorable outing. Unlike many towns in eastern Connecticut, kayak and SUP access is restricted for non–Greenwich residents. However, launch options do exist—see below.

Primary Launches: Greenwich Point Park. For Greenwich residents the primary launch, with a town permit (www.greenwichct.org), is from the large kayak

Curt Anderson exploring Shell Island and the Greenwich coast. **PHOTO DAVID FASULO**

launch/beach at the northeast section of Greenwich Point Park. The park is free to nonresidents November through April. Directions: GPS Tod's Driftway Road, Greenwich. Follow Tod's Driftway Road to the entrance gate to Greenwich Point Park. The launch is just under a mile from the entrance gate, on the north side of Tod's Driftway Road. Park in the lot to the east of the kayak racks, and launch from the beach just east of the kayak racks.

Edith G. Read Wildlife Sanctuary. Although it will take some prior planning, for nonresidents the Edith G. Read Wildlife Sanctuary in Rye, New York, is a good option. From the Read Sanctuary, Captain's Island is just over 2.5 miles from the launch (one way), and Greenwich Bay/Greenwich Point is about 6 miles (one way). It is a nice beach launch on the south side shortly after entering the sanctuary. To gain access to the launch, you need to become a member of the Friends of Read Wildlife Sanctuary (www.friendsofreadwild lifesanctuary.org). The yearly fee is $20 and the grounds are open 365 days a year from dawn until dusk. Members are provided with a bar-coded FRWS card that allows vehicular access through the Playland Amusement Park.

Directions, according to the website: "From I-95, Northbound or Southbound, take Exit 19 (New York) Playland Parkway to Playland. If you are a member of the sanctuary, your barcoded membership card will allow you to open the yellow automatic gate in the *left* lane at the ticket booths at Playland's main entrance. Continue driving to the back right side of the main parking lot by the Dragon Coaster ride. You'll see another automatic gate. Scan your card again, and continue straight down the road into the sanctuary. Manursing Lake is on the left and Long Island Sound and Kayak Launch area are on the right. There is a parking area in front of the nature center. *Note:* Please do not park on the grassy areas."

Secondary Launches: As of 2017, the town of Greenwich is issuing a limited number of nonresident launch permits for their ramp facilities at Cos Cob and Grass Island. Permits are available at the Parks and Recreation office beginning on April 15, or the following business day if April 15 falls on a weekend. The permits are good for the entire season and the cost is $80 for each vessel, with a limit of one permit per person.

Cos Cob Marina. The dockmaster's office can be reached at (203) 618-9698. The marina is located on River Road just south of the I-95 overpass. Cos Cob Marina to Great Captain's Island is 4.3 miles one way, or 2.5 miles one way to Greenwich Point Park.

Grass Island Marina. The dockmaster's office can be reached at (203) 618-9695. The marina is located off Shore Road in central Greenwich just south of I-95. Grass Island Marina to Great Captain's Island is 2.3 miles one way, or 2.6 miles one way to Greenwich Point Park.

Drew Schoudel playing in the waves off Great Captain's Island. **PHOTO DAVID FASULO**

Landing on Great Captain's Island or Little Captain/Island Beach. Obtaining a beach pass or a kayak launch pass in season (May through October) is rather complex, so it is best to navigate the town website, www.greenwichct.org, for details.

Cruising Paddler

Circuit from Playland/Read Sanctuary Rye, New York. This circuit provides a pleasant tour of the westernmost islands of Connecticut. Launch from Playland/Read Sanctuary and make your way to Great Captain's Island (2.6 miles), around Little Captain Island/Island Beach (4 miles total), to Bowers Island (5.3 miles total), around (or past) Calf Island (6.5 miles total), and then back to Playland (8.8 miles total).

Circuit from Greenwich Point. Greenwich Point to Little Captain Island/Island Beach (2 miles), to Great Captain's Island (3 miles total), to Calf Island midpoint (4 miles total), around Calf Island to Bowers Island (5 miles total), with a return along the Greenwich shore to Greenwich Point launch (8 miles total).

Distance Paddler

From Playland/Read Sanctuary in Rye, head past Great Captain's Island and Little Captain Island/Island Beach to the northwest end of Greenwich Point Park (5.5 miles). Paddle across Greenwich Cove and into Cos Cob Harbor around Goode Island. Head back (west) along the coast to Tweed Island (8 miles total). Continue across Smith Cove and follow the coastline to Calf Island (9.5 to 10 miles total). Head around the island (north or south) and return to Rye (13 miles total).

Rough Water Paddler

At certain tides and winds, the northern tip of Great Captain's Island can produce fun waves to play in.

SUP Friendly

Greenwich Cove, north of Greenwich Point, has protected waters, and Great Island (small island in the center) provides some scenery. From Playland, Rye, you can head south and check out the protected waters in the Rye Town Park area, or paddle north along the coast of Manursing Island.

Something Fishy

The islands, and Newfoundland Reef, outside Cos Cob are popular. Cormorant Reef, located northwest of Great Captain's Island and before Jones Rocks, is rumored to hold fish. Trolling a tube and worm along Greenwich Point, from Flat Neck Reef to Woolsey

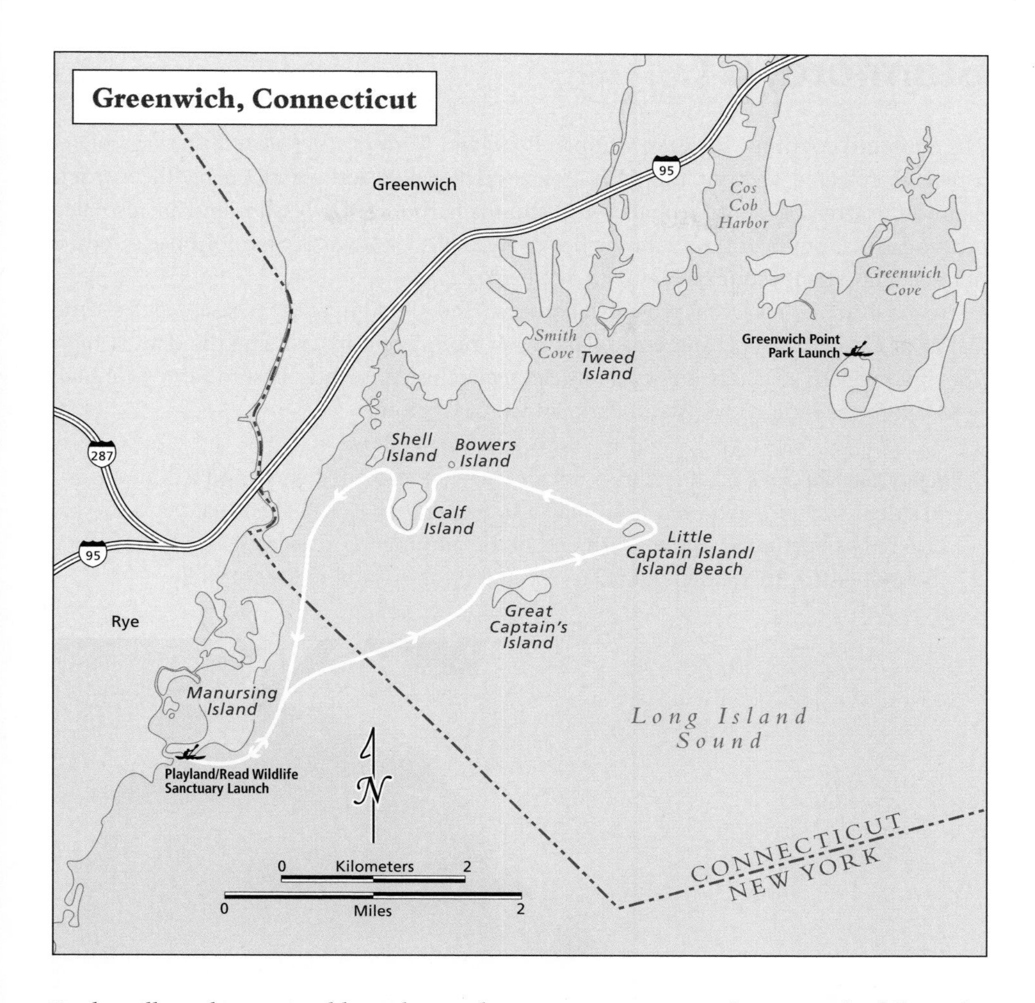

Rock, will produce striped bass during the spring migration and again in the fall. In the waters east of Woolsey Rock, the characteristically uniform sandy bottom is a proven fluke haven in midsummer.

Stamford, CT

The Stamford coastline, between Shippan Point and Nash Island (town of Darien), offers a nicely protected area for the recreational sea kayaker and stand up paddleboarder. Stamford Harbor (west of Shippan Point) and the harbor east of Nash Island are also nice cruising areas, but boat traffic can be heavy. Access is via town of Stamford parks, and a nonresident pass is required May 1 to September 1.

Aside from the relatively protected harbors, Holly Pond is a very pleasant area for the SUPer or casual kayaker. Some paddlers reach Holly Pond by crossing the dam at high tide, but exposed structure and currents can make this dangerous. Best to carry your SUP or kayak to the inner Cove Island Park launch (see below).

Primary Launch: Cove Island. This is a really nice town-owned park, and a non-resident sticker is required from May 1 to September 1 ($25 at the gate). There is a boat ramp at the south end of the parking lot to access Long Island Sound, and a small beach launch is located on the island to access Holly

Igor Pounov returning to the Cove Island launch. **PHOTO DAVID FASULO**

Pond. If using the boat launch, be courteous of boaters navigating the channel due to currents—kayaks do not have the right-of-way. To reach the Holly Pond access, cross the bridge and head to the building on the northeast side of the island. There is a small beach north of the building (near kayak racks), west of the dam, from which to launch.

Directions: From I-95 North, get off at exit 9, East Main Street (Route 1), and make a right onto Seaside Avenue. Follow Seaside Avenue to Cove Road, then make a left onto Cove Road to Cove Island Park. From I-95 South, get off at exit 9, East Main Street (Route 1). Make a left onto East Main Street and then right onto Weed Avenue to Cove Island Park.

Secondary Launch: Cummings Park. This is a town-owned park, and a nonresident sticker is required from May 1 to September 1 ($25 at the gate). There is a very nice beach launch on the west end of the beach, north of the building, leading into the small harbor. Be courteous of boat traffic when coming in and out of the channel. Directions: GPS Elm Street (exit 8 from I-95 South). Follow Elm Street to Shippan Avenue and bear right; Cummings Park will be on the left side, past the fire station. Follow the road past the rotary to the parking area on the northwest side (harbor side).

Cruising Paddler

Leave the Cove Island Launch and head west to Greenway Island and then to Vincent Island (1 mile). Continue around Vincent Island, then head back towards the launch and the beach in front of Cove Island and paddle into the harbor going into Holly Pond (3 miles). (***Note:*** At this point the tour of the shoreline continues, but depending on tides and current, it is fun to explore the edge of the Holly Pond dam—but do not cross over it.) Continue into Darien and along Weed Beach (harbor can be shallow) to Pratt One Island (3.5 miles total), and then around Nash Island to Pear Tree Point Beach (4.3 miles total). Take a break at the beach (near the kayak racks) and return to the Cove Island launch (6.4 miles total).

Distance Paddler

From the Cove Island Launch, head past Cove Harbor, past Nash Island, to Long Neck Point (see Darien map for Long Neck Point and points east). Paddle north past Hay Island, then cross over to Crab Island and the Fish Islands to a break on a small beach (access at low tide) on north Fish Island (3.3 miles). Head south around south Fish Island and return (about 7 miles total) with some more exposed crossings.

David Appleman rigged and ready to search for keeper fluke. **PHOTO DAVID FASULO**

Rough Water Paddler

Depending on winds and tides, Shippan Point/Shippan Point Shoal can provide some rough water play. There is also a reef (Smith Reef) about 1 mile offshore (southeast) off Greenway Island.

SUP Friendly

From the Cove Island Park inner launch (cross the bridge and launch from the small beach west of the dam and northeast of the buildings), cruise along the shores of Holly Pond. Be careful to avoid the dam area on an ebb tide. For more salty waters, launching from Cummings Park and exploring the coast east of the beach, up towards Greenway Island and Vincent Island, is a pleasant journey. There is a small beach (tidal) on the breakwater just south of Greenway Island (about 2 miles round-trip).

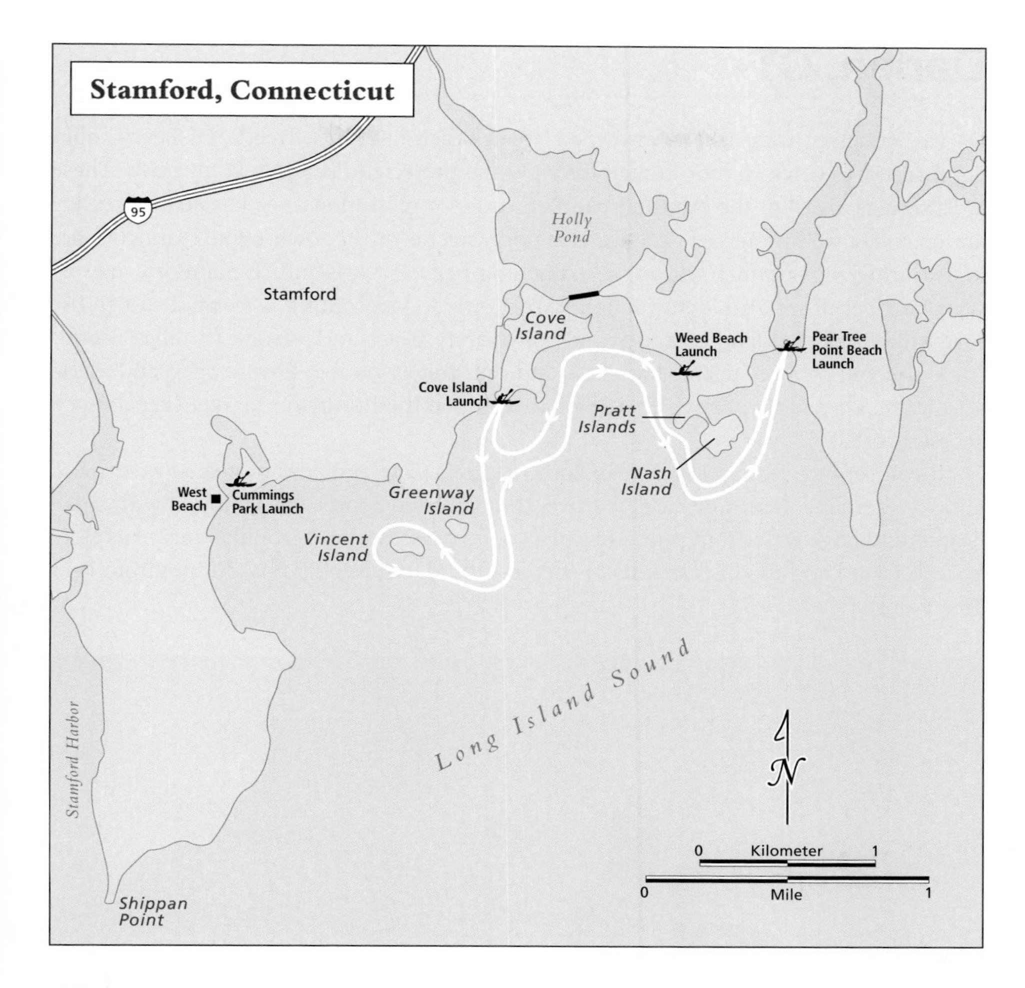

Something Fishy

The sandy bottom of the harbor areas is decent for fluke, and in the fall the bluefish come in. Stripers can be found along the edges of the shore at night. Drifting eels inside the breakwater off Shippan Point, when the wind and tide allow, along the cobble bottom to the west of the breakwater is a good bet. When the seasons allow, tautog (blackfish) can be found tight to bottom structure along the breakwater and will gladly take a crab or clam presented properly. Later in the season, scups will occupy the same spots and will accept bloodworms and squids on appropriately sized hooks. Shippan Point is known to produce large stripers.

Darien, CT

Darien launches, from the town-owned Weed Beach and Pear Tree Point Beach, offer good access to Cove Harbor in Stamford and the protected Pear Tree Point Cove. These are also nice areas for the stand up paddleboarder or recreational sea kayaker since they are relatively well protected. The fees for nonresidents at the town-owned launches are high during the summer season, so launching from Cove Island in Stamford may be your best bet if not a resident (Stamford section). A good outing is to head east to the Five Mile River and land at Rowayton Community Beach in Norwalk (8 miles round-trip). You will pass interesting coastline, and can stretch/stroll in Rowayton to add to the adventure. Or paddle upriver a bit more to a stop at the Rowayton Market (kayak/dock access as of 2017).

If you venture around Long Neck Point, Zieglers Cove provides protected waters and a rocky shoreline. North of Zieglers Cove, the protected Scott Cove is dotted with small islands and large waterfront properties in a suburban seascape. A popular area to explore is Crab Island and the Fish Islands (1.5 miles from Long Neck Point, 3 miles from Pear Tree Point).

Katharine Fulk and her daughter exploring the waters of Darien. **PHOTO DAVID FASULO**

Primary Launches: There are two town-owned beach launches: Weed Beach and Pear Tree Point Beach. Weed Beach is less congested with boat traffic, and Pear Tree Point is better protected from ocean waves when launching and landing.

According to the town website, beach/park permit and boat launch stickers are required from Memorial Day weekend through Labor Day at Pear Tree Point Beach and mid-April through early October at Weed Beach (or when gatehouses are staffed). Passes can be purchased at the gate ($40 per day for nonresidents). The town also states, "Both Weed Beach and Pear Tree Beach are designated launching sites for light (Optimist, Sunfish, Laser, etc.) and ultra-light (sail board and wind surfer, boats and kayaks). . . . Any water craft carried on or within a motor vehicle requires a current vehicle permit only. . . . Except for unusual and/or unforeseen emergencies, beaches shall be open to the public every day of the year from sunrise to 10:00 p.m."

Directions to Weed Beach: GPS Nearwater Lane and follow for 0.4 mile. Weed Beach will be on your right.

Directions to Pear Tree Point Beach: GPS Pear Tree Point Road and follow for 0.6 mile. Pear Tree Point Park will be on the right.

Cruising Paddler

Pear Tree Point to Fish Islands. Launch out of Pear Tree Point and head southeast along Long Neck Point. From the point (1 mile), head northeast along the point to Zieglers Cove (2 miles). Paddle across the entrance of Scott Cove (east) to Coyler Point (2.5 miles), then past the point to the Fish Islands, just past Crab Island (2.7 miles one way). There is a small beach on north Fish Island. Return the same route, or explore the coves as you head back to the launch (about 6 miles round-trip).

Weed Beach to Westcott Cove. This is a good cruise since it is typically well protected with some nice scenery. Head west out of Weed Beach along Cove Island, then around the point of land (watch for boats) to Greenway Island (see Stamford map; 1.25 miles). Paddle around the breakwater and around Vincent Island to a rest stop on the north side of the breakwater, depending on conditions (2.3 miles total). Head back to the launch (about 4 miles round-trip).

Distance Paddler

Pear Tree Point to Rowayton Community Beach: Head east around Long Neck Point and on to the Fish Islands (2.7 miles). Continue heading east along the shore to the Five Mile River and Rowayton Community Beach (3.8 miles total). The beach is on the east side of the river, 1,668 feet from the mouth of the river, and has a seven car parking lot adjacent to the road. Stretch your legs in Rowayton, then head back to the launch (about 8 miles round-trip). (***Note:*** While the Rowayton Community Beach is located in Norwalk,

Heading into Rowayton Community Beach, a nice landing spot, for a stroll. **PHOTO DAVID FASULO**

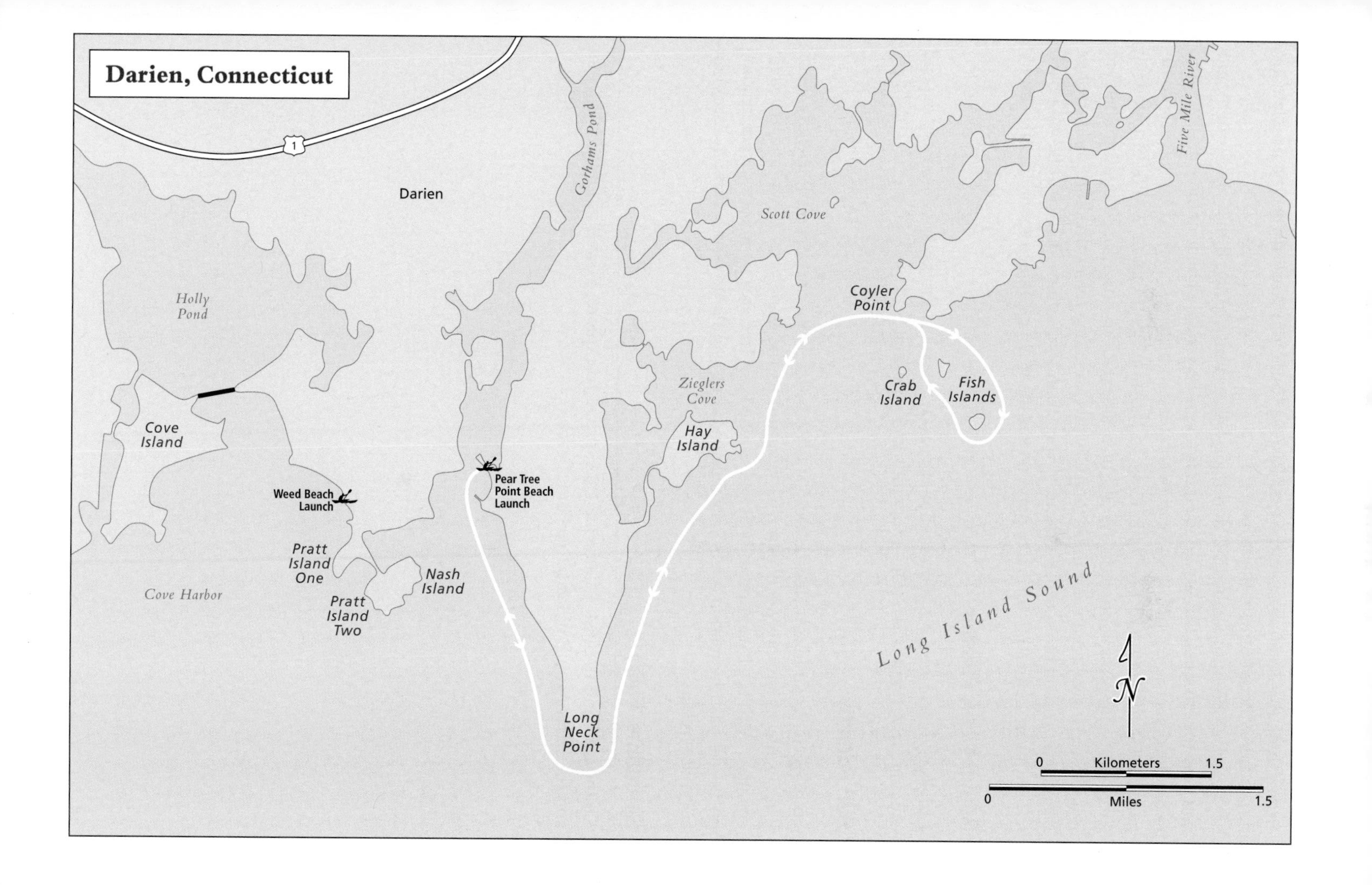
Darien, Connecticut
1
Darien
Gorhams Pond
Scott Cove
Five Mile River
Holly Pond
Cove Island
Weed Beach Launch
Pear Tree Point Beach Launch
Zieglers Cove
Hay Island
Coyler Point
Crab Island
Fish Islands
Pratt Island One
Pratt Island Two
Nash Island
Cove Harbor
Long Neck Point
Long Island Sound
N
0
Kilometers
1.5
0
Miles
1.5

approaching this location from the Calf Pasture Launch in Norwalk can be problematic due to heavy boat traffic in the summer.)

Pear Tree Point to Sheffield Island (Norwalk Islands chain). If the wind is light and you time the currents, this is a good circuit— just be careful of boat traffic when crossing to Sheffield Island. Launch from Pear Tree Point and head east around Long Neck Point, past the Fish Islands and Five Mile River to Noroton Point (about 4 miles if following shoreline). Cross the harbor (be careful of boat traffic) to Southwest Point on Sheffield Island (see Norwalk map; 4.6 miles total). Head east, along the north shore, around Shea Island to a stop on the southeast shore of Shea Island (6.8 miles total). Paddle west back to Southwest Point (8.5 miles total) and return the way you came (about 13 miles total).

Rough Water Paddler

Ledges and reefs are scatted throughout the area. The most accessible is probably the end of Long Neck Point when tides and winds are opposing.

SUP Friendly

Both Weed Beach (Cove Harbor area) and Pear Tree Point are very SUP-friendly areas. Late in the afternoon Weed Beach is beautiful as the wind dies down and the light changes. With the exception of boat wakes, the Pear Tree area is protected, and heading north just past the marina offers very nice paddling (similar to North Cove in Essex) for a 3-mile stretch.

Something Fishy

Crab Island and the Fish Islands are good places to explore, as well as Long Neck Point and the harbor south of Pear Tree Point Beach.

Norwalk, CT

The Norwalk Islands are one of the most interesting paddling venues in Connecticut. They offer many protected areas, and portions of some of the islands allow public access and camping. The boat traffic can be a bit heavy in the summer, but it is manageable. A unique paddling adventure is to land on Sheffield Island and tour the lighthouse grounds—but see below for restrictions. The primary launch is from Calf Pasture Town Beach at a designated cartop boat launch area, but the Saugatuck River State Boat Launch (free) in Westport is also a popular option. However, low water and current can make the return up the Saugatuck River a slog on an ebb tide. Popular stops include Cockenoe Island (Westport) and Shea Island (southeast side of island).

Aside from the well-known Norwalk Islands, other adventures include the Five Mile River in Rowayton and the Bermuda Lagoon. The Five Mile River provides access to downtown Rowayton and is 4 to 4.5 miles from the Calf Pasture launch. There is a landing (Community Beach) at the corner of Rowayton Avenue and Cook Street, and landing is possible at the dock at the Rowayton Market (just before reaching Pinkney Park on the right). The Bermuda Lagoon is an interior bay, and mellow circuit, north of Sprite Island; the entrance is 1.5 miles from the Calf Pasture launch.

Enjoying the day at the popular Norwalk Islands. **PHOTO ERIK BAUMGARTNER**

With regard to access to the Norwalk Islands, according to the City of Norwalk website (www.norwalkct.org), "Chimon Island: Day use of Chimon Island is available only in the designated beach area. No overnight camping or use of the island's interior is allowed. Access to Chimon Island is restricted from April 1 to August 15 because of the bird nesting season. Grassy Island/Shea (Ram) Island: During the open season from May 1 through Columbus Day (October 12), Grassy Island and Shea (Ram) Island are open to the general public for daytime and overnight camping."

Landing areas summarized:

Cockenoe Island—north side, inside of harbor; camping is allowed (with permit)
Grassy Island—north and south sides
Chimon Island—northwest side
Shea Island—southeast side beach; camping is allowed (with permit)
Sheffield Island—near lighthouse for a $5 fee May–September
Crow Island—land bridge between Chimon and Copps Island at lower tides

Sheffield Island is comanaged by the Norwalk Seaport Association (3 acres of land the lighthouse is on) and the Stewart B. McKinney Wildlife Refuge (52 acres). From May through September a ferry departs the mainland for guided tours of the lighthouse and self-guided tours of the island. For kayakers and SUPers paddling to the island, there is a fee/donation for landing, which is $5 for adults and $3 for children.

According to Jim Rose, the lightkeeper and island manager, "While there is no 'designated area' to land on the island, the area just to the right of our dock is a popular landing spot for kayakers that wish to visit the lighthouse grounds. Visitors are typically welcomed and get information from island staff as they land. We typically ask them what their intentions are and provide information they find useful while on the island, as well as providing a few ground rules during their stay. The landing fee includes the use of our facilities, including restrooms, and lighthouse tours (as long as visitors are dry!) upon request if time and staff are available. The landing fee is viewed as a much-appreciated donation to help preserve and restore the lighthouse. Bottom line is, we welcome all comers to visit our lighthouse and grounds; you will never be turned away." Please be aware that unless Norwalk Seaport Association (NSA) staff are present upon visitors' arrival, the island is considered "closed" anywhere above the high-tide mark. This rule is strictly enforced by US Fish & Wildlife officials. There is also private property immediately adjacent to the NSA property to the west—do not trespass.

Primary Launch: Calf Pasture Beach (town-owned). The southern beach, off Calf Pasture Beach Road, has a designated kayak/SUP launch area. Ask the gate attendant about parking once the boat is dropped off. During the summer season the nonresident parking fee is $25/car on weekdays before 5 p.m., $30/car on weekends before 5 p.m., and $10 after 5 p.m. Passes are available at the

Passing ruins in the Norwalk Islands. **PHOTO DAVID FASULO**

beach. Directions: GPS Calf Pasture Beach Road (I-95 to exit 16). Follow to the end to the park entrance.

Secondary Launches: Saugatuck River State Boat Ramp (Westport). This is a free public launch, but make sure to carpool and keep the ramp clear when launching. The current and low water can make the return back to the launch a bit strenuous. Directions: GPS Elaine Road, Westport. You will be heading south on Route 136 (South Compo Road). Go under I-95 and make a quick right onto Elaine Road, then continue to the launch.

Rowayton Community Beach. This is a small launch on the Five Mile River. The parking is very limited and the launch is best used as a landing destination from Calf Pasture. Boat traffic can be heavy if approaching from Norwalk Harbor. Directions: GPS 62 Rowayton Avenue (across from Cook Street).

Veterans Park in Norwalk is an area to keep an eye on, as renovations may include cartop boat access. Off season, November through April, Compo Beach in Westport is a possibility as well. In season, Compo Beach is a great launch, but expensive for nonresidents (see Westport section).

Cruising Paddler

For a nice tour, launch from Calf Pasture Beach and head to the northeast side of Betts Island (1 mile). Continue around the east side of Grassy Island and past the south side of Chimon Island (2 miles total). Cross the sandbar/Crow Island (short carry, or go around Copps Island and add a little more distance). Head to Shea Island and take a break on the beach (2.8 miles total). Continue along the island chain to Sheffield Island and around the point (can be rough) to an optional stop/tour at the Sheffield Lighthouse ($5 donation; 4.6 miles total). Continue along the island past the north side of Shea Island to Chimon Island (possible rest stop; 6.8 miles total). Head past Betts Island and back to the launch (8 miles total).

Extras: You add mileage (but some open water) by landing on Cockenoe Island (Westport), which has a great beach to land on in the harbor. If you prefer to stay along the coast, to the east (1.4 miles from the Calf Pasture launch) is the entrance to the Bermuda Lagoon. The lagoon offers a sheltered excursion. To the west you can paddle about 4.5 miles up into the Five Mile River and stop for a walk or lunch in Rowayton, but boat traffic can be heavy the entire trip.

Distance Paddler

The Norwalk Islands (including Cockenoe Island in Westport) make for one of the best distance paddles in Connecticut—especially off-season if you have the proper equipment. From the Saugatuck River State Boat Launch (Calf Pasture Beach can shorten the distance), head to the landing area on Cockenoe Island for a stretch (3 miles); leave the harbor and paddle between Grassy and Goose Island to Chimon Island (6.5 miles total). From here either head out around Copps Island or carry boats across the small sandbar of Crow Island. Take a lunch break on the southeast corner of Shea Island (7.3 miles total). Head down the south side of Sheffield Island to the southwest point (9.1 miles total) and continue up the north side of Sheffield and Shea Islands. Paddle to Betts Island, then continue north to Calf Pasture Island (12.5 miles total). Head past Sprite Island to the mouth of the Saugatuck River (14 miles total), then upriver to the launch (about 16.2 miles total). Ebb tide, low water, and north wind can make the return upriver a slog. This circuit out of Calf Pasture Beach is about 12.5 miles total.

Rough Water Paddler

The southwest point of Sheffield Island will kick up at times, as will Cockenoe Reef (northeast section of Cockenoe Island).

SUP Friendly

If the conditions are right and you have the proper equipment, Chimon Island (1.26 miles one way from the Calf Pasture Beach launch) is within reason. Otherwise, a nice

Claudine Burns, paddling a Greenland-style kayak, passing Sheffield Lighthouse. **PHOTO DAVID FASULO**

loop consists of heading east to Sprite Island (1 mile), paddling around the island, and returning to the launch—a 2.6-mile round-trip. A safer island expedition is heading east, around Calf Pasture Island, and back—a 1.5-mile round-trip from the launch.

Something Fishy

According to "Norwalk Fishing Information," by Tom Schlichter, on the New England Boating website (www.newenglandboating.com), "Pecks Ledge, just north of Goose Island, is one of the most reliable spots for connecting with fluke in the 2- to 4-pound class. Fish here on the incoming water and use large squid strips for bait. Also worth investigating is the 25-foot-deep hole, located just north of Pecks Light." The article advises that blackfish can be found along the rocks off Norwalk Harbor and along the islands when in season, and Cockenoe Reef can be productive in the spring and fall. The article also advises that Norwalk Harbor, and the mouth of the harbor near Peach and Calf Pasture Islands, can be productive for schoolie bass and bluefish. The eastern and western ends of the island chain, Sheffield and Cockenoe, are productive for a variety of fish.

While overridden with the ubiquitous skate, whose wings are an absolute delicacy worth trying, the waters of Sheffield Harbor also hold enormous fluke during the

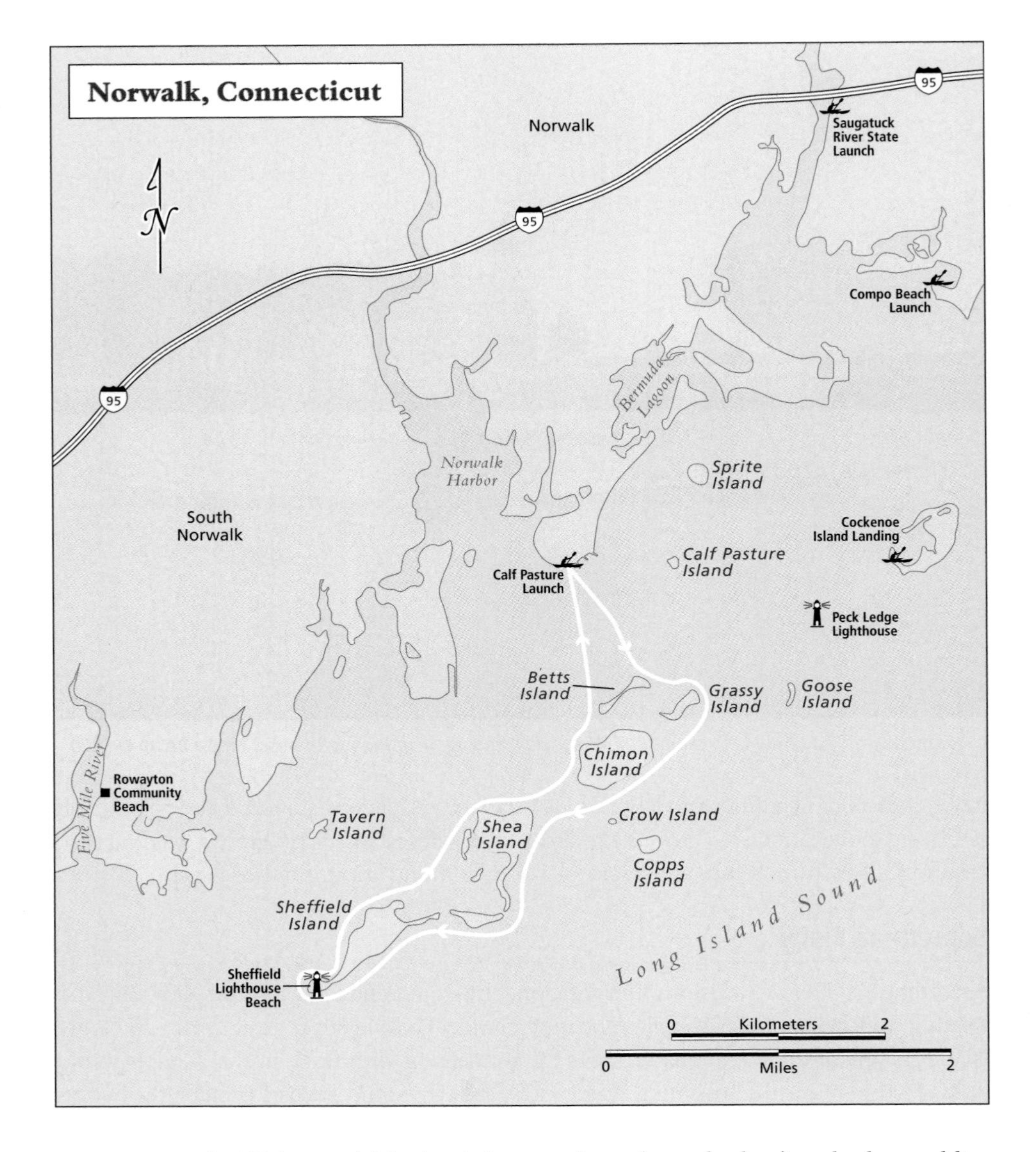

summer months. Fish a variable-depth bottom (i.e., channel edges) and where eddies and currents may leave the ocean's surface a bit rippled. This variable bottom is usually passed over by the crowds, while holding fluke use the distinct bottom changes to ambush prey. This same bottom can also be utilized in the pursuit of striped bass during the spring migration and fall run.

Westport, CT

The coastline along Sherwood Island beach, and east to Fairfield, is a pleasant wide-open beachscape to enjoy while cruising along the Connecticut shore. The most interesting, for the paddler prepared to venture away from the Westport coastline, is the 28-acre Cockenoe Island. According to the Westport Historical Society (www.westporthistory.org), "In 1967, the United Illuminating Company wanted to build a nuclear plant perceived as a clean and inexpensive source of energy. Opposition to the plan was swift and the town preserved the natural beauty of the island. *Life* magazine heralded Westport's acquisition of Cockenoe as one of the most significant conservation victories in the nation."

From the Saugatuck River State Boat Launch (free), Cockenoe Island harbor/beach is 3 miles one way. From Sherwood Island State Park, Cockenoe Island is 3.5 miles, and from the Compo Beach launch, 1.6 miles. Camping is allowed on Cockenoe Island; see the town website (www.westport.gov), under the Conservation Department.

Suzanne Timerman, Nancy Breakstone, and Val Rahmanl touring Compo Beach. **PHOTO DAVID FASULO**

Primary Launches: Saugatuck River State Boat Launch. This is a free public launch, but carpool and keep the ramp clear when launching. The current and low water can make the return back to the launch a bit strenuous. Directions: GPS Elaine Road, Westport. You will be heading south on Route 136 (South Compo Road). Go under I-95 and make a quick right onto Elaine Road, then continue to the launch.

Sherwood Island State Park. This is a beautiful state park, with a cartop boat launch on the east side of East Beach (southeast corner of parking lot, beyond the nature center). The fees are: $13 weekends, $9 weekdays, $6 after 4 p.m. Directions: From I-95, take exit 18. From Route 1, take the Sherwood Island Connector into the park.

Secondary Launch: Compo Beach. This is a well-located town-owned beach that has a nice cartop boat launch area, but fees for nonresidents during the summer season can be prohibitive. A pass is required to enter the park May 1 to October 1. For non-residents admission fees are $30 for weekdays and $50 for weekends and holidays. To launch a kayak or SUP, along with a day pass,

Carolyn Zeiss and Ron Gautreau exploring Sherwood Point early in the season. **PHOTO DAVID FASULO**

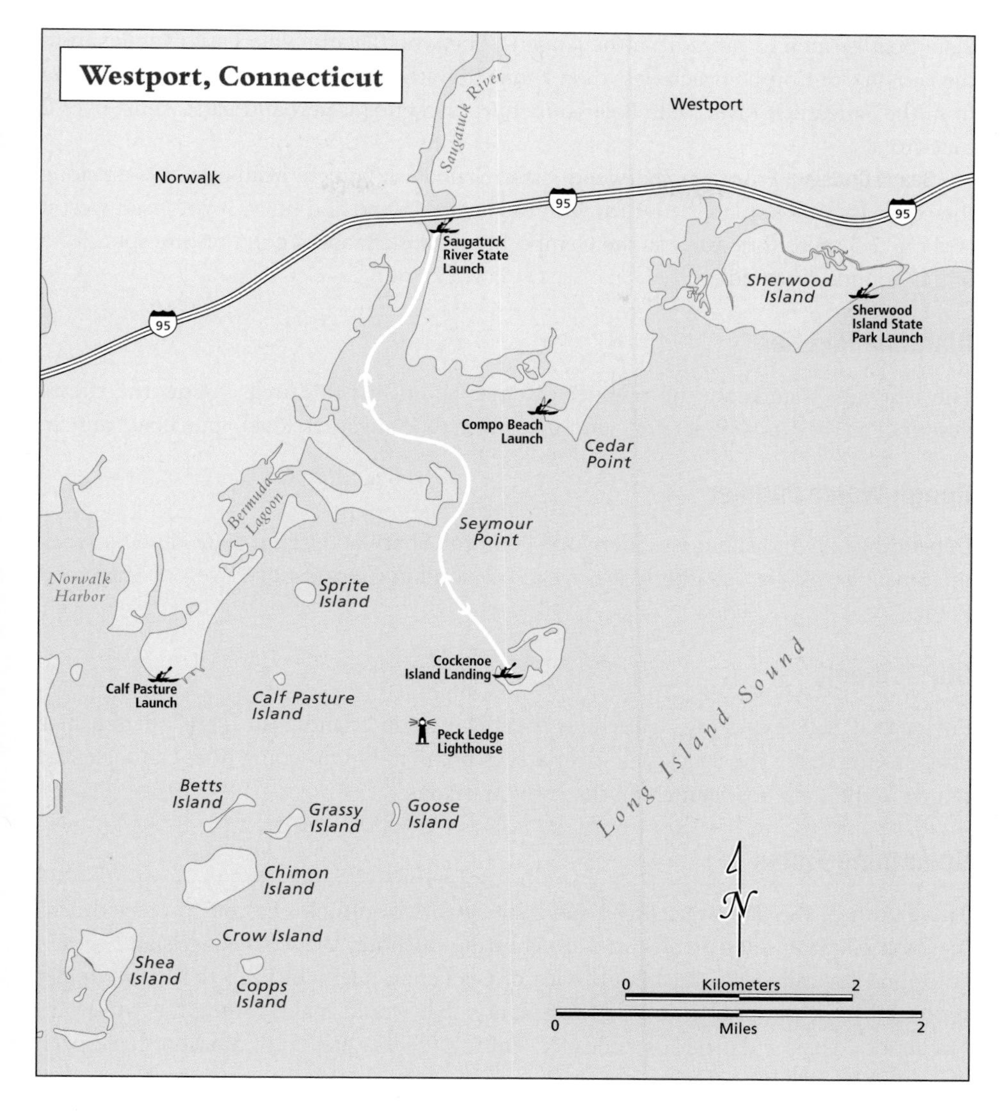

a launch permit is required. The cost for a launch permit is $10/day for residents and nonresidents. Directions: GPS Compo Road South, Westport. Turn right onto Compo Beach Road. The launch is located at the northwest end of the park at a small boat ramp.

Cruising Paddler

From the Norwalk side of the Saugatuck River (Seymour Point), the crossing to Cockenoe Island is 1 mile (one way). This point can be reached from the Saugatuck River

State Boat Launch (2 miles from the launch); Sherwood Island State Park (3 miles from the launch); or Compo Beach (less than 1 mile from the launch). For example, launching from the Saugatuck River State Boat Launch to Cockenoe Island and back is just over 6 miles total.

Beach Cruising: From the Sherwood Island State Park launch, head east or west along the coast. It's best to plan the return with the favor of wind and tides. If you head west it is about 2.5 miles (one way) to the Compo Beach launch, and a good resting spot, for a 5 mile round-trip paddle.

Distance Paddler

The Norwalk Islands are the premier distance circuit for this area. Follow the circuit described in the Norwalk section, launching from the Saugatuck River State Boat Launch.

Rough Water Paddler

Depending on wind and tides, Sherwood Point (off Sherwood Island State Park) can kick up. Small waves, on a southerly wind, can be found in Compo Cove (west of Sherwood Point).

SUP Friendly

For coastal SUP exploring, launching from Sherwood Island State Park offers a nice cruise to the west. The Saugatuck River area is popular, but outgoing tides can make the return to the state boat launch on the river strenuous.

Something Fishy

The mouth of the Saugatuck River (and the small island/rock pile) has protected fishing (watch current and wind), and if venturing offshore, the Cockenoe Island area is an option for calm days. Fishing the lee of Cockenoe Reef will keep the kayak angler protected from the prevalent southwest winds that would make fishing the windward Cockenoe Shoals a dangerous endeavor. During the late fall, false albacore have been known to be caught in these waters.

Fairfield, CT

The Fairfield area, especially late in the day, offers pleasant touring along the mile-long beachfront. Penfield Reef helps protect this area and is therefore great for SUPs, and it is also a focal point for kayak anglers. If heading east from Ash Creek, Fayerweather Island is about a mile crossing (Black Rock Harbor), and the beach extends for several miles. For the nonresident, the Ash Creek launch is best. However, great care must be taken when navigating the narrow channel due to current and boat traffic.

Primary Launch: Ash Creek Open Space. This is a very nice launch site for this part of Connecticut. According to correspondence with the town, "The parking is free, but is limited to 30 spaces. This area is accessed via the Turney Road entrance to the South Benson Marina. Inform the security guards you are launching at Ash Creek. Once you've launched, please be very careful crossing the channel entrance to the South Benson basin, as the current is swift and on weekends and holidays the boat traffic is substantial. It's a narrow channel and the bigger boats can't steer away from smaller craft. The big boat launch ramps are off-limits to SUPs and kayaks." The Ash Creek kayak/SUP launch is at the southeast corner of the parking area. It is a bit muddy at low tide, but

The Ash Creek public launch provides free access for nonresidents, but be careful negotiating boat traffic in the narrow channel. **PHOTO DAVID FASULO**

is a good launch. There is a sandy beach northeast of the narrowest side of the channel. Hug this shore (or get out of your watercraft) if boat traffic is heavy.

Directions: GPS Turney Road. Take Turney Road southeast to the marina. Turn left on the access road (sign indicating ASH CREEK OPEN SPACE parking) to the parking area. There is a sign marking the Ash Creek Public Access Canoe Launch.

Secondary Launch: The primary launch for Fairfield residents is the town-owned Jennings Beach. Jennings Beach is free and open to the public, but a beach sticker is required Memorial Day weekend through Labor Day. The kayak and SUP launch area is at the north end of the beach; the daily fee for nonresidents is $150/year or $50/day, purchased at the town Parks and Recreation Department. Directions: GPS 880 South Benson Rd.

Cruising Paddler

From Ash Creek, cruise eastward across Black Rock Harbor to Fayerweather Island (1 mile). Continue along the Seaside Park beach to the Bridgeport Harbor breakwater (3.5 miles total). Carefully cross to the other breakwater (commercial boat traffic) to a stop at Pleasure Beach Park (4.3 miles total). If landing at Pleasure Beach, avoid the swimming area. Round-trip 8.6 miles.

Distance Paddler

The coastline is mostly devoid of islands if heading east or west. A longer trip depends on wind and tides (as always), but westerly to Sherwood Island State Park in Westport is a nice run (7 miles one way), with the only "obstacle" being Penfield Reef.

Rough Water Paddler

Outer Penfield Reef, just over a mile from the launch, has potential for rough water play depending on tide and wind.

SUP Friendly

From Jennings Beach, cruise southwest along the Fairfield beachfront to Penfield Reef (1.15 miles one way), and return the same route.

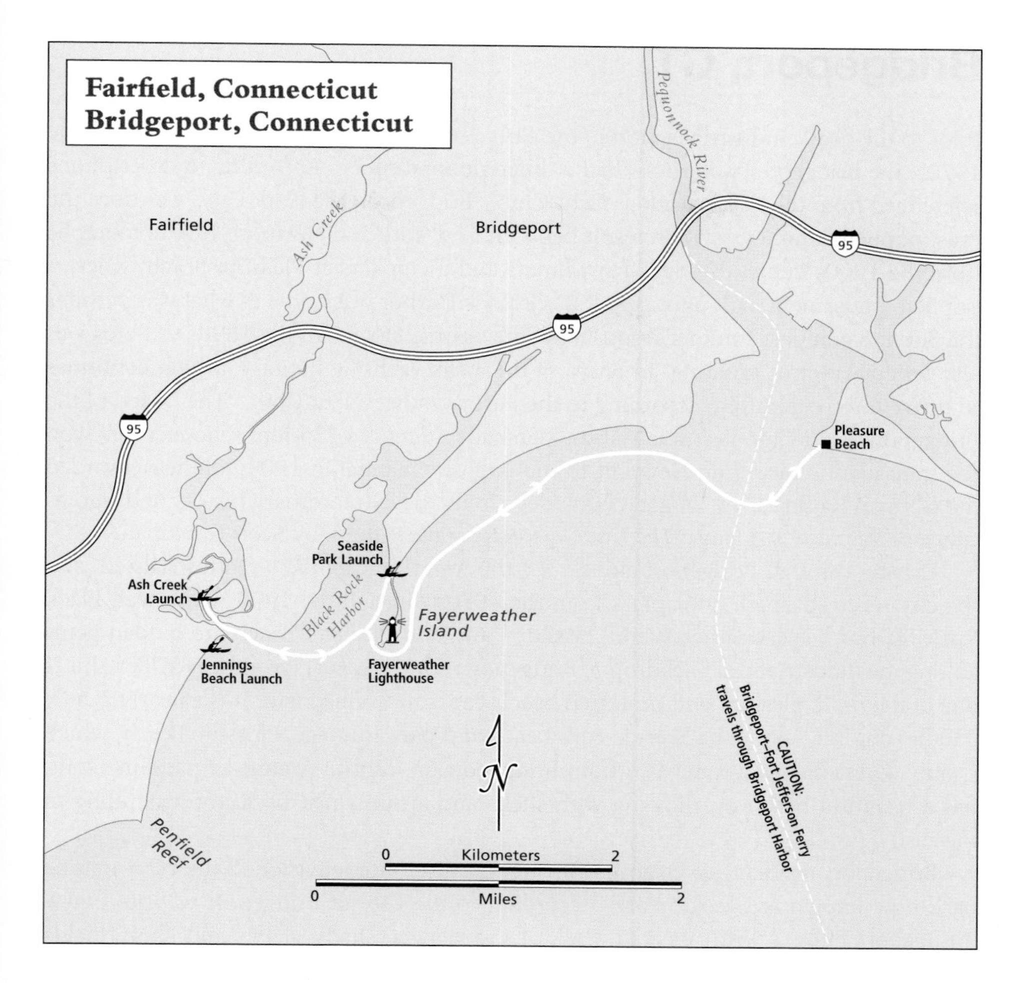

Something Fishy

While Fairfield lacks some of the more-abundant bottom structure afforded to anglers to the west and east, a more concentrated and variable catch can be found along Penfield Reef. The reef is a popular area for a variety of fish from large stripers to porgies (scups). When drifting at the reef, extended drifts that take you into deeper waters to the northeast should not be ignored, as they may present a depth where you will find the majority of your catches. This method of zeroing in on a productive depth is as important as finding an effective-color jig. Cruising along the beachfront can also be productive for those who want to troll for longer distances with a tube and worm rig to find a hump or hollow holding a hungry striped bass.

Bridgeport, CT

Prior to the heavy industrialization in the early 1900s, and the deindustrialization in the 1970s, the Bridgeport waterfront had a different appearance. According to descriptions referenced from the Fayerweather Yacht Club, "Bridgeport, the 'Park City,' was once the most popular summer vacation resort between New York and Newport, RI. Photographs from the 1900s depict throngs of swimmers and picnickers at Pleasure Beach, where a popular amusement park once stood. Black Rock Harbor was home to what was perhaps the Sound's grandest summer resort hotel, the George Hotel." In the 1890s this area was also an epicenter of yachting. In terms of the area's yachting heritage, which continues to thrive into present day, according to the Fayerweather Yacht Club, "The queen of the Bridgeport Yacht Club fleet was Wilson Marshall's *Atlantic*, a 185-foot schooner that won the transatlantic race from Newport to the English Channel in 1904, and was awarded the German Kaiser's Cup." A great book describing the extraordinary history and significance of this race is *Atlantic: The Last Great Race of the Princes*, by Scott Cookman.

Driving through Bridgeport along I-95, the waterfront looks too industrialized, and the city received much poor press from the 1970s through the 1990s. However, Black Rock Harbor, Fayerweather Island, Seaside Park, and Pleasure Beach are hidden gems among the industrialized backdrop of Bridgeport. For the casual kayaker or SUPer, this is one of the more pleasant and protected beachscapes in Connecticut. It is a nearly 2-mile paddle, one way, along the Seaside Park beach and park frontage. Pleasure Beach, which is only accessible via a water taxi from Bridgeport on Central Avenue or paddling craft, has a beautiful beach overflowing with shells and an untamed backdrop extending to the east.

Bridgeport resident, the well-known P.T. Barnum, first envisioned the rural marine park now known as Seaside Park. According to the City of Bridgeport website (www.bridgeportct.gov), "With its 325 acres of lush lawns, shady glades and sports fields rolling toward Long Island Sound, Seaside Park is a park without peer on the Eastern Seaboard. Visitors are delighted by the beaches, surf and sunshine along three miles of sparkling coastline. The park was laid out just after the Civil War by Calvert Vaux and Frederick Law Olmsted, whose other efforts include Manhattan's Central Park and Prospect Park in Brooklyn. Their 19th-century landscapes have proved timeless as they entice each new generation of park-goers."

Primary Launch: Seaside Park. This is a city-owned park, and parking fees are in effect Memorial Day through Labor Day ($20/day for nonresidents). The typical launch is at the far end (west) of the beach, next to the harbor side of the breakwater. Directions: I-95 to exit 27, GPS Barnum Boulevard. Continue to the far west end of the park to the launch. The beach launch is on the south end of the parking area, and there's a nice ramp launch on the north end.

While it has not served as an aid to navigation since 1932, the picturesque Fayerweather Island Lighthouse is thought to be America's oldest cut brownstone lighthouse. Ron Gautreau passes Fayerweather Island. **PHOTO DAVID FASULO**

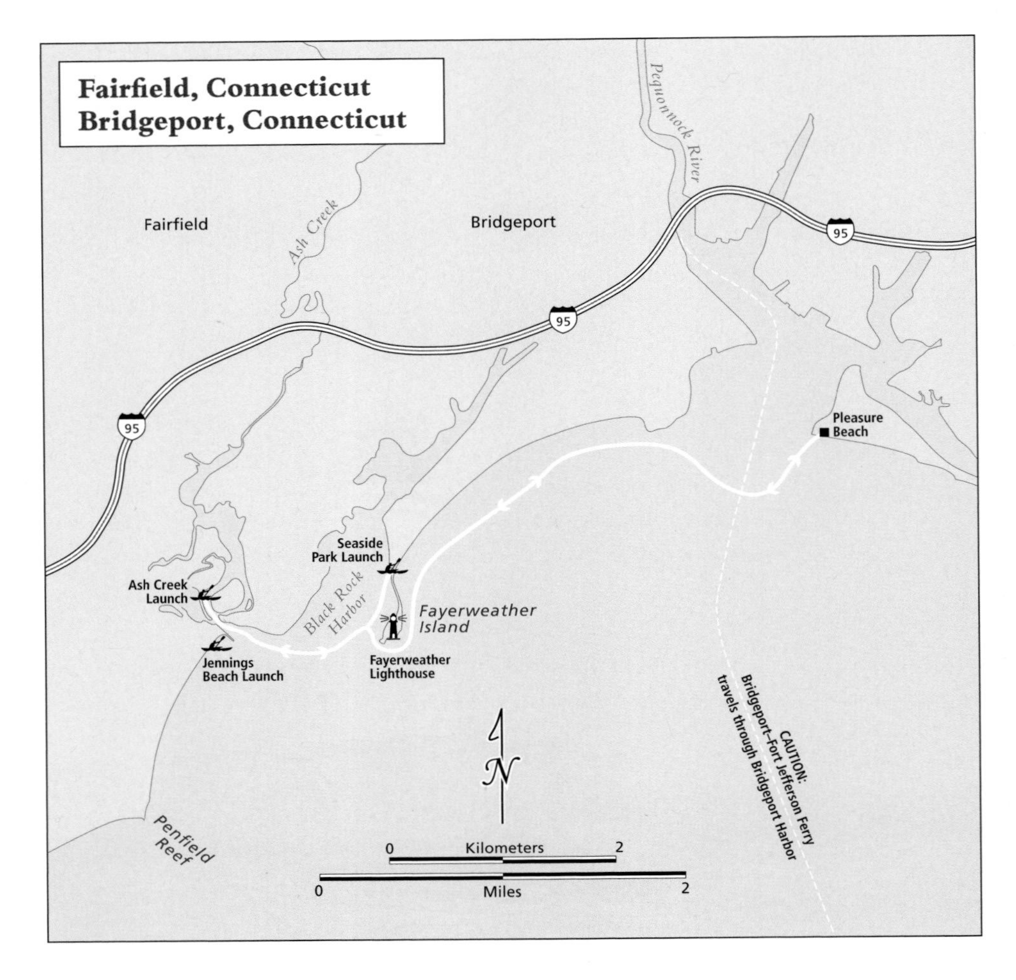

Secondary Launch: Ash Creek Open Space (Fairfield). This is a free launch, and only one mile from Fayerweather Island and 4.3 miles from Pleasure Beach Park. Directions: GPS Turney Road (Fairfield). Take Turney Road southeast to the marina. Turn left on the access road (sign indicating ASH CREEK OPEN SPACE parking) to the parking area. There is a sign marking the Ash Creek Public Access Canoe Launch.

Landing Area: Pleasure Beach. According to correspondence with the town, "You can land a kayak at Pleasure Beach but it has to be at the beach access area (southern end, away from swimmers). You cannot land near the boating docks. The water taxis are for passengers and small items only, so kayak/

paddleboards are not allowed on the boat. There is no fee for access via the water taxi for residents or nonresidents."

Cruising Paddler

From the Seaside Park launch, head out of Black Rock Harbor to Fayerweather Point (just under 1 mile). Continue east along the Seaside Park beach to the Bridgeport Harbor breakwater (3 miles total). Carefully cross to the other breakwater (commercial boat traffic) to a stop on Pleasure Beach Park (3.8 miles total). If landing at Pleasure Beach, avoid the swimming area. Round-trip 7.6 miles.

Distance Paddler

From the launch, head south around Fayerweather Island and then east along Seaside Park. Cross the Bridgeport Harbor entrance (be careful of the ferry and boat traffic) and continue along the beaches and breakwaters of Long Beach (see Stratford Map) to a break on the east end of the beach (5.5 miles one way). Return along the coast (11 miles total).

Rough Water Paddler

This is a generally protected area. Rough water potential is at the end of Penfield Reef (Fairfield), about 1.5 miles south/southwest of Fayerweather Island.

SUP Friendly

Cruising the long beach is a nice journey, and a circuit around Fayerweather Point (if the southern point is not rough) is a good circumnavigation (1.8 miles total).

Something Fishy

The mouth of Black Rock Harbor and Fayerweather Point can be productive. Keep an eye on the telltale birds working the area. Kayak anglers should take note of the dangerous wave run-ups that occur from large vessels on the flats bordering the navigational channel and jetties.

Stratford, CT

Long Beach, the primary coastline in Stratford, is distinctive in that it has the feel of a beach you would encounter south of New England. According to the town website, "Long Beach, approximately 1.5 miles in length, is Stratford's coastal barrier beach lying between the waters of Long Island Sound and the Lewis Gut. The middle sections of Long Beach are maintained as shorebird nesting areas. These areas are considered to be some of the best nesting habitats in the state for piping plovers and least terns."

Long Beach has a good access point and is perfect for the beginner coastal cruiser or SUPer that wants to put on some distance along a safe coastline. Short Beach is well protected, but a bit shallow at low tide. Locals report good surfing (probably good for SUPs), but my guess is you are surfing boat wakes—which can be fun. The Birdseye Street launch provides good access to the Housatonic River (watch for strong current), as well as a interesting circuit through the Charles Wheeler Wildlife Management Area.

Primary Launches: Long Beach Park. According to the town of Stratford website, "The beach is easily reached by car (parking permit required from May 31st until Labor Day), and is located at the end of Oak Bluff Road in the Lordship section of Stratford. Long Beach is considered an 'unimproved' beach; that is, there are no food concessions or permanent restroom facilities. The eastern end of Long Beach is designated as a public beach area and is used for bathing, sailboarding, and fishing. Nonresident fee is $20 per day, purchased at gate. Launch on either side of the swimming area." Directions: GPS Oak Bluff Avenue. The parking and access is at the foot of Oak Bluff Avenue.

Short Beach. This is a town beach located adjacent to the mouth of the Housatonic River. Short Beach fees for nonresidents are $20/day or $150 for the season. Kayaks and SUPs can launch at the southern end of Short Beach, but not in the designated swimming area. Directions: GPS Dorne Drive and follow it to the end.

Birdseye Street Boat Launch. This is a free launch on the Housatonic River. However, the current can be strong in this area and boat traffic heavy. Plan for the tides accordingly if accessing Long Island Sound. Directions: GPS Birdseye Street. Follow Birdseye Street to the end, where the launch is located. There is a fee for trailered boats, but cartop boats can park north of the trailer parking near the pier. The author has launched a kayak without a fee, but that may change over time.

Stratford Point. **PHOTO DAVID FASULO**

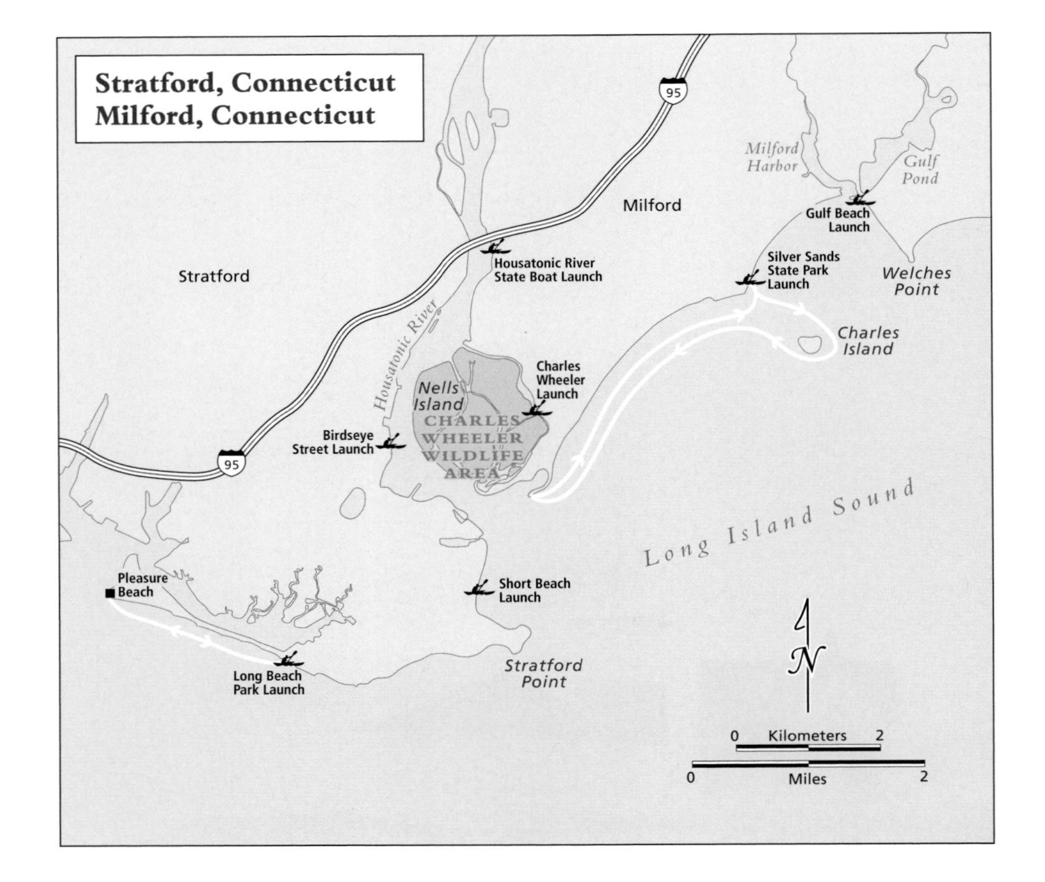

Cruising Paddler

Long Beach/Pleasure Beach tour. A nice stretch of beach to cruise. From the Long Beach launch, head west along the beach to Pleasure Beach. Take a break, and then return to the launch (4 miles total).

Charles Wheeler Wildlife Management Area. From the Birdseye Street launch, head north up the Housatonic River about 1.13 miles to the second entrance on the right. Paddle downriver to the small boat launch in Milford on the left (2.1 miles). Just past the launch, head right (southwest) and make your way through the disconnected waterways (best at higher tides) past Milford Point (3.03 miles total). Head into the Housatonic River (3.2 miles total), then upriver back to the launch (4 miles total).

Distance Paddler

From the Birdseye Street launch, head down the Housatonic River and then southwest around Stratford Point to the Pleasure Beach breakwater (6.5 miles one way). You can shorten the route by stopping/turning around at the eastern end of Long Beach Park (5 miles one way).

Rough Water Paddler

If you head south from the Birdseye Street launch, there is potential play just south of the breakwater (2 miles) depending on conditions.

SUP Friendly

For the SUP, the best bet is to launch from Long Beach Park and cruise along the beautiful beach. Another option is Nells Island. From the Birdseye Street launch (exposed to current and boat wakes), on a rising tide, head upriver 1 mile and then take a right (south) at the opening around Nells Island. Head down the narrow waterway to the Housatonic (2 miles), then back upriver to the launch (2.4 miles total).

Something Fishy

The Housatonic presents some considerable currents (3–4 knots) that keep many kayak anglers from transiting the river in the pursuit of fish outside the mouth. The end of Stratford Point and the sandbar off Short Beach attract bluefish and stripers. The waters between the Devon Bridge (Route 1) and the I-95 bridge offer striped bass a large source of forage during most of the spring, early summer, and fall.

Milford, CT

The Milford coast is a relatively well-protected body of water, with the nearby Charles Island dominating the scenery. According to the Connecticut DEEP website, "The Island is connected to the mainland by a sand/gravel bar (tombolo) that is submerged at high tide. Captain Kidd is reputed to have buried his treasure on the island in 1699. The only remains on the island are of a Catholic retreat center from the 1920s–30s. The island's interior is closed May 1 through August 31 to protect heron and egret rookeries." The Milford coast has interesting coastal cruising for kayaks and SUPs, good launches, and productive fishing. As long as you pay attention to the wind (be careful of a strong offshore wind) and tide, Charles Island is a good destination with an "offshore" feel for the intermediate kayaker.

The breakwaters and points of land help to calm the seas and make this a nice area for SUPs and kayakers of moderate abilities. The area is also a good locale for kayak anglers in the early fall. Oyster farms just west of Charles Island are also of interest. The downside of this area is that the launches are primarily beach launches, but a couple sheltered options do exist. Care must be taken due to strong currents and boat traffic

The tombolo (sandbar) extending to Charles Island at low tide. **PHOTO DAVID FASULO**

in the Housatonic River, and especially the narrow entrance to Milford Harbor. Beach wheels, if kayaking alone, will help if launching or landing at low tide.

Primary Launches: The main launch site is Silver Sands State Park. As of 2017 there is no fee, but that may change due to a proposed renovation project. There is a kayak and SUP launch area at the east end of the beach. A little walking to the parking area is required after dropping off your boat; beach wheels are helpful if kayaking alone. Directions: I-95 to exit 35, GPS Silver Sands Parkway. Follow the parkway across Meadowside Road and continue to the parking area.

Housatonic River State Boat Launch. This launch provides free access to the Housatonic River. On a rising tide, north of the launch is a pleasant area to explore. There is a rest stop about 4.2 miles north on a small island, or 5.6 miles north on Wooster Island. Directions: GPS Naugatuck Avenue. The launch is under the I-95 bridge (***Note:*** The launch was recently renovated and scheduled to be reopened in 2017).

Charles Wheeler Wildlife Management Area. This is a free, protected, year-round launch area (if clear of snow) with access to the waterways through Nells Island. These waterways also provide protected access to the Housatonic River and an interesting one-hour-plus circumnavigation of Nells Island and surrounding waterways. Directions: GPS Milford Point Road. Turn right onto Court Street and follow it to the end.

Secondary Launches: Gulf Beach. A decent launch area. During the season, May 15–September 30, there is a nonresident fee of $5 per day. The far northern end has protected access to Milford Harbor next to the bridge, and the southern end has a rocky/sand launch (depending on the tide). Directions: GPS Gulf Street and follow it to the intersection with Old Field Lane (just south of Milford Harbor).

Milford Public Library. A protected launch from concrete ramps, but there can be a lot of boat traffic in Milford Harbor and the narrow area leaving the harbor has strong currents. A permit is required. Daily permits are $15 for residents and $25 for nonresidents and can be purchased from the ramp attendant. Yearly permits are also available. Directions: GPS 57 New Haven Ave. Follow Shipyard Lane to a launch behind the tennis courts.

Cruising Paddler

Charles Island circumnavigation and beach tour. Charles Island, especially at low tide, is accessible to the cruising paddler. The low tide exposes the path leading to the island and offers more protection (depending on the wind direction). Even at high tide, when conditions permit, the island is less than a mile offshore (3,390 feet) from Silver Sands State Park. The island can be circumnavigated, but at low water the boat will need to be carried over the sand/gravel bar at some point. A nice circuit leaves from Silver Sands State Park and goes around Charles Island. Continue west to the beach just before the Housatonic River (4 miles), then back along the sandy coast to the launch (carry boat over sandbar at lower tides); 6.8 miles total.

Tina Prichard paddling along the Milford coast with Charles Island in the background. **PHOTO DAVID FASULO**

Nells Island waterways circumnavigation. In a sea kayak, without exploring or getting lost, this route takes about an hour. If exploring, or you get lost, or in adverse conditions, it will take longer. It is best to paddle this route towards the top of the tide, as it can get shallow in areas. From the launch head left, then take a quick right. Trend right at the first split, then make your way southwest to a beach and the Housatonic River (1 mile). Head upriver (1.5 miles total), then take a right into the waterway heading into Nells Island. Stay in the main waterway (trend left) to the Housatonic River (2.5 miles total). Head right (northeast) to another waterway marked by a no-wake sign. Follow this waterway back to the launch site (3.7 miles total). Your best bet is to use a picture from Google Maps (satellite view) or Bing Maps (bird's-eye view) to help navigate.

Distance Paddler

A good circuit heads east out of Silver Sands and explores the Milford Harbor entrance for rough water (1.1 miles). Cruise past Gulf Beach to Welches Point (2 miles total), then past the southern side of Charles Island (3.15 miles total) to a breakwater by a small island (at lower water 5.25 miles total) just off a beach near Milford Point. Continue to Milford Point (6 miles total) and investigate the northern (smaller) breakwater to the large breakwater (6.5 miles total), then make your way back along the coast to Silver Sands State Park (10 miles total). If the water is low, you will need to go around Charles Island again, or carry your boat (easy carry) over the sandbar connecting Charles Island to Silver Sands State Park.

Rough Water Paddler

Depending on conditions, the shallow areas extending from the beaches can provide interesting small surf. At times, just outside the channel leaving Milford Harbor, the water is very turbulent.

Practice area:

Just past the narrow entrance to Milford Harbor is a waterway leading to Gulf Pond (under the bridge). At ebb tides classic circular eddies appear between the breakwater and the water moving past. It's a good spot to practice boat-handling skills, but only if the area is unoccupied by anglers or powerboats.

SUP Friendly

The Nells Island waterway is fun to explore, but only at a rising tide to offset the current. The beauty of the Milford coast is that it is well protected, with a lot of shallow beaches to land if the wind is not cooperating. There is even small surf that is well suited for SUPs due to the shallows.

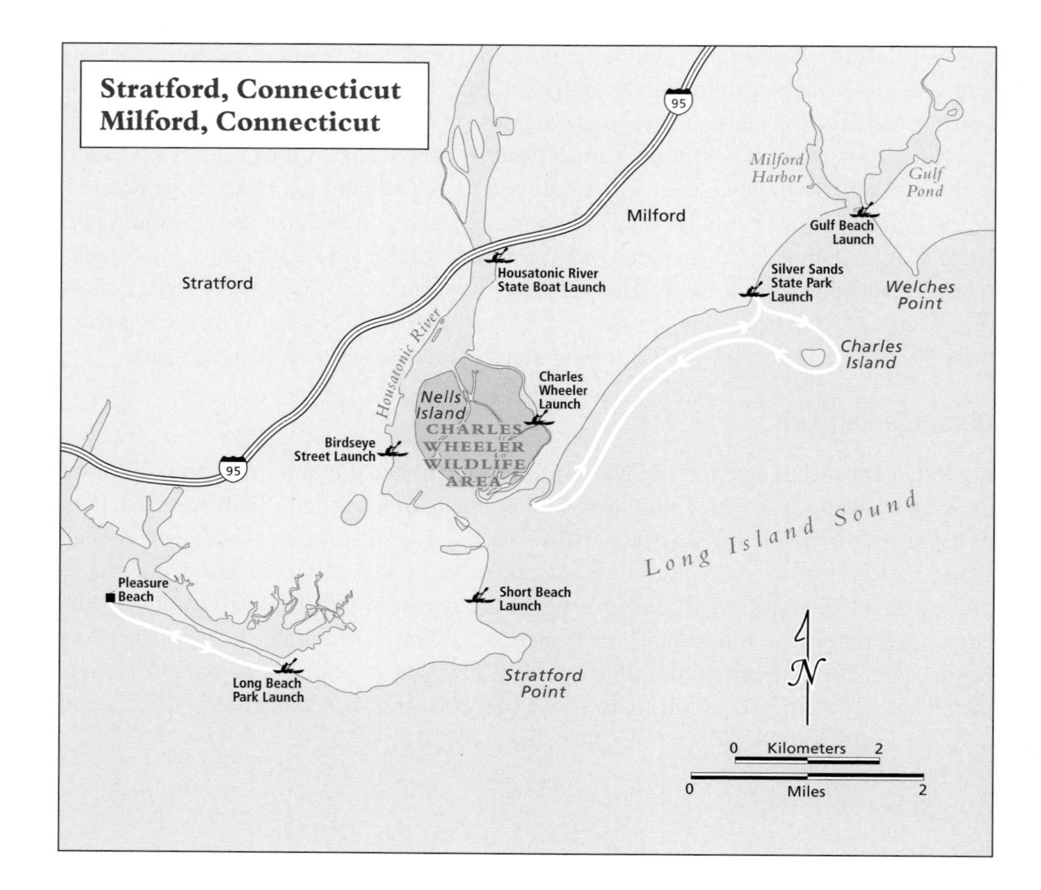

Something Fishy

The waters around Charles Island contain good fishing for several species; the tip of the island itself is best at higher tides when the rocks are submerged. Kayak anglers will find blues, stripers, and even false albacore abundant in the fall. The inner harbor of Milford also offers abundant striped bass fishing opportunities along the east shore where bait-fish congregate during the early summer and fall.

West Haven, CT

The coastline offers over 3 miles of beachfront, and breakwaters help protect the waters from large waves. Because of the protected nature, the West Haven coast is great for late-day SUP cruising. While access points are plentiful, parking for nonresidents is not. When there are parking spaces available, the Bradley Point beach is probably the best bet.

The West Haven shore is also well-known for birding. According to the Long Island Sound Study website (www.longislandsoundstudy.net), "Over 60 acres of barrier beach, tidal creek and marsh, and mudflats at Sandy Point and adjacent Morse Beach provide excellent habitat for water birds. These City of West Haven–owned properties provide some of the most important beach habitat in Connecticut for piping plovers (a federally endangered species), least tern, and common tern." The exceptionally beautiful black skimmer shorebird once bred at Sandy Point, but according to the Connecticut Audubon Society, are now only seen there occasionally.

A winter paddle along the Sandy Point Bird Sanctuary. **PHOTO DAVID FASULO**

Primary Launch: Bradley Point Park city beach. Since there is a short carry, bring beach wheels. The area is well protected and a good SUP launch. Daily parking fee is $10, $5 after 5 p.m. Parking can fill up quickly. Directions: GPS Captain Thomas Boulevard. The parking area is located between the intersection of Ivy Street and Kelsey Avenue.

Secondary Launches: Morse Park city beach: You will need to carry your boat across the street, and the launch area is rocky. Daily parking fee is $10, $5 after 5 p.m. Directions: GPS Beach Street and follow it until it crosses Morse Avenue.

South Street city beach. A good location on the western end of West Haven, but the parking lot is for residents only. Directions: GPS South Street and follow it to Ocean Avenue. Additional parking across from Linwood Avenue.

Dawson Avenue city beach. This is a nice beach launch, but the parking lot is for residents only. Directions: GPS Dawson Avenue and follow it to the intersection of Ocean Avenue.

City Boat Ramp. Quick access to Sandy Point, but parking for city residents only May through September. Directions: GPS April Street. The launch and parking is just to the right of April Street, where Monahan Place ends.

Cruising Paddler

From Bradley Point Park, head east along the coast to the end of the Sandy Point Sanctuary (2.2 miles). Continue along the shore until you reach City Point, New Haven, and the marina. Enter the marina to access a public beach to land on next to South Water Street (3.7 miles total). There are restaurants at the marina, or bring your own snacks. Return the way you came, avoiding commercial boat traffic (7.4 miles total).

Distance Paddler

While paddlers do cross the harbor and head over to Lighthouse Point, it is in the path of large commercial traffic and not advised. For a tour of the shore, much of it in Milford, head west along the shoreline to Silver Sands State Park (8.2 miles). Return along the coastline (16.4 miles total).

SUP Friendly

Bradley Point town beach is probably the best area for SUPs, as it is better protected and there is nice cruising along the beach and up to the Sandy Point Sanctuary.

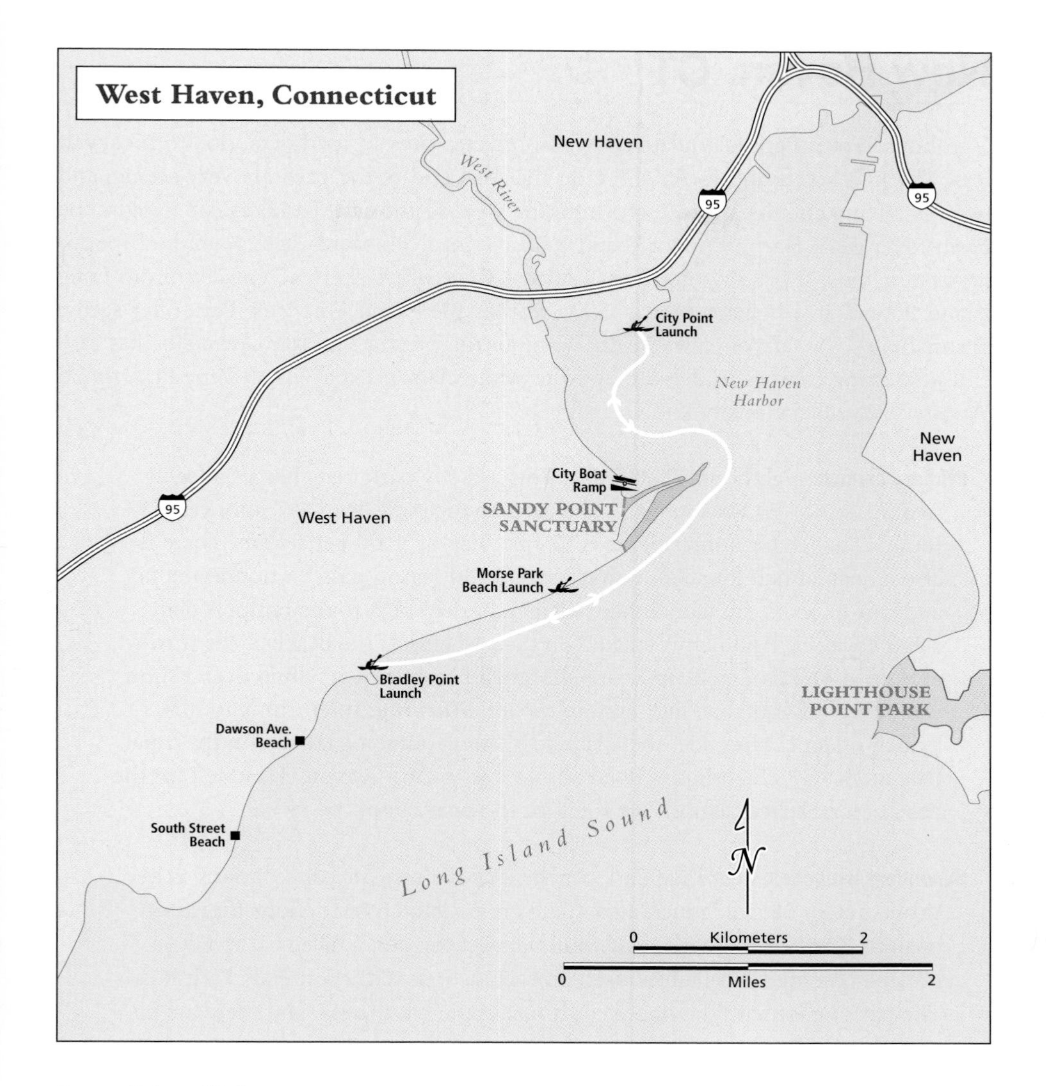

Something Fishy

The reef and rocks south of Bradley Point have structure for fish, as do the large breakwaters for New Haven Harbor. Looking for birds, as they mark blues and potentially false albacore, is also worth the time in the fall.

New Haven, CT

Lighthouse Point Park is a relatively well-protected area for paddlers, due to breakwaters. The lighthouse and rocky shore on the west end of the park are very scenic, and two interesting circuits are accessed from the area. To the east, paddlers can explore the Farm River (East Haven/Branford) and Kelsey Island (Branford), which are both popular destinations. If heading northwest, Morris Cove offers shelter (typically) from Long Island Sound. Just beyond Morris Cove, Forbes Bluffs and Fort Hale Park offer scenic destinations. The city of New Haven, home to the prestigious Yale University, has several interesting eateries to debrief, and the white clam pizza at Frank Pepe Pizzeria on Wooster Street is nationally known.

Primary Launch: Lighthouse Point Park. This is a city park that charges a fee in season, April 1 to November 1. The gates to the park open at 7 a.m. year-round. The fee for nonresidents is $20 per day or $100 per season. There is also a boat launch for small powerboats ($130 season pass for nonresidents), and cartop boats can launch here (daily park fee) next to the ramp. A dedicated kayak/SUP launch is located on the east side of the beach at the turnaround at Morris Creek. To access the small beach launch, climb over a short wall, drop off you boat, and park in the lot. ***Warning:*** If returning to this launch on an ebbing tide, there can be a strong outgoing current in the canal. Directions: GPS Lighthouse Road and follow to Park Avenue. Head left for the beach/Morris Creek launch, or right for the boat ramp.

Secondary Launches: Fort Hale Park beach. This is a nice area and parking is free. While not an official launch area, there are no launch restrictions for cartop boaters. The beach is a bit rocky but manageable, and a nice spot to take a break if coming from Lighthouse Point. Directions: GPS Fort Hale Park Road. The parking lot with the bocce court marks the beach area, and there are historical artifacts on the northern end of the park.

Dover Beach Park. This is a city park with on-street parking. The park has a ramp leading to the Quinnipiac River. While in an industrialized area, a mile north upriver leads to the Quinnipiac River Marsh Wildlife Area and extends for 3 miles north (be careful of current near the bridge). If heading south, the waters offer views of streetscapes. Directions: GPS Front Street. The park is at the intersection of Front Street and John Williamson Drive. When parking, pay attention to the street sweeping signs to avoid getting your car towed.

Lighthouse Point Park. **PHOTO DAVID FASULO**

Cruising Paddler

Lighthouse Park to Farm River and Kelsey Island. This is a pleasant coastal paddle with a very cool stop at Kelsey Island, as well as nice scenery along the Farm River. Leave the lighthouse canal (Morris Creek) and head east along the New Haven/East Haven coastline. After 2,000 feet you will pass Morgan Point (which can have large waves). Continue past beach homes and beaches to the wide Farm River entrance on the left (north). You will see Darrow Rocks to the east and Kelsey Island to the northeast (2.5 miles). You can take a break at the east end of the first beach/bay, staying waterward of the mean high-water line when landing (be respectful of the islanders). Circumnavigate Kelsey Island and return to the Lighthouse Park launch (6.5 miles round-trip).

Local kayaker Martin Torresquintero taking a break in January at Fort Hale Park beach. **PHOTO DAVID FASULO**

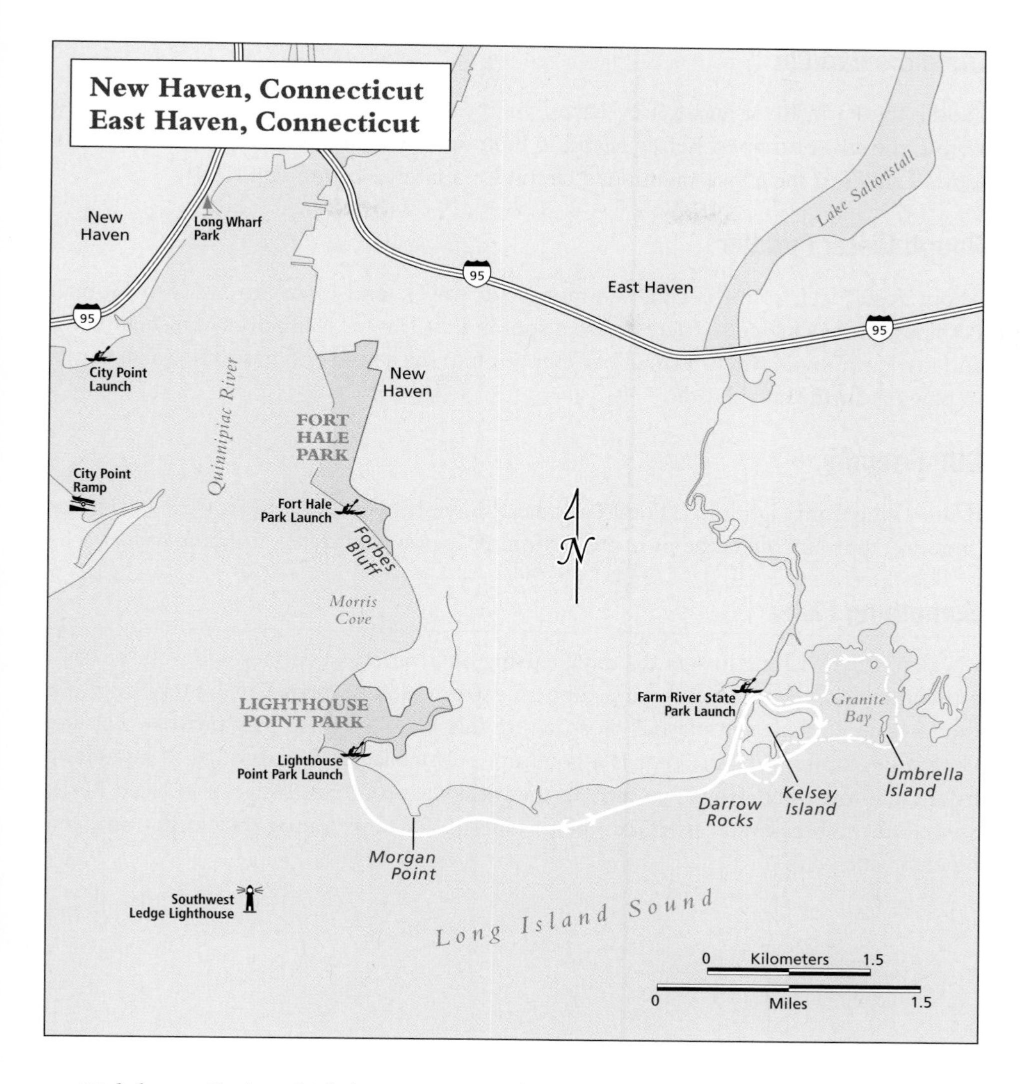

Lighthouse Park to Lighthouse Point and Fort Hale Park. This paddle is more protected and provides interesting scenery (Forbes Bluffs) as well as a unique point of interest (Fort Hale). Leave the lighthouse canal (Morris Creek) and head west along the park beach to the lighthouse (1,700 feet). Follow the coastline past the beach on the east side of Morris Cove (1.5 miles), then past the basalt crags of Forbes Bluffs (1.9 miles). Stop at the rocky beach at Fort Hale (2 miles one way). Return via the same route (a little over 4 miles round-trip).

Southwest Ledge Light. For those willing to go offshore a bit, from Lighthouse Park head south to the breakwater. Cruise along the breakwater to the end (1.2 miles one way) to check out the lighthouse.

Distance Paddler

Paddle the Farm River and Kelsey Island circuit in the "Cruising Paddler" section, but extend the adventure past Kelsey Island to Branford Cove, and then explore Granite Bay (adds 2 miles to the above-mentioned circuit for a 6 miles round-trip total).

Rough Water Paddler

About 2,000 feet from the canal entrance/exit, waves tend to set up between Morgan Point and the rocks/reefs. There is also a spot in East Haven, just before Mansfield Point and the Farm River, where a small bay empties into the sound and has some small waves to play on during an ebb tide.

SUP Friendly

If launching from Lighthouse Point Park, heading northwest into Morris Cove (1.5 miles one way) typically offers the most protection. Be aware of currents and boat wakes.

Something Fishy

Kayak anglers wishing to spend a day focusing on a variety of species will troll the eastern shore along East Haven with a tube and worm along Morris Cove. Stopping from time to time to drop soft plastics on structure that is holding fish may provoke a strike. Continuing on to Morgan Point is a good option for blackfish and scups. If launching from Lighthouse Park, the areas around the breakwater (Quixes Ledge, Old Head Reef), as well as the breakwater itself, can be productive for large tautog (blackfish), stripers, bluefish, and scup.

East Haven, CT

In terms of launching a cartop boat, the East Haven coastline is essentially inaccessible. However, with some prior planning, Farm River State Park in East Haven provides access from May 1 to November 1 to the Farm River outlet. This launch provides quick access to Kelsey Island, Granite Bay, and several beautiful seascapes. The Farm River outlet, where it meets Long Island Sound, is a great area for the recreational kayaker or SUPer.

The popular Kelsey Island area and nearby Granite Bay provide interesting scenery in a relatively protected setting. Kayak and SUP landing is common on Kelsey Island, waterward of the mean high-water line, but *be respectful* of the island residents and their property. Paddlers can also head up the Farm River, but when the river jogs left (west), care must be taken (and should be avoided by SUPs) due to the narrow causeway that produces strong current and exposed dangers at certain tides. As with any river area, keep an eye on the current. Tidal current (ebb and flow), combined with river current, can create fast-moving water at certain moon cycles and after heavy rains. On calm days, the beachfront along the East Haven coast can be a pleasurable cruise as well.

Taking a break at Farm River State Park, with Kelsey Island in the background. **PHOTO DAVID FASULO**

Primary Launch: Farm River State Park provides a protected beach launch to a very pleasant stretch of coastal waters. Historically, car-top access for the Farm River State Park was managed by Quinnipiac University. A key card was provided for car-top boaters to drive past the gate to access the launch site. However, as of January 2017 the contract with Quinnipiac University has been terminated. The DEEP is working on a plan to manage the site, and will communicate more information as they have it. Please visit the Connecticut Department of Energy & Environmental Protection website, Farm River State Park section, for the latest updates at www.ct.gov/deep.

Secondary Launches: Off-season, the primary launch is from Lighthouse Point Park in New Haven. Otherwise, the Branford River State Boat Launch is popular. To reach the north side of Kelsey Island, both launches require about a 3-mile paddle. The Branford River launch is better protected and free, but is crowded with boat traffic in the summer.

Launch Restrictions: The East Haven city beach (intersection of Coe Avenue and Cosey Beach Avenue) is open Memorial Day through Labor Day, and parking is free for residents and nonresidents. However, launching is not allowed on beach areas.

Cruising Paddler

A nice circuit is to leave the Farm River launch and head east, passing the northern end of Kelsey Island. Head north along the shore of Granite Bay to the Branford shoreline (1 mile). Paddle south down the coast and around Umbrella Island (1.76 miles), then west across the bay to Kelsey Island (2.2 miles total). Head west along the south shore of Kelsey Island to a break in a cove (just around the rocky point at the beach bordering the rocks). Continue around Darrow Rocks and back up the Farm River to the launch (3.5 miles total).

Distance Paddler

To add distance, and combine coastal beach cruising with a rocky coast, head out of Lighthouse Park in New Haven. Cruise east along the coast to the Farm River basin (2.3 miles), then up the river and east across the north side of Kelsey Island (3 miles total). Paddle along the coast of Granite Bay, then south to Umbrella Island (4.4 miles total). Cross the bay to a rest stop on the south shore of Kelsey Island (5.4 miles total). Head back west through Darrow Rocks and back to the launch (8.3 miles total).

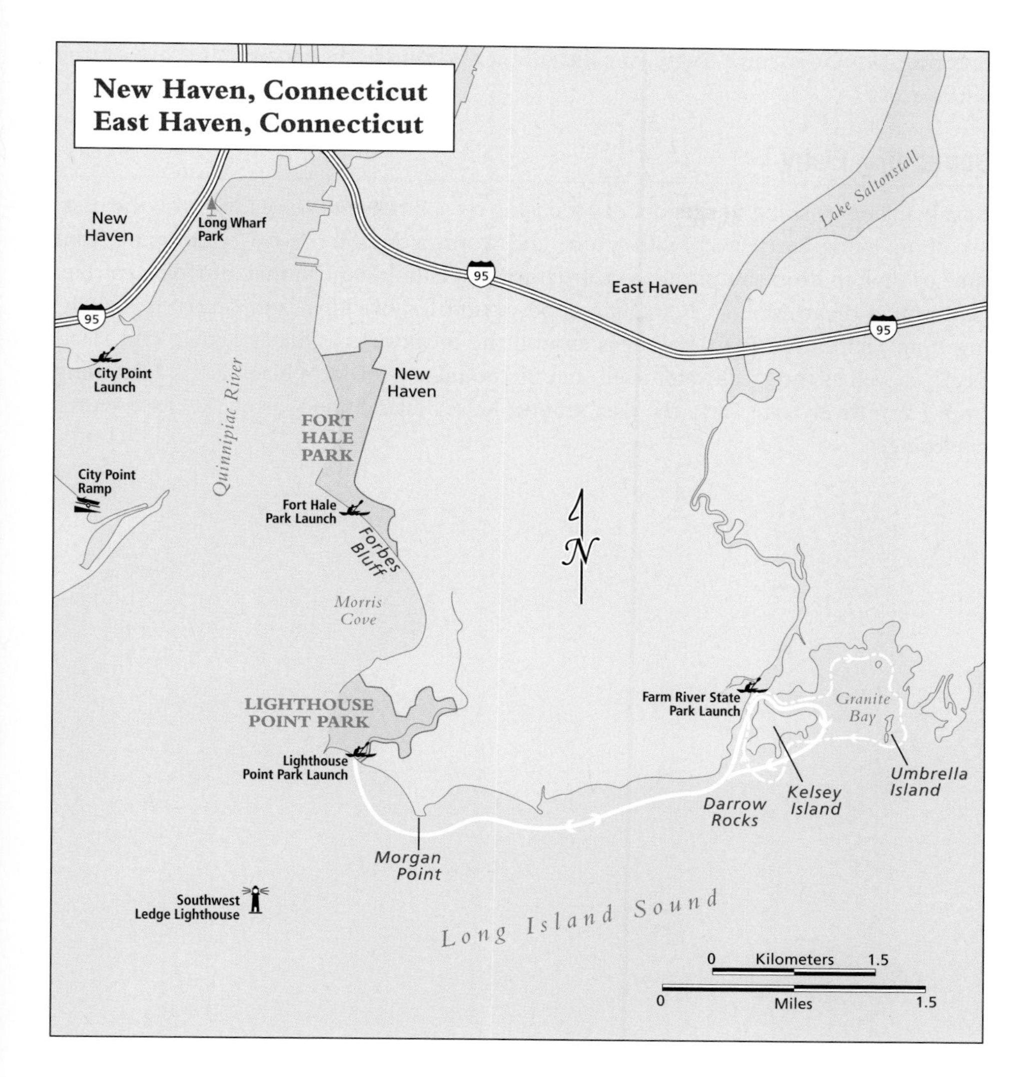

Rough Water Paddler

The south end of Darrow Rocks can produce waves during certain conditions.

SUP Friendly

Farm River Gut, located north of Kelsey Island, and the adjoining Granite Bay are very pleasant outings. Circumnavigating Kelsey Island is a 1.5-mile route, but if paddling a SUP, it should be done on a rising tide so as to not be swept by the current. Another nice circuit is up the Farm River to the East Haven Marsh Wildlife Area, just under 1 mile one way. Do not attempt to go over the submerged bridge that guards the cove on the left (west).

Something Fishy

Kayak anglers wishing to spend a day focusing on a variety of species will troll the eastern shore along East Haven with a tube and worm along Morris Cove. Stopping from time to time to drop soft plastics on structure that is holding fish may provoke a strike. Continuing on to Morgan Point is a good option for blackfish and scups. If launching from Lighthouse Park, the areas around the breakwater (Quixes Ledge, Old Head Reef), as well as the breakwater itself, can be productive for large blackfish. If launching from Farm River State Park, the area around Kelsey Island and Darrow Rocks is worth exploring.

Branford, CT

The entire Branford coast has many small cliffs, intriguing granite islands, and interesting bays to explore. The famed Thimble Islands, the pink and orange granite archipelago located relatively close to shore, are an immensely popular destination for sea kayakers. There are about twenty-five inhabited islands and several small protrusions. The closer islands, and rocky bays, can also be reached by SUPs on calm days. Legend has it that Captain Kidd sought refuge from pirate hunters and may have stashed some loot on some of the islands.

There are several interesting paddling circuits, but landing on Outer Island (see restrictions) is one of the most rewarding adventures; the shortest route is 1.75 miles from the Stony Creek Town Dock launch. Be forewarned that parking near the Stony Creek launch can be difficult in the summer.

Primary Launches: Stony Creek Town Dock. This is the most popular launch because it has quick access to the Thimble Islands. However, parking is a problem in the summer and on weekends. According to the Town of Branford website (www.branford-ct.gov), "Stony Creek Beach is located in the southeast section of town and is open to the general public. This beach is staffed with lifeguards Memorial Day through Labor Day daily during peak tides. Small boats, canoes and kayaks maybe launched from the boat launch located on the other side of Madera Park." There is short-term drop-off parking at the dock

Dale Geslien enjoying the distinctive scenery in the Thimble Islands. **PHOTO ERIK BAUMGARTNER**

While overshadowed by the Thimble Islands, Branford Harbor and Granite Bay offer unique scenery. Oliver Bloch exploring Granite Bay. **PHOTO DAVID FASULO**

Outer Island, Stewart B. McKinney National Wildlife Refuge, is a great destination when the conditions are favorable. **PHOTO DAVID FASULO**

and on-street parking south of the launch on Thimble Island Road. In the summer, historically, there is also parking across the street (small fee) behind a church, along with on-street parking past the launch on Thimble Island Road. Directions: GPS Thimble Island Road. The launch is near the split at Thimble Island Road and Island Point Road (across from Three Elms Road).

Branford River State Boat Launch. This is a good launch to access Branford Harbor. If continuing west, Granite Bay and Kelsey Island (7 miles round-trip) is a common destination, and in good conditions Outer Island is a 10-mile round-trip (with an open crossing). However, boat traffic can be heavy through the relatively narrow marina channel. Directions: GPS Goodsell Point Road. From the intersection with Harbor Street, follow Goodsell Point Road to the launch on the left.

Secondary Launches: Parker Park. This town-owned park has a very nice kayak/SUP launch into Lindsey Cove and is perfect for SUP cruising. However, parking is only permitted for Branford residents. Directions: GPS Parker Memorial Drive. Parker Memorial Drive is located in the park, just off of Harbor Street.

Guilford Town Dock. While more for the distance paddler, this launch is an option (along with other launches in Guilford) to reach the Thimble

Kate Powers meandering through the many rocks and ledges along the Thimble Islands. **PHOTO DAVID FASULO**

Islands. From the town dock, the Thimble Island chain is about 6 miles one way. Fees are $6/day for cartop boats and $20 for a season pass. Directions: Exit 58 off I-95. GPS Old Whitfield Street, Guilford. The Guilford Town Marina is at the end of Old Whitfield Street.

Primary Landing: Outer Island, Stewart B. McKinney National Wildlife Refuge. There is a designated beach in front of the pavilion for kayak/SUP landing, about 1.75 miles from the Stony Creek Town Dock. According to the Friends of Outer Island (www.friendsofouterisland.org), "Outer Island is open for visitation by individuals and families from the end of May until on or about September 25th. Reservations are not required. The island is open and staffed by Island Keepers on weekdays from 8 a.m. until sunset. On weekends and holidays, Visitor Services Volunteers from the Friends of Outer Island staff the island from 10 a.m. until 3 p.m. Extended hours may be offered depending on volunteer availability. The island may be closed at any time due to inclement weather. Pets are not permitted on the island." Check www.outerisland.org for up-to-date information on landing restrictions.

Could this be a marker for buried treasure? Legend has it Captain Kidd buried treasure throughout the Thimble Islands in the 17th century. This peculiarity can be found at low tide just off the northeastern end of Governor Island. **PHOTO RON GAUTREAU**

Outer Island. When conditions allow, this is a favorite destination. Be aware that if you choose to go around the island, the southern tip tends to have much rougher water. It is fun to just meander around the islands; the following is just one recommended circuit. From the Stony Creek Town Dock, head south to Governor Island (less than 1 mile); continue between the Crib Islands and between High Island and Pot Island (1.2 miles). Continue past Horse Island to the landing at Outer Island (1.7 miles total). After a break and a tour, head north past the east side of Horse Island and Exton's Reef Island, then paddle along the southeast side of Money Island and meander over to Bear Island (3 miles total). Paddle around Bear Island and between the Cut-in-Two Islands (3.8 miles total). Head back to the launch; just under 5 miles total.

Shell Beach. This route stays closer to shore and is better protected if the wind is up. Head east along the shore, then over to Bear Island (1.2 miles). Continue along the coast to a break on Shell Beach (2.6 miles one way). Return the same route, or explore a few islands on the return (5.2 miles total).

Granite Bay tour. Another common outing is to launch at the Branford River State Boat Launch or Farm River State Park Marina in East Haven (see East Haven) and explore

Julie and Jennifer exploring the Thimble Islands. **PHOTO DAVID FASULO**

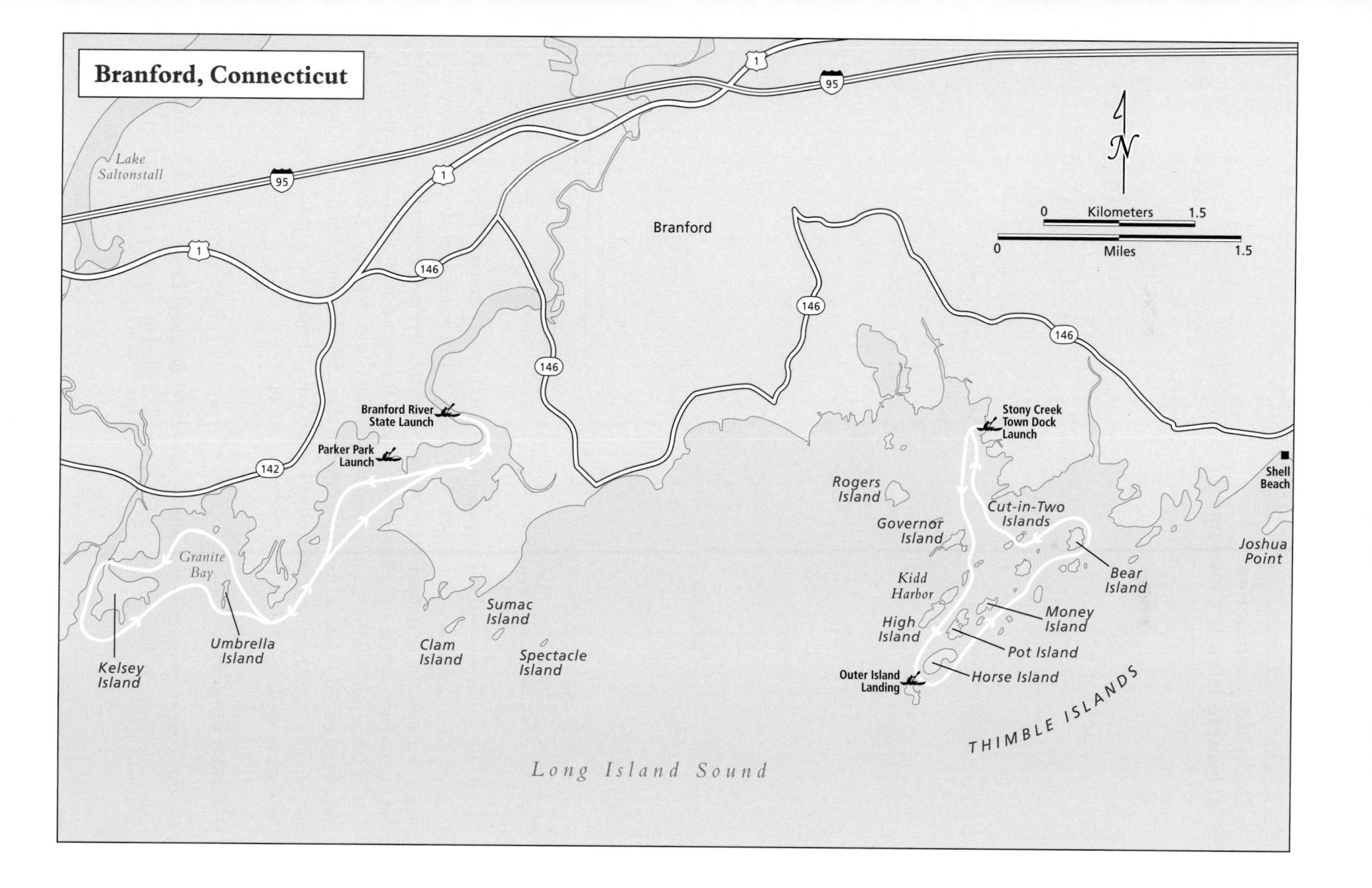
Branford, Connecticut
Lake Saltonstall
95
1
146
142
Branford
N
0
Kilometers
1.5
0
Miles
1.5
Branford River State Launch
Parker Park Launch
Granite Bay
Kelsey Island
Umbrella Island
Clam Island
Sumac Island
Spectacle Island
Long Island Sound
Stony Creek Town Dock Launch
Rogers Island
Governor Island
Kidd Harbor
High Island
Outer Island Landing
Cut-in-Two Islands
Bear Island
Money Island
Pot Island
Horse Island
THIMBLE ISLANDS
Shell Beach
Joshua Point

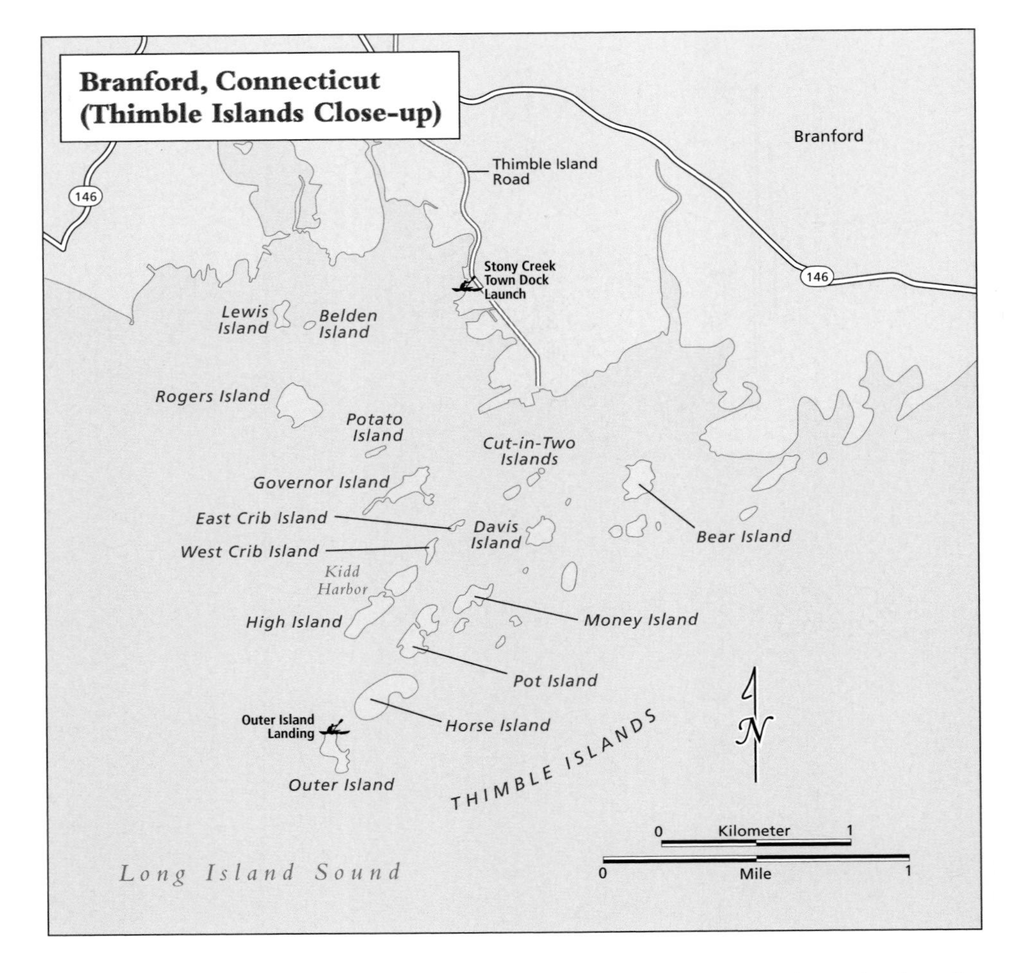

Granite Bay and Kelsey Island. A popular spot to land for lunch is Kelsey Island, at the eastern end of Johnson Point Beach near rocks. While landing is allowed at low tide, please be respectful to homeowners on the island by leaving no trace and keeping noise to a minimum. From the Branford River launch, it is about an 8-mile round-trip.

Great Harbor Wildlife Management Area/Trolley Road landing. A scenic outing is to launch out of Stony Creek, meander through the Thimble Islands, and go to Great Harbor Wildlife Management Area/Trolley Road (Guilford map) for lunch. Then return via the shortest path (8 to 10 miles, depending on tour).

Distance Paddler

To add some mileage, you can launch out of the Branford River State Boat Launch to access the Thimble Islands. Be careful of surprisingly big seas at times between Linden

Point/Spectacle Island and the main Thimble Island chain. It is also best to time the tides if going this route (just over 5 miles one way to Outer Island with an open crossing).

Guilford Town Dock launch. A pleasant long-distance outing is to launch out of the Guilford Town Dock (6 miles to the Thimble Islands). There are several interesting rocks, ledges, and coves to explore along this route. This launch also has ample parking, which is not the case for the Thimbles in the summer months.

Rough Water Paddler

Depending on conditions, rough water can be found all over the Thimble Islands. Larger waves also set up outside Linden Point, around Spectacle Island, on flood tides against westerly winds.

SUP Friendly

The Stony Creek Town Dock and surrounding waters are very SUP friendly, with Governor Island within reach. The best times are early in the morning, or late in the day during the summer months.

Something Fishy

There are plenty of fish to be found along the islands and rocky ledges. For the kayak angler, if dressed for conditions, tautog (blackfish) fishing is good along the entire Indian Neck area, where numerous visible rock outcroppings replicate themselves in the subsurface. The abrupt break in slope southwest of Sumac and Spectacle Islands offers a mixed bag for spring and summer fishing. The Bear Island area may be the most accessible. The western shore along Johnson Point should also not be overlooked for late summer eel drifts along the 8- to 14-foot break in slope. The mouth of the Branford River can be loaded with bluefish in the fall.

Guilford, CT

The coastline heading west around Sachem's Head is varied and interesting, and the East River offers a protected option if the conditions are too rough. If you plan to frequent this area, it is worth getting a yearly pass to the Guilford Town Marina, or look into keeping your kayak on a rack at Jacob's Beach. For the distance paddler, the Thimble Island chain is about 6 miles from the Guilford Town Marina. This launch is a decent option since the coast leading to the Thimbles is interesting, and the parking can be very difficult in the Thimbles during the summer.

The real highlight of this area is Faulkner's Island, as it is one of Connecticut's classic moderate distance paddles. According to the Faulkner's Light Brigade website (www.faulknerslight.org), "Built in 1802, Faulkner's Island Lighthouse is Connecticut's second oldest lighthouse tower, and is the only active light station on an island in the state. Faulkner's Island is about three and one half miles offshore from Guilford, Connecticut. Faulkner's Light Brigade is charged with the care, education and preservation of the island and its celebrated lighthouse."

Bill Hills on his way to tour Faulkner's Island during an open house. **PHOTO DAVID FASULO**

Full moon over Sachem's Head. **PHOTO DAVID FASULO**

The website further states, "More than 150 species of birds use Faulkner's Island, which is part of the U.S. Fish and Wildlife Service's Stewart B. McKinney National Wildlife Refuge, as a migratory rest stop. The island has one of the northeast's largest breeding colonies of roseate terns, an endangered species." Access to the island is restricted. However, there is an open house a few days each year, typically in September, when kayaks are allowed to land next to (north of) the ferry dock and guided tours are provided.

Aside from Faulkner's Island, about 1 nautical mile (heading 270 degrees magnetic) from Faulkner's is Goose Island. This is a privately owned island that is a relatively small collection of rocks at high tide. Seals frequent this area year-round. Please see "Respecting the Sea and Coastal Wildlife" in the introduction for general guidelines on observing seals.

Primary Launch: Guilford Town Dock. A very good launch site. Fees are $6/day for cartop boats, $20 for a season pass. Directions: Exit 58 off I-95. GPS Old Whitfield Street, Guilford. The Guilford Town Marina is at the end of Old Whitfield Street.

Secondary Launches: East River State Boat Launch. This free launch is located just across the East River from the Guilford Town Dock. However, it floods at high tides and can damage your vehicle. Directions: Exit 60 off I-95. GPS Circle Beach Road, Guilford. At the end of Ridgewood Avenue, turn right onto Circle Beach Road. After 0.3 mile on Circle Beach Road, turn right on the dirt road to the entrance.

Jacob's Beach. This is a town-owned beach that during the season (Memorial Day to Labor Day) charges nonresidents $10 per vehicle. The park is open year-round 7 a.m. to dusk. The beach has a nice kayak ramp next to a breakwater, and is a very pleasant setting for a family outing. Directions: Exit 58 off I-95. GPS 198 Seaside Ave., Guilford. Drive 0.5 mile on New Whitfield Street and take a right onto Seaside Avenue. Jacob's Beach is 0.3 mile on the left.

Chaffinch Island Park. There is a rock/ledge launch on the northeast side of the park—more suitable for the advanced paddler. The park is free, but the gate closes at dark. Directions: GPS Chaffinch Island Road and follow it 0.7 mile to the park.

Great Harbor Wildlife Management Area/Trolley Road. This small beach launch has very limited parking and is not appropriate for groups. There is a breachway that provides rough water (reversing falls) at certain tides for experienced kayakers only. Directions: GPS Trolley Road to the small parking lot at the end of the street.

Cruising Paddler

From the Guilford Town Dock, head west along the coastline past Mulberry Point (1.4 miles) to Sachem's Head Yacht Club (3.4 miles total). Continue west along the coast (or tour Sachem Harbor) to the point and then head north to Horse Island in Joshua Cove (4.36 miles total). Continue up the cove to a break on the Great Harbor Wildlife Management Area/Trolley Road beach 200 feet east of the breachway (4.7 miles total). Return the same route (9.4 miles total).

Distance Paddler

Faulkner's Island and Goose Island are approximately 3.5 miles from the shore and 4 miles from the Guilford Town Dock launch. While not too far away, the water is abnormally rough heading to and from Faulkner's Island and the Goose Island area. There are reefs extending north of Faulkner's Island that seem to kick up the water due to the east–west flow of tidal water. Boat wakes also add to the unpredictable water in this area. Landing on Faulkner's Island is not permitted, so be prepared. Also, keep a reasonable distance from the seals around Goose Island for their protection. When returning to shore, look past the coast to the mountain/ridge line in the background. A good waypoint for the return paddle is where the ridge (looking at the coastline) drops down 45 degrees.

Rough Water Paddler

There is a reef that extends north from Faulkner's Island a couple hundred yards that has a tidal race. It should be noted that the water surrounding Faulkner's Island is known, during certain tides and winds, for being uncommonly rough for Long Island Sound.

Rapids formed by changing tides (reversing falls) near the inlet separating Joshua Cove and the Great Harbor Wildlife Area can be found on certain tides, but parking is very limited. Also, the potential for getting trapped/injured/killed in the inlet during certain tides is a serious concern. This exercise is only for very experienced paddlers with proper equipment, solid rolls, rescue skills, and a spotter.

SUP Friendly

Guilford Harbor is pleasant to explore, and Chaffinch Island Park is a nicely protected launch about 0.75 mile from Jacob's Beach. The East River and Grass Island are also

The Guilford coastline provides miles of interesting scenery. John Lathrop off of Hatch Rock, Guilford.
PHOTO DAVID FASULO

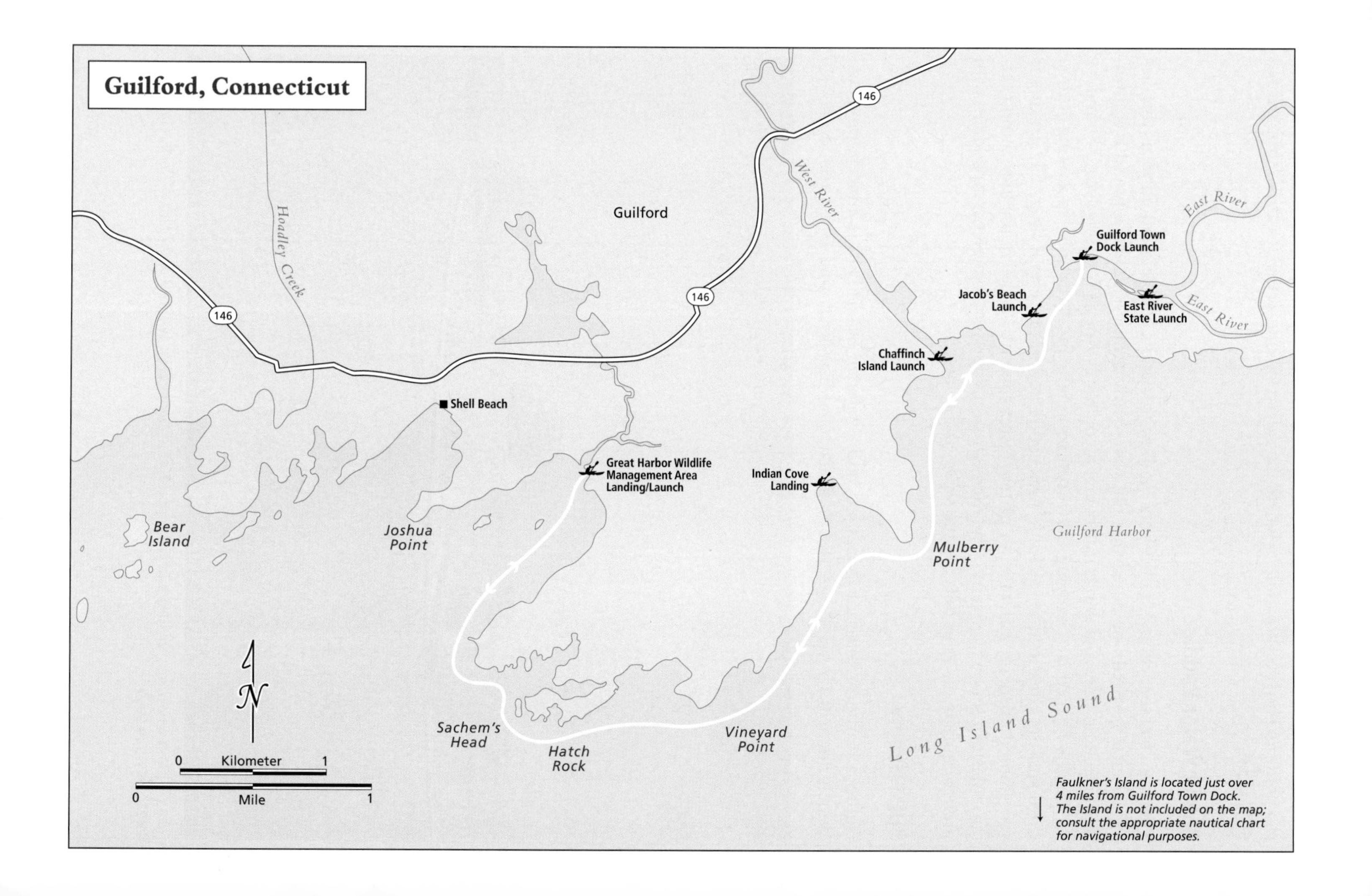

Guilford, Connecticut
Guilford
146
146
146
Hoadley Creek
West River
East River
East River
Guilford Town
Dock Launch
Jacob's Beach
Launch
East River
State Launch
Chaffinch
Island Launch
Shell Beach
Great Harbor Wildlife
Management Area
Landing/Launch
Indian Cove
Landing
Bear
Island
Joshua
Point
Guilford Harbor
Mulberry
Point
Sachem's
Head
Hatch
Rock
Vineyard
Point
Long Island Sound
0
Kilometer
1
0
Mile
1
Faulkner's Island is located just over
4 miles from Guilford Town Dock.
The Island is not included on the map;
consult the appropriate nautical chart
for navigational purposes.

Nick Shade playing in the turbulent water at the Great Harbor Wildlife Area (Trolley Road) breachway. **PHOTO DAVID FASULO**

pleasant, but the harbor can be rough on the eastern end and you will need to keep an eye on the current/tide for the East River.

Something Fishy

Guilford Harbor, and the point where the East and West Rivers meet the sound, sees a lot of action. There are also numerous rock outcroppings along the shore. Many kayak anglers find Guilford Harbor to be a great introductory fishery, where boat traffic is considerably less than other fisheries to the east and west. Long drifts with a southwest or south wind will afford the opportunity to drift across variable sand/cobble/rock bottom.

Madison, CT

The Madison shore is a relatively wide-open expanse of water. The Hammonasset Beach State Park launch, at Meigs Point, offers quick access to a variety of venues. Hammonasset Beach is also an enjoyable family outing, where folks can share boats while others explore the beach (Connecticut's largest shoreline) or fish/crab off the breakwater. The nature center and the trails heading along the eastern end of the point are fun to explore. From the Hammonasset launch recreational kayakers and SUPers can access the protected Clinton Harbor, and rough water play for the experienced paddler can be found off the tip of the Meigs Point launch breakwater (watch for exposed rocks).

The cruising paddler can explore the nearly 2-mile-long Hammonasset Beach to the west, or head east for some added distance and check out Duck and Menunketesuck Islands (about 8 miles round-trip). From the town beaches (Surf Club, West Wharf, East

Kyle Fasulo exploring Meigs Point, Hammonasset Beach State Park. **PHOTO DAVID FASULO**

Wharf), the small Tuxis Island makes for a scenic paddle, but access is more restrictive. However, West and East Wharfs offer nicely protected launches off-season.

Primary Launch: The Hammonasset Beach State Park launch at Meigs Point offers the easiest public access point. Once you enter the park, head east towards Meigs Point Nature Center. Drive past the nature center to a beach launching area at the very end of the road. Fees are $13 for Connecticut residents, $22 for nonresidents, $6 after 4 p.m. Directions: I-95 to exit 62. Head south off the exit for 1 mile. Go straight through the traffic light, crossing Route 1 into the park.

Secondary Launches: The three town beaches—Madison Surf Club, East Wharf, and West Wharf—offer cartop launching for residents and nonresidents. For nonresidents, a daily parking pass can be purchased at the town-owned Surf Club. Memorial Day through Labor Day, the fee is $25 Monday through Thursday and $40 Friday through Sunday and holidays. The Surf Club is open from 8:30 a.m. to dusk.

Madison Surf Club. The town-owned Madison Surf Club has a nice beach launch for cartop boats on the western end of the park at Garvan Point. Directions: GPS Surf Club Road. Once in the park, the launch is west of the second parking lot (look for small sailboats and kayaks in a dirt parking area).

East Wharf and West Wharf. These town beaches offer cartop launches with better protection (really nice for SUPs), but parking can be limited and a parking pass must be purchased at the Surf Club. Directions: For West Wharf, GPS West Wharf Road and follow it to the end of the road to the sound. For East Wharf, GPS East Wharf Road and follow it to Middle Beach Road; the entrance is at the intersection.

Cruising Paddler

The beach cruise. From Meigs Point, head west along the beach to a stop near the beach/breakwater at the western end of Hammonasset just before Webster Point (2 miles), or continue west to East Wharf Beach (3.1 miles). Return the same route.

Clinton Harbor area. This is a very pleasant paddle—just be careful of waves near Hammonasset Point. From Meigs Point, head east along the shore then north past the Hammonasset Nature Preserve towards Cedar Island. There is a beach 1.5 miles from the launch for a break. (***Note:*** You can carry over the beach to access the harbor quicker.) Continue to the end of Cedar Island (2.1 miles total) and either explore the inner harbor or head over to the Clinton Town Beach for a break. Return the same route, watching for boats in the channel (4.2 miles total, plus extra miles for exploring).

Kayak fishing off of Meigs Point, Hammonasset Beach State Park, with Faulkner's Island in the background. **PHOTO DAVID FASULO**

Distance Paddler

From Meigs Point, go east and cross the harbor to Kelsey Point (2 miles). Continue on relatively open water to the inner harbor of Duck Island (3.8 miles total). Return the same route (7.6 miles total).

Rough Water Paddler

Just south of the breakwater at Meigs Point (beware of rocks) is an area that has rough water play during certain conditions.

SUP Friendly

Clinton Harbor is relatively protected, but the area around Meigs Point/Hammonasset Point can be rough. The well-protected harbor north of Cedar Island is typically calm (with the exception of boat wakes and some current), and is a good place to explore via SUP (see Clinton launches if too far for comfort from Meigs Point/Hammonasset). After

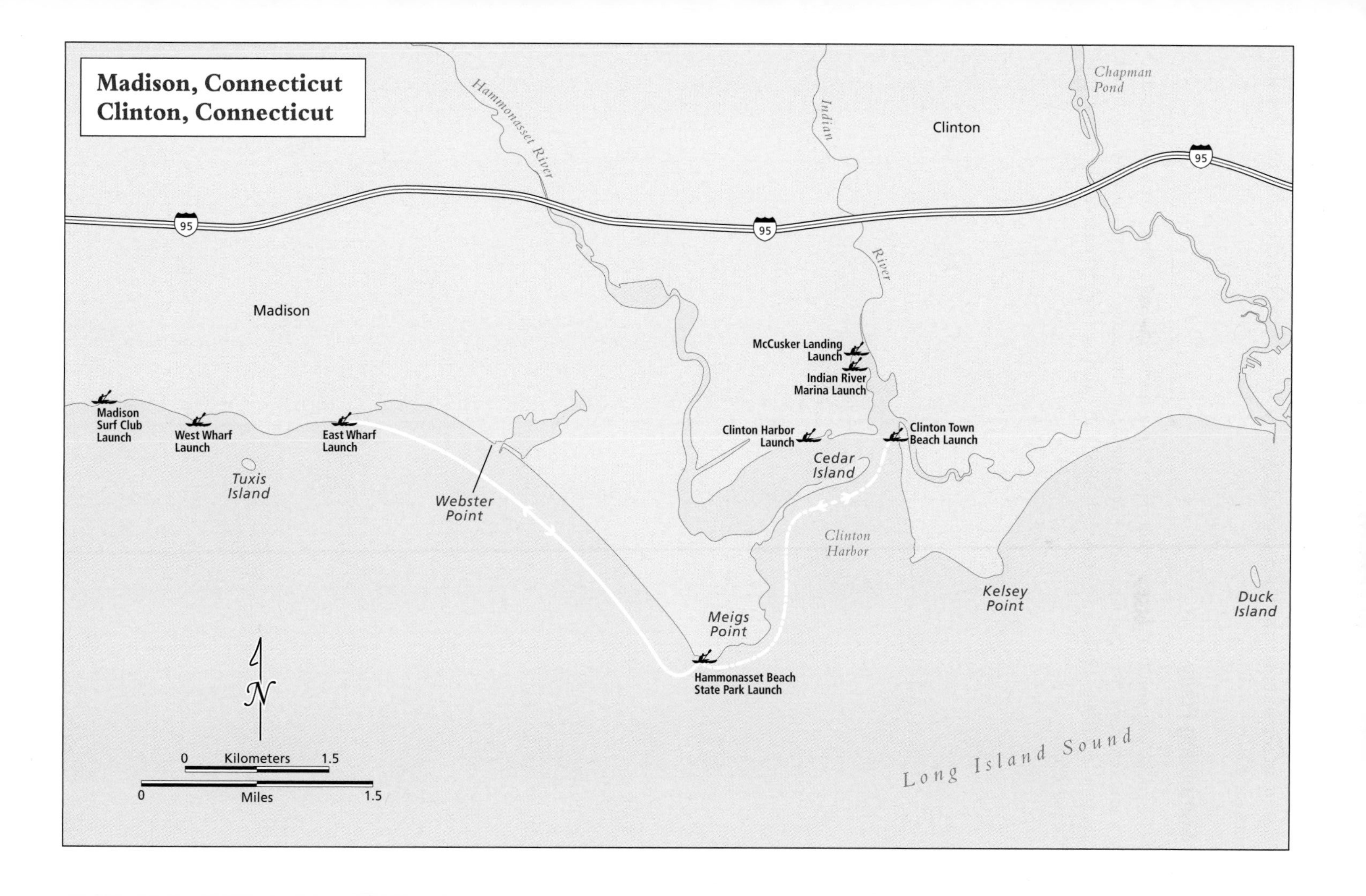
Madison, Connecticut
Clinton, Connecticut
Hammonasset River
Indian
River
Chapman
Pond
Clinton
95
95
95
Madison
McCusker Landing
Launch
Indian River
Marina Launch
Madison
Surf Club
Launch
West Wharf
Launch
East Wharf
Launch
Clinton Harbor
Launch
Clinton Town
Beach Launch
Cedar
Island
Tuxis
Island
Webster
Point
Clinton
Harbor
Kelsey
Point
Duck
Island
Meigs
Point
Hammonasset Beach
State Park Launch
N
0
Kilometers
1.5
0
Miles
1.5
Long Island Sound

5 p.m. in the summer, the town-owned East and West Wharf beaches offer nice late-day cruising.

Something Fishy

The rocks just south of Meigs Point, Hammonasset Beach State Park, are a popular and productive spot. You can also troll along the beachfront area, before and after the beach is open, for fluke. Fluke and other fish also tend to chase baitfish near the breakwater at Meigs Point.

Clinton, CT

The Clinton Harbor area is well protected and offers excellent opportunities for the SUPer as well as the beginning to intermediate sea kayaker. The waters between the Clinton breakwater and Hammonasset are generally calm and shallow near the Clinton Town Beach (except for boat wakes). Paddling up the Indian River is pleasant, as well as exploring the small beach and waterways on the western side of Clinton Harbor by kayak or SUP. The harbor is also a fun place to explore in the summer on a full moon. If you want to add a few miles to your paddling, beyond the Clinton breakwater you can access Duck Island in Westbrook, or cruise past Hammonasset Beach in Madison.

Restaurants are located on the water next to the Clinton Town Marina, and SUP and kayak rentals are conveniently located in this area. The Clinton Town Beach is great for small children, and paddlers can also access the downtown area utilizing the McCusker Landing floating dock/launch located off the Indian River.

Jessica Lavigne, co-owner of Paddleworks (SUP rentals and sales on Clinton Harbor), paddling in Clinton Harbor. **PHOTO DAVID FASULO**

Enjoying a sunset, and soon to be full moon, paddle in Clinton Harbor. **PHOTO DAVID FASULO**

Primary Launches: Clinton Harbor Launch. The Clinton Harbor Launch (not the Clinton Town Marina boat ramp) offers free access from a protected launch to residents and nonresidents alike. The parking is limited, and it is not a good destination for large groups. At low tide the launch is muddy. Directions: GPS Riverside Drive. The parking area is across from the intersection of Maplewood Drive. The town boat ramp is on the east side of the parking lot; the small beach launch is on the west side of the parking lot.

Indian River Marina. This is a pleasant small marina that rents kayaks and SUPs. The access ramp to the Indian River is excellent, and the facilities are clean. The ramp fee is $10, and it is a good option in the summer season (Memorial Day to Labor Day). A short paddle up the Indian River gains access to the harbor and Long Island Sound. Directions: GPS 58 Commerce St.

Paddleworks at Harborside Marina. Located in Harborside Marina, next to the Clinton Town Marina boat ramp and close to the Clinton Harbor Launch, Paddleworks rents SUPs and offers SUP launching (reservation requested) from the dock for $5 per launch or $50 for the season. Directions: GPS 131 Grove Street.

Clinton Town Beach. This is a very convenient beach launch that has ample parking. From Memorial Day through Labor Day, for nonresidents the charge is $25 for the day, collected at the gate from 9 a.m. to 3 p.m. There is no parking from 10 p.m. to 6 a.m. After 5 p.m., during the summer season, the fee is typically not collected. During the winter months, the gate to the beach may be locked. Directions: GPS Waterside Lane and follow it south to the beach.

McCusker Landing/Clinton Landing. This is a town launch located behind Clinton Town Hall that offers free access to the Indian River. The Indian River provides access to Clinton Harbor (1 mile) and Long Island Sound (1.6 miles total). The site has ample parking and a floating dock. The ramp is tricky to access for kayakers (due to a sharp turn getting to the dock) but well suited for SUPs. If paddling in Long Island Sound, it provides access to downtown Clinton. Directions: GPS 54 East Main St. and park behind the town hall.

Cruising Paddler

Outer Harbor/Meigs Point. From the Clinton Town Beach, head west across the harbor and cruise along the coast of Cedar Island. There are rest stops along the way. Continue

Stone Island breakwater, with Kelsey Point in the background. **PHOTO DAVID FASULO**

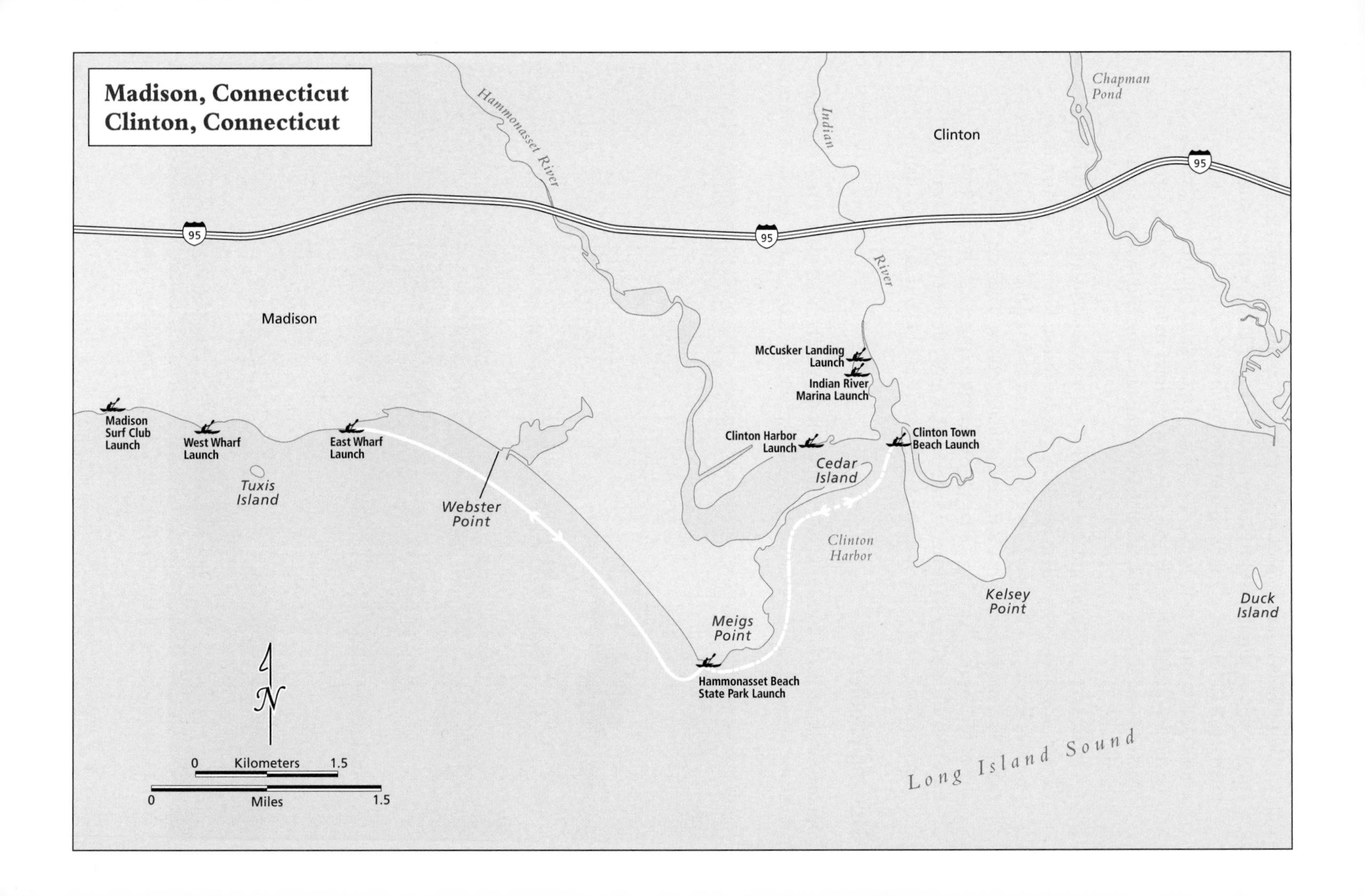
Madison, Connecticut
Clinton, Connecticut
Hammonasset River
Indian
River
Chapman
Pond
Clinton
95
95
95
Madison
McCusker Landing
Launch
Indian River
Marina Launch
Madison
Surf Club
Launch
West Wharf
Launch
East Wharf
Launch
Clinton Harbor
Launch
Clinton Town
Beach Launch
Cedar
Island
Tuxis
Island
Webster
Point
Clinton
Harbor
Kelsey
Point
Duck
Island
Meigs
Point
Hammonasset Beach
State Park Launch
N
0
Kilometers
1.5
0
Miles
1.5
Long Island Sound

to Meigs Point (2.25 miles) and a break at the beach. Return the same route (4.5 miles total).

Inner Harbor Cruise. From the Clinton Harbor Launch, head west along the harbor (stay out of channel) to the Hammonasset Preserve Area (1 mile). Explore the area by heading north up the river or investigating the inlets in the preserve (shallow). Continue along the shore to the north side of Cedar Island and a small beach (1.87 miles total, not including exploring the river and inlets). Cruise along the shore of Cedar Island and return to the launch (2.5 miles total).

Distance Paddler

From the Clinton Town Beach, paddle along the eastern coast to Hammock Point, then east to Kelsey Point (1.5 miles). Follow the shoreline to the Menunketesuck River/breakwater (3.6 miles total). Head south to the inner harbor of Duck Island in Westbrook (4.5 miles total), then cross the open water back to Kelsey Point, returning to the town beach (8 miles total).

Rough Water Paddler

Just south of the breakwater at Meigs Point, Hammonasset Beach State Park, provides wave action, but be careful of rocks.

SUP Friendly

Wherever you launch, the Clinton Harbor area is a good SUP destination because it is well protected. Be aware of current in the rivers and harbors, as well as boat wakes and boat traffic. The Indian River is also interesting because you can take a break and go for a walk in downtown Clinton, from the McCusker/Clinton Landing.

Something Fishy

The Clinton Harbor area, although relatively shallow, can be productive. The breakwater off Kelsey Point is a good option, and a prime spot to search for tautog (blackfish). The trick to fishing the breakwater for tautog is to bring a small anchor for the rocks. If in Clinton Harbor, checking out Meigs Point off Hammonasset Beach is worth the effort.

Westbrook, CT

The Westbrook islands, including Salt, Menunketesuck, and Duck, are popular areas for shorebirds and provide charming vistas while touring the shoreline. Each of these islands was once a frequent destination to land and explore, but are now restricted. Salt Island is still accessible at low tide (south side), but Menunketesuck and Duck Islands are now closed to protect breeding birds. Throughout Westbrook the beaches, harbors, and rivers (Menunketesuck and Patchogue) are all pleasant areas to explore.

According to the US Fish & Wildlife Service, "Duck Island, a natural preserve owned by the State of Connecticut, once served as a hospital for smallpox victims. Today a chimney from a long-abandoned building and a set of stairs are all that remain of a human existence there. Duck Island hosts a major colony of long-legged waders including egrets, herons and ibises. In the summer, the bird population is quite evident and people often observe the white plumage of great egrets and snowy egrets nesting in the treetops. Other important species, such as dunlin, appear in winter."

As for the popular Salt Island, Fish & Wildlife says, "In the late 1800s, salt and fish oil were produced on the island. Sailing ships were loaded and unloaded here while their cargo of lumber, fruits, vegetables and the like was carted to and from the mainland at low tide. At that time, the island was described as the heart of commerce for the town."

Primary Launches: Westbrook Town Beach (West Beach). This is a very nice location. Launching is allowed on the north end of the beach just past a breakwater. Nonresident passes are $20 per day and are sold at the gate Memorial Day through Labor Day. The town typically stops charging after 5 p.m., which is the best time to be on the water in the summer due to the calmer seas. At the bottom of the tide, the water is low and will require a carry over the sand/mud. Directions: GPS 405 Seaside Ave. The beach and parking is across the street from this location.

Westbrook Town Hall/Mulvey Center kayak launch. This is an anticipated fishing/kayak launch located behind the Westbrook Town Hall with access to the Patchogue River. The completion date has yet to be determined. From this launch it is about 1.52 miles, past Bill's Seafood and through the marinas, to Long Island Sound. Directions: GPS 866 Boston Post Rd.

Pier 76 Marina. This is a private marina, and as of 2017 cartop launching into the Patchogue River is $5. Located behind the very popular Bill's Seafood, the ramp has access to the Patchogue River, which is less than 1 mile from Long Island Sound, meandering under the "singing bridge" and through marinas. Directions: GPS 54 Old Boston Post Rd.

Kirtland Landing. This is a good launch for the Menunketesuck River—a pleasant 2-mile paddle to the Route 1 bridge, and 2.5 miles (total) to Long

Lisa Fasulo exploring Salt Island, a popular destination for beachgoers from the nearby Water's Edge Resort during low tide. **PHOTO DAVID FASULO**

Island Sound. Directions: I-95 to exit 64. Head south on Route 145 for about 1.5 miles. Turn right on Old Clinton Road (Route 145) and continue for 0.4 mile to a small parking area (carpool, please) and launch on the Menunketesuck River.

Cruising Paddler

Duck Island cruise. From the town beach (West Beach), paddle southwest along the coast to Menunketesuck Island. Cruise along the island to the southern end, watching for rough waves (1 mile). Head across the bay to the north end of Duck Island (1.8 miles total). Continue along the north side of the breakwater, then south alongside the breakwater to the beach (3 miles total). Head west along the breakwater, then after rounding it east along the breakwater, and return to the town beach (5.3 miles total).

Salt Island cruise. From the town beach (West Beach), cruise east along the shore to Salt Island (1.4 miles). At low tide you can explore the island (many folks walk from Water's Edge Resort at low tide). Cruise around the island, and return along the coast (3 miles total).

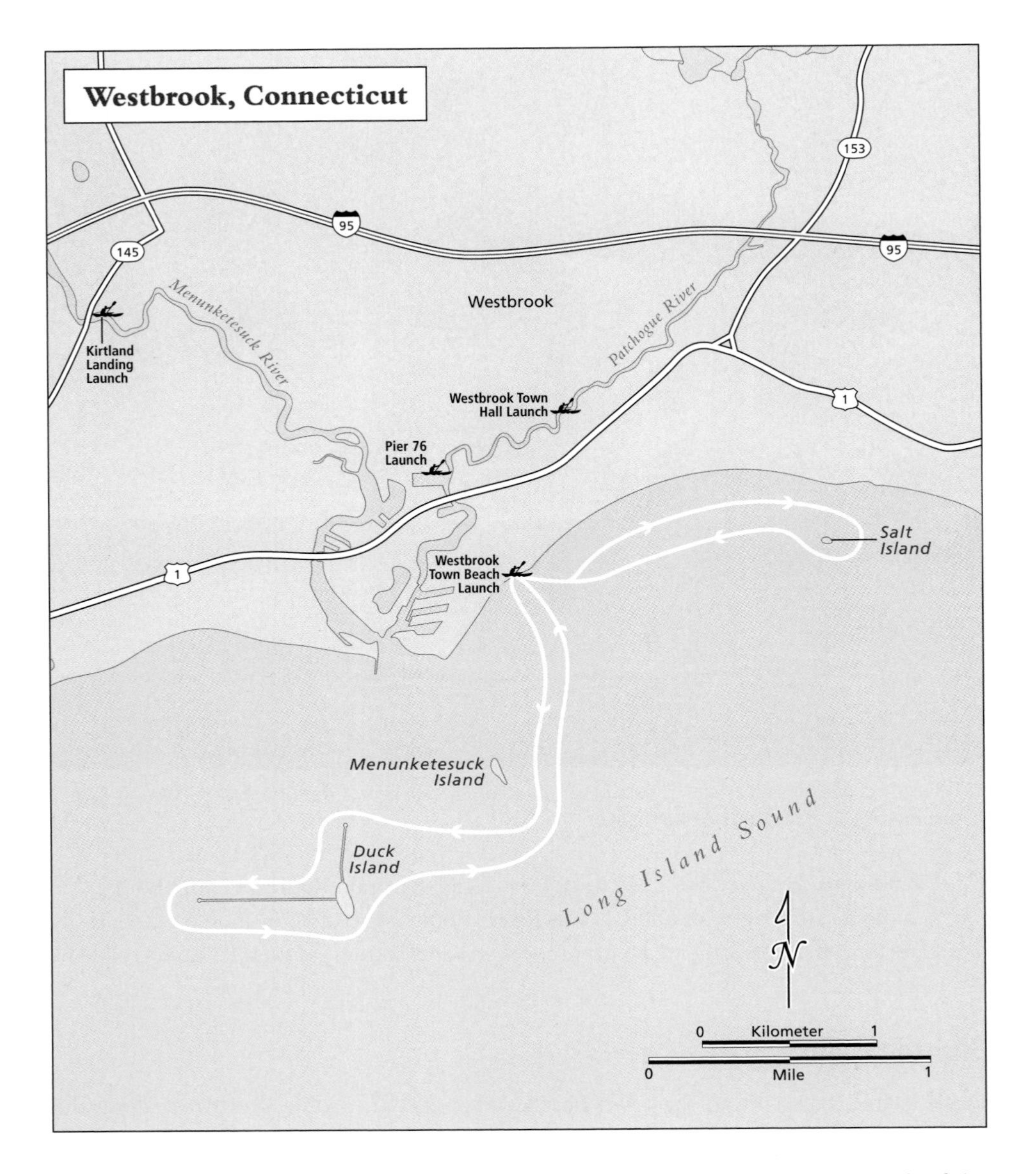

From Kirtland Landing, paddle down the Menunketesuck River to the mouth of the sound (2.5 miles). Return, or if time and tides allow, explore Menunketesuck Island or Duck Island (5 miles total).

Distance Paddler

From the town beach (West Beach), combine the above two cruising paddler routes out of West Beach (8.3 miles total).

Rough Water Paddler

At certain tides the south end of Menunketesuck Island will have rough water to play in.

SUP Friendly

From the town beach (West Beach) it is a 1.4-mile coastal cruise east along the shore to Salt Island. If you proceed a bit farther up the coast, you can stop at the Water's Edge Resort and grab a snack at the restaurant.

From the Kirtland Landing launch, the Menunketesuck River is a pleasant 2-mile paddle to the Route 1 bridge (plan tides to help with the return).

Something Fishy

Westbrook has a good variety of fishing. Fluke can be found on the sandy bottom, and if you venture out to the islands (Duck, Menunketesuck, Salt), they attract tautog (blackfish) as well as stripers. Tautog (blackfish) can be found along the breakwater at Duck Island. Blues and stripers patrol the shoreline, especially in the fall, with the telltale birds showing the way. An area that is best accessed by kayak anglers is the mouth (east side, out of the channel) of the Menunketesuck River. The mouth, especially in the fall, is loaded with bunker, and you can set up between the mouth and Menunketesuck Island. Pier 76 Marina (fee) is a convenient launch.

Some very large stripers have been caught in this area. According to "Fishing Westbrook, CT," by Tom Richardson, on the New England Boating website (www.newengland boating.com), "By now most anglers know Westbrook as the place where the world-record striped bass was landed in 2011 by Greg Myerson. While Myerson won't reveal exactly where he landed the 81-pound leviathan, his catch has striper fishermen flocking to Westbrook like miners to the Yukon." If you venture out to the Hens and Chickens Reef, the scup are plentiful.

Old Saybrook, CT

Old Saybrook contains some beautiful waters and is a pleasant town to explore. However, there are no public access points for the Old Saybrook coastline along Long Island Sound. If approaching the shoreline from the Connecticut River, outgoing tides/currents and boat wakes will make the return upriver very difficult (always keep this in mind when on the river). The access options for Old Saybrook include North Cove and the Connecticut River. North Cove is a pleasant spot for SUPs, and you can poke around the

Kyle Fasulo paddling protected waters in North Cove. **PHOTO DAVID FASULO**

river if conditions allow. The Connecticut River access is a great spot to head upriver to Essex (best to plan tides and keep an eye on the wind), land at the Essex town dock, and stroll around town.

From late August to early October, a very interesting paddling experience is to head upriver from the Baldwin Bridge launch to the east (popular with boaters) or west side of Goose Island (Old Lyme). For an hour or so leading up to sunset, hundreds of thousands of tree swallows converge each night. On the best nights they will form an enormous funnel (see photo in Old Lyme section) just before sunset, and all at once withdraw into the reeds where they roost for the night. Another popular Connecticut River/Old Lyme tour is to head a short ways upriver and explore the meandering backwaters (which eventually dead-end) of Lord Cove Wildlife Area (see photo in Old Lyme section) via the eastern end of Goose Island. In this area, Calves Island has a pleasant beach to explore.

Primary Launches: Baldwin Bridge State Boat Launch. Directions: GPS 218 Ferry Rd., Old Saybrook. This will bring you to the marina next to the launch. The cartop launch is located on the north side of the boat ramp next to the marina.

North Cove/Sheffield Street Town Launch. There is a public launch at the end of Sheffield Street that provides easy access to the protected North Cove and is pleasant for SUPs. Nonresident parking is allowed back up Sheffield Street (700 feet) at the middle school parking lot when school is not in session. The new sign states that the area is for residents only, but as the author understands it, that is in terms of parking (not access) only. Directions: GPS 199 Sheffield St. Drop off boats and park at the middle school.

Cruising Paddler

Due to lack of public access, cruising along the shore is difficult. However, there are some great circuits that head north upriver from the Baldwin Bridge State Boat Launch. Just be sure to *check the tides* (especially in the early spring) since an ebb tide along with river current can be strong.

Essex and Old Lyme tour. From the Baldwin Bridge launch, head across the river towards the southern end of Calves Island (Old Lyme) near a marina. Round Calves Island and then head into the Connecticut River along Goose Island and upriver to the east side of Nott Island (2.4 miles). Paddle around the east side of Nott Island and then around to the west side (nice small beach at the northwest side of the island). Head across the river to the western shore to the Essex Town Dock (next to the Connecticut River Museum) and walk around the town—ice cream, lunch and dinner options, and beverages are a short walk from the dock. After a pleasant stroll, return along the western shore back to the launch (6.6 miles total).

The Swallow Paddle. In the late summer and early fall, hundreds of thousands of swallows (a new group each night) gather over Goose Island to roost for the night. The gathering at dusk is spectacular. The best launch, in terms of access as well as plentiful parking, is the Baldwin Bridge State Boat Launch. It is about a 1-mile paddle to the prime viewing area (either side of Goose Island). Bring a white light for the return.

Distance Paddler

Distance is easy, or difficult, on the Connecticut River if you time the tides correctly. In the late summer and fall, the flood tide can be very strong and offsets the river current. One longer paddle is to follow the route mentioned above (cruising paddler to Essex), but extend the journey upriver up and around Brockway Island (about 10 miles total). During lower tides there is a nice sandbar on the northern end of Brockway Island.

Super Distance Paddler

Connecticut River from the Massachusetts border to Old Saybrook. To the author's knowledge, he is the only paddler to have paddled this stretch of water in a single day. The author paddled from the Massachusetts border to Middletown solo, then, with partner Steve Fagin, continued to Old Saybrook. It is a 70-mile paddle that was completed in 13 hours (with the help of the spring current).

While located in Old Lyme, the Baldwin Bridge launch is a good launch to access the spectacular late summer/early fall swallow show on Goose Island in Old Lyme. **PHOTO ERIK BAUMGARTNER**

Late day fishing on the Connecticut River. **PHOTO DAVID FASULO**

Rough Water Paddler

When the wind is howling out of the north, some kayakers shuttle cars (leave a car at the launch and a car at the end of the paddle) and ride the wind waves while paddling downriver. Upriver launches include the Deep River town dock, Haddam Meadow State Park, and as far as the Massachusetts border area.

SUP Friendly

North Cove offers a protected area for SUPs. You can also venture out into the Connecticut River, but be careful of wind and current.

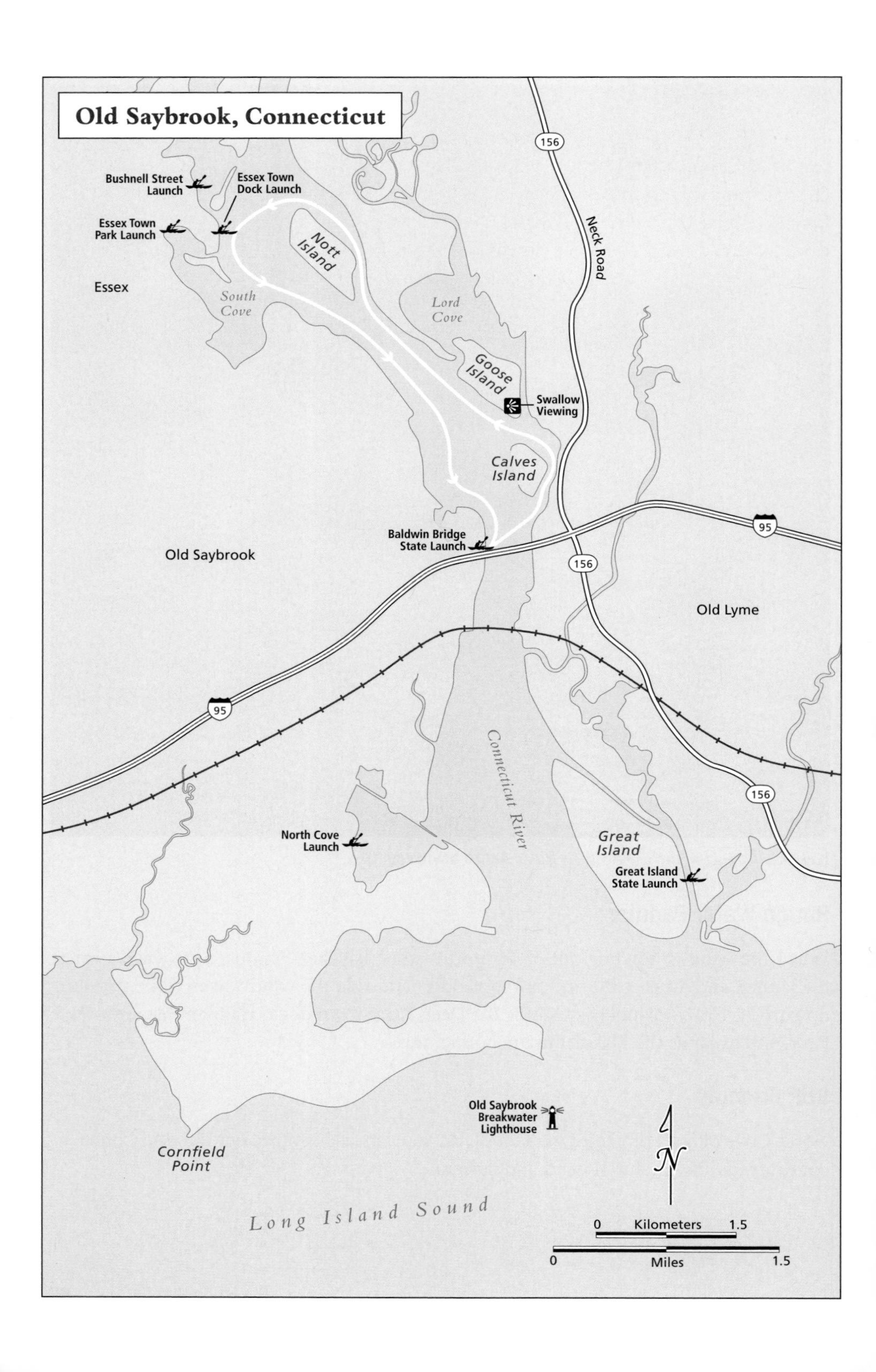
Old Saybrook, Connecticut
Bushnell Street Launch
Essex Town Dock Launch
Essex Town Park Launch
Essex
Nott Island
South Cove
Lord Cove
Goose Island
Swallow Viewing
Calves Island
Neck Road
156
95
Baldwin Bridge State Launch
Old Saybrook
Old Lyme
Connecticut River
North Cove Launch
Great Island
Great Island State Launch
Old Saybrook Breakwater Lighthouse
Cornfield Point
Long Island Sound
N
0 Kilometers 1.5
0 Miles 1.5

Something Fishy

The Old Saybrook area of the Connecticut River holds bluefish and stripers, and fluke can be found between North and South Coves (sandy part of river, on the edge of the channel near the middle of the river). The mouth of the Connecticut River is a well-known area for bass and blues, and can swarm with bunker in the evening. The mouth of the Lieutenant River (Old Lyme side) is also productive with bass in the spring. Cornfield Point is a good area for a variety of fish if you can reach it.

Essex, CT

For the recreational kayaker or SUPer looking for protected waters in a beautiful setting, Essex is hard to beat. Essex, which is composed of the villages of Essex, Centerbrook, and Ivoryton, was dubbed "The Perfect Small American Town" in the *1,000 Places to See Before You Die* travel guide and achieved the top rank in *The 100 Best Small Towns in America*. The town of Essex is also access friendly, with multiple shoreline access sites. The picturesque downtown is easy to access from the parking areas, so spending time on the water then exploring Essex by foot are easy to manage. The Griswold Inn is a recommended destination after paddling, as it has been in operation since 1776 and is one of the country's oldest continuously operated inns. If the Gris is too crowded, head up the street to the Black Seal.

The best launch for kayakers and SUPers is Bushnell Street (although a bit muddy at lower tides). This spot has ample parking and convenient access to the scenic North Cove as well as the Connecticut River. It is best to paddle North Cove at high tide because the cove can be shallow. During the summer, there is a channel that you can follow (typically marked with stakes) that is very helpful. The foot of Main Street, next to

Jessica Weinstein touring North Cove from the Bushnell Street launch. **PHOTO DAVID FASULO**

the Connecticut River Museum, is also an option, with quick access to the river but very limited parking. There is also the town park, with parking behind the post office or on the street. The town park is a nice launch for a family that wants to picnic and play in the shallows of Middle and South Coves or easily access the Connecticut River. The floating dock (if in place) can be tricky to launch a kayak from, but is great for SUPs.

Please note that the lower Connecticut River can have strong current, especially in the spring. The combination of river current and tidal current can be strong when in sync with each other. Your best bet when paddling in the Connecticut River is to head north for the first leg of your journey, so your return trip is downstream. In late summer and early fall, depending on rainfall, the flood tide (going north) can actually be strong.

Primary Launches: Bushnell Street. This is a good launch for kayaks and SUPs to access North Cove and the Connecticut River. There is plenty of parking and a dirt/sand launch. It is also within walking distance of downtown. ***Note:*** North Cove is shallow, so if heading north into the cove, first head to the pilings, then follow the channel markers (temporary white stakes in the summer) to

The town of Essex is access friendly, and a perfect spot for SUP and casual kayak tours. Getting ready for a tour of Middle Cove and the Connecticut River from the Essex Town Park launch. **PHOTO DAVID FASULO**

stay in deeper water. To access the Connecticut River, after launching take a right into the marina and follow the channel to the river. You can also access the river by heading northeast from the launch to an outlet, but it can be very shallow. Directions: GPS Bushnell Street. The launch is on a dirt road off the street heading to the water behind the marina.

Essex Town Dock. This is a nice launch, but there is limited on-street parking. Quick access to the Connecticut River and Nott Island is just across the river (be careful of current and boat traffic). Directions: GPS Main Street and follow it to the end (next to the Connecticut River Museum).

Essex Town Park. This is a great place for causal SUP touring in Middle and South Coves, or access to the Connecticut River and Nott Island Wildlife Area. There is a floating dock for SUPs, but is awkward for kayaks to launch. Directions: GPS Nott Lane (behind the post office at 12 Main St.).

Cruising Paddler

Hamburg Cove (Lyme). A very pleasant tour, with a rest stop on the north end of Brockway Island at lower tides (or southern end if the tide is up). From the Essex Town Dock,

Steve Seely passing Joshua Rock, just north of Brockway Island and near the entrance of Hamburg Cove. **PHOTO CARL TJERANDSEN**

At low tide there is a great sandbar on the northern tip of Brockway Island, which is just upriver from Essex. Hamburg Cove is in the background. **PHOTO DAVID FASULO**

or one of the other Essex launches, head into the Connecticut River. From the town dock, head up the western shore of the river to the north end of Brockway Island (1.75 miles). (Note that there is shallow water in this area; you may have to go farther north than planned.) Head east into Hamburg Cove (narrow channel; 2.5 miles total). Continue up the narrowing waterway northeast until you enter a nice cove with a marina and yacht club (3.6 miles total). Return to the launch, passing the eastern side of Brockway Island/eastern shore of the river (boat traffic converges here) and cross over to the western shore and launch (6.8 miles total).

Nott Island Circumnavigation. This is not too difficult, but river current must first be assessed, as well as the amount of boat traffic. It is a no-wake zone, so boats are typically not traveling too fast. From the Essex Town Dock, or one of the other Essex launches, head into the Connecticut River. From the town dock, head east across the river to a beach on the northwestern end of the island. Paddle downriver along the island, then head west at its end and then north (can be shallow) to the top of the island. Head back to the beach for a break, or return to the launch. From the town dock, just under a 3-mile round-trip.

Distance Paddler

The classic circuit is the Selden Neck State Park (Island) loop from Bushnell Street. Head along the dock on the right and then take a right into the marina. Follow the channel out past boats to the Connecticut River. There is a more-direct option that heads northeast across North Cove to a cut that allows you to get into the river; however, at low tide it can be difficult to get through. Once in the river, head north to Brockway Island (1.73 miles). It is best to stay west of the island to stay out of the channel. From the southern end of Brockway Island, head north about 1.42 miles. On the western shore is the Selden Creek entrance (about 140 feet wide and just north of a house on the water with a cliff behind it). Head up the creek, passing cliffs and beautiful scenery, into Selden Cove. Paddle west along the shore (watch for angry swans) to a creek on the left (nice beach/camping area), which leads to the Connecticut River. Head south down the river (be careful of boat traffic) to the launch (just over 11 miles for the total trip).

SUP Friendly

North Cove, launching from Bushnell Street, is a nice SUP area. Follow the channel past the windmill to a hidden cove on the left. You can also access the Connecticut River from

Heading up the Connecticut River, towards Selden Creek and a circumnavigation of Selden Neck State Park, during a full-moon paddle. **PHOTO DAVID FASULO**

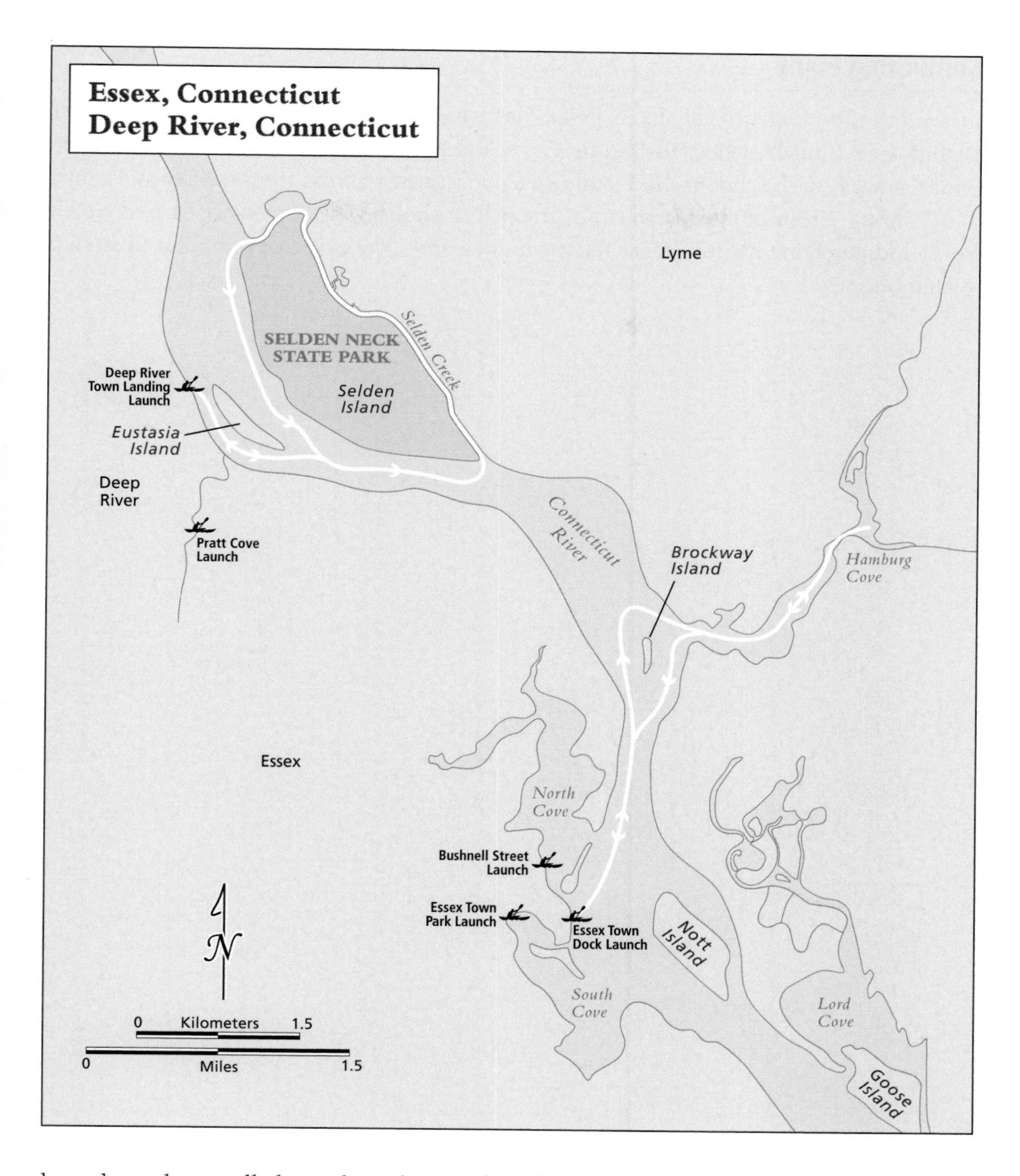

here through a small channel northwest of the launch, or through the marina channel to the south, but be careful of boat wakes and river current. It can be shallow, so follow the channel, which is typically marked with small stakes.

Middle and South Coves are fun to explore from the beautiful Town Green, but there are shallow areas and be careful of current where South Cove joins the Connecticut River. A channel leading to the river, past the Essex Yacht Club, is marked with stakes. Once past the yacht club, it is fun to meander along the moored boats and shoreline.

Something Fishy

In the fall the bluefish heat up in Essex Harbor (between downtown Essex and Nott Island), and bunker collect in Middle Cove. From June through the fall, bass can be found as well, with schoolies in Hamburg Cove (upriver across from Brockway Island) in the spring. Fresh bunker seems to be the bait of choice. There are huge carp in North Cove, and perch are plentiful near the town dock and were once very popular upstream in Hamburg Cove.

Deep River, CT

This area is the farthest from the coast, but it has one of the best circuits for the kayaker or motivated SUPer in Connecticut—the Selden Neck State Park circumnavigation. Camping is allowed on Selden Island (check the CT DEEP website), and the combination of paddling, staying overnight on the island, and swimming is an enjoyable outing in the summer for cartop boaters and small powerboats. In the interior of the island there is rock climbing for those inclined, and is described in the Falcon Guide *Rock Climbing Connecticut* (also written by the author). However, take precautions against Lyme ticks if exploring the island. There are cliffs along Selden Creek that were once popular for diving—check out the Billy Joel video "River of Dreams" on YouTube.

Primary Launches: Deep River Town Landing. This is a great launch spot to access Selden Neck State Park, which is a really fun island to circumnavigate. During the summer, there may be a nonresident parking fee. Directions: GPS 161 River St. Continue a short distance on River Street to the launch entrance.

Kevin Fasulo exploring a side creek, off the main Selden Creek, on the east side of Selden Island.
PHOTO DAVID FASULO

Pratt Cove. This is a free launch, but getting under the bridge can be tricky at high tide, and getting out of Pratt Cove can be tricky at low tide. It is a 3,500-foot paddle from the launch to the Connecticut River/protected area near Eustasia Island. Directions: GPS Essex Street. From the intersection of Middlesex Turnpike/Route 154 (downtown Deep River), follow Essex Street about 0.5 mile to a bridge and small parking area on the right.

Cruising Paddler

Selden Island Circumnavigation. From the Deep River Town Landing, head south along the river on the western side of Eustasia Island. After less than a mile, you will join the main Connecticut River. As soon as practicable, cross the river to the other side. Continue downriver to the entrance of Selden Creek on your left (1.8 miles from the launch), and head northwest up the creek. About 2.7 miles total from the launch, you will pass cliffs lining the creek on your right. Continue upriver (at 3.3 total miles there is a creek on the right and an island you can land on) to a right turn into Selden Cove (3.6 total miles). Enter Selden Cove (beware of angry swans) and trend left around the point to a beach/campground on the left (4.1 total miles). Continue down the creek back to the Connecticut River. Head downriver along the shoreline of Selden Island until in line with the southern end of Eustasia Island (5.4 miles total). Paddle across the Connecticut River (beware of boat traffic) and then back up to the launch (6.4 miles total). ***Note:*** You can shorten the trip by cutting over at the northern end of Eustasia Island, but you will miss some interesting island scenery.

The Connecticut River side of Selden Island. **PHOTO ERIK BAUMGARTNER**

Exploring the cliffs in Selden Creek. **PHOTO DAVID FASULO**

Gillette Castle. Another unique trip is to head upriver to Gillette Castle, overlooking the river from the eastern shoreline, about 1.8 miles upriver from Deep River Landing. There is a small beach to land on. Just before the landing, on the right, is the entrance to Hadlyme Cove (marked with a channel marker), which is also pleasant to explore.

Distance Paddler

The Selden Island circumnavigation is also completed out of Essex from the Bushnell Street launch; about 11 miles total.

SUP Friendly

You can SUP around Selden Island, but it's only for the experienced paddler. Wind, current, and boat wakes can make it very difficult on the western end of the island. The interior creek is pleasant and protected, and sometimes folks powerboat into the area and then SUP the interior creek.

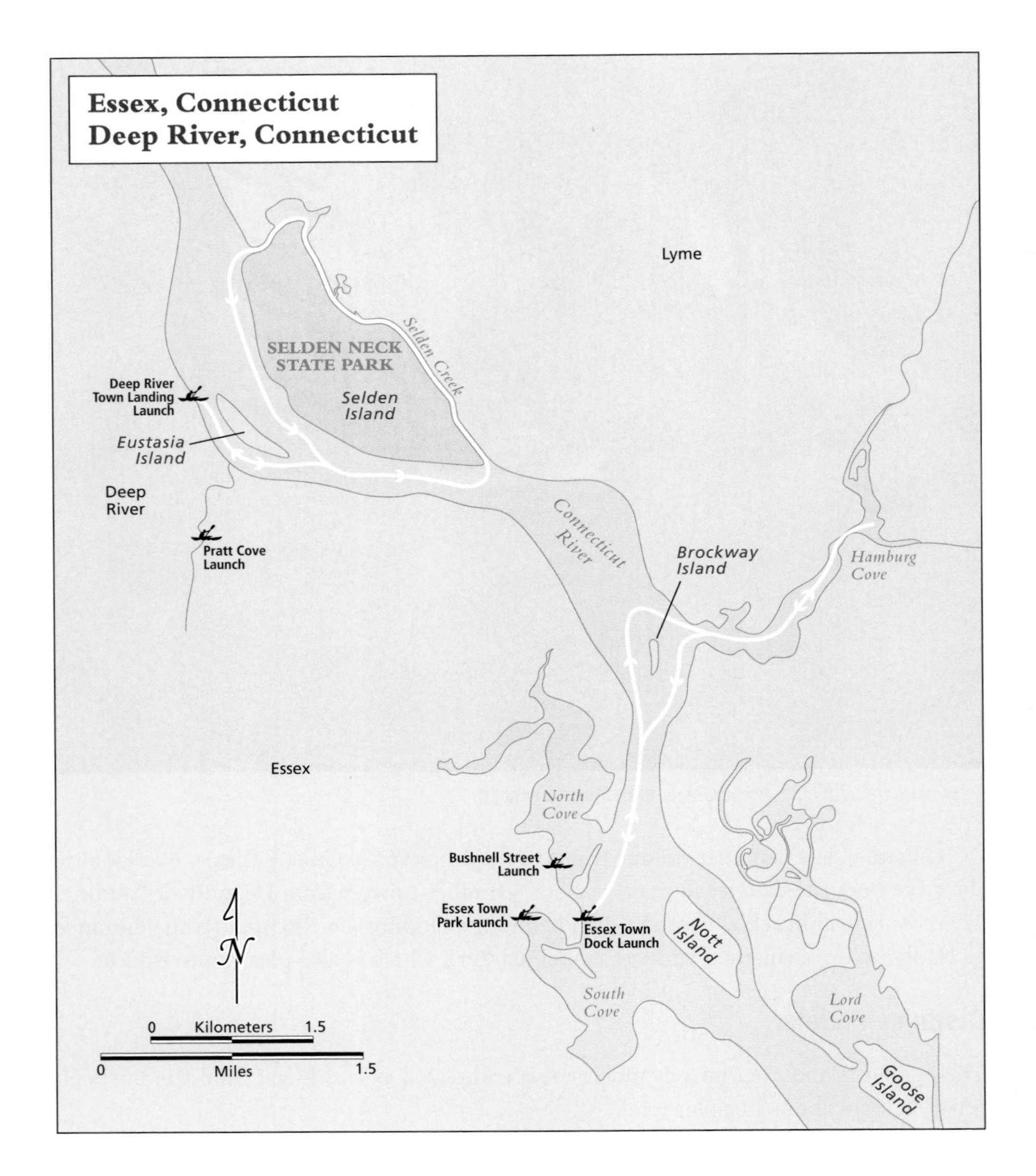

Something Fishy

Bass and bluefish occupy the area, and in the fall the southern end of Selden Creek, where it meets the Connecticut River, can be productive on fresh bunker. Catfish can also be caught as the sun begins to set.

Old Lyme, CT

Old Lyme has several good launches for SUPers, cruising kayakers, and advanced kayakers. For SUPers, the Lord Cove area and Lieutenant River offer protected exploration of marsh areas. Paddlers can easily access the mouth of the Connecticut River as well as the Old Lyme shoreline from the Great Island State Boat Launch. The Four Mile River State Boat Launch, a favorite among many paddlers, provides perfect access for the eastern Old Lyme shoreline as well as the interesting islands and waters around Rocky Neck State Park (East Lyme).

There are several historical sites throughout Old Lyme. If paddling up the Lieutenant River, you will pass the grounds of the Florence Griswold Museum. If paddling up to the Lieutenant River from the Great Island launch, you will pass the Watch Rock Preserve on your right. According to the Old Lyme Land Trust, "There are signs of continuous habitation from 2500 BC to Contact (between Europeans and Native Americans). Watch Rock was an important spot in the Contact period. From this vantage point, the local Indians could look north, south and also west towards Saybrook. Hostile Indians could not approach unseen."

Thomas Svinlland exploring Lord Cove. **PHOTO DAVID FASULO**

Leaving from the Four Mile River launch. **PHOTO DAVID FASULO**

Primary Launches: Four Mile River State Boat Launch. This is a great launch with ample parking and access to interesting waters. There is good birding right near the launch, and at times fun surfing just after you paddle under the train bridge. Unload boats near the ramp, then park in the main parking lot. Directions: GPS Oakridge Drive. Follow it to the first right down a road to the ramp.

Great Island State Boat Launch. This is another great launch with ample parking and access to interesting waters, including the lower Connecticut River and Black Hall River. SUP friendly, but pay attention to current. Directions: GPS Smith Neck Road and follow it to the end.

Lieutenant River State Boat Launch. This is a nice spot if you wish to explore the Lieutenant River (casual kayak or SUP), and you can also make your way to the Great Island ramp or Connecticut River (watch for current making the return difficult). Directions: GPS Ferry Road. The launch is off Shore Road, on the northwest side of the bridge, next to Ferry Road.

Secondary Launches: Ferry Road. This is a nice sandy launch that provides access to the Connecticut River. It is a good location to access the Lieutenant River to the south or explore Lord Cove to the north. Parking for about eleven cars. Directions: GPS Ferry Road and follow it to the first sandy beach on the right. Parking is just past the beach.

Pilgrim Landing. A good launch for Lord Cove, but parking is very limited. It is a nice area to SUP, but is crowded in September due to paddlers watching the swallows nesting in the evening. Directions: GPS Pilgrim Landing Road (less than a mile north from I-95 on Neck Road). The launch is on the immediate left.

Cruising Paddler

There are several enjoyable tours to explore. One of the most popular is to explore the East Lyme coast, past Rocky Neck, from the Four Mile River launch—but that paddle is placed in the East Lyme section.

In the late summer and early fall, hundreds of thousands of swallows (a new group each night) gather over Goose Island to roost for the night. The gathering at dusk is spectacular, as the birds funnel all at once into the reeds at sunset. PHOTO DAVID FASULO

Great Island to Lieutenant River to Connecticut River. This cruise is better towards the top of a rising tide due to some shallow water. From the Great Island launch, head north up the river. In a little over 1,000 feet, the river will split. Continue straight/right into the shallow cove area. Head towards a gap between a shore point on the left and small island on the right (Watch Rock Preserve and Duck River will be on your right). Trend left into the entrance of a narrow creek through tall grasses (best to use a picture from Google Maps to help you navigate). In just under 2 miles, you will reach the Lieutenant River. Head west on the Lieutenant River to the Connecticut River (2.2 miles total). Continue south down the Connecticut River along the eastern shore, then around the southern tip of Great Island and back to the launch (5.3 miles total).

Lord Cove Wildlife Area. From the Ferry Road, Pilgrim Landing, or Baldwin Bridge State Boat Launch (Old Saybrook), paddle over to the north side of Calves Island (nice beach landing). Continue up Lord Creek, past the eastern side of Goose Island, into Lord Cove. From here meander up the creek to Rat Island. It is fun to explore the curving creek (dead-ends eventually); however, it is best to have an accurate chart or Google Maps image to figure out the twists and turns, and not get too lost.

Stand up paddling in Lord Cove, as seen from a drone, with Coults Hole in the center/background.
PHOTO DAN RENNIE

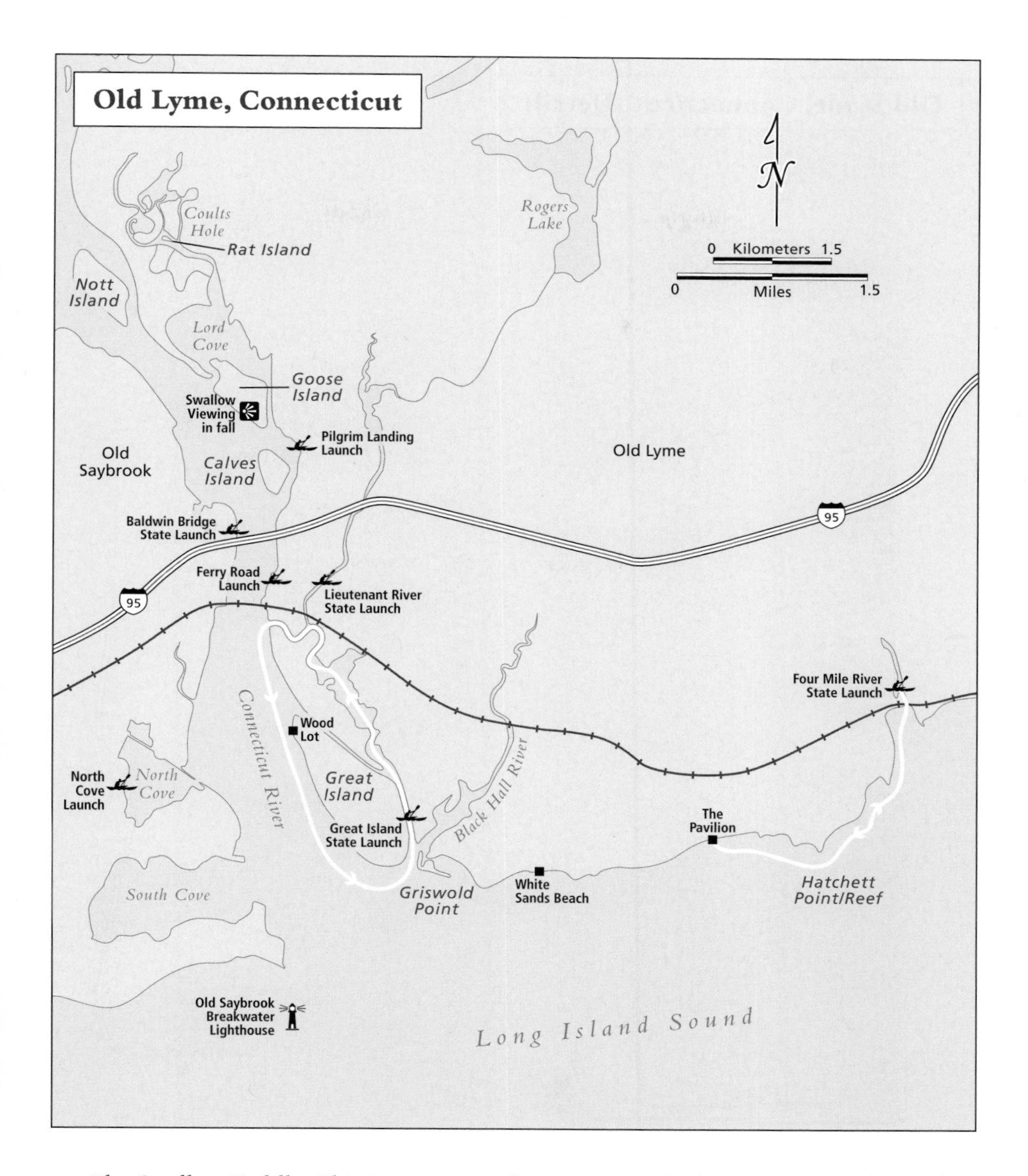

The Swallow Paddle. This is an outstanding event. In the late summer and early fall, hundreds of thousands of swallows (a new group each night) gather over Goose Island to roost for the night. The gathering at dusk is spectacular. The best launch, in terms of access as well as plentiful parking, is the Baldwin Bridge State Boat Launch (Old Saybrook). It is about a 1-mile paddle to the prime viewing area (either side of Goose Island). Bring a white light for the return.

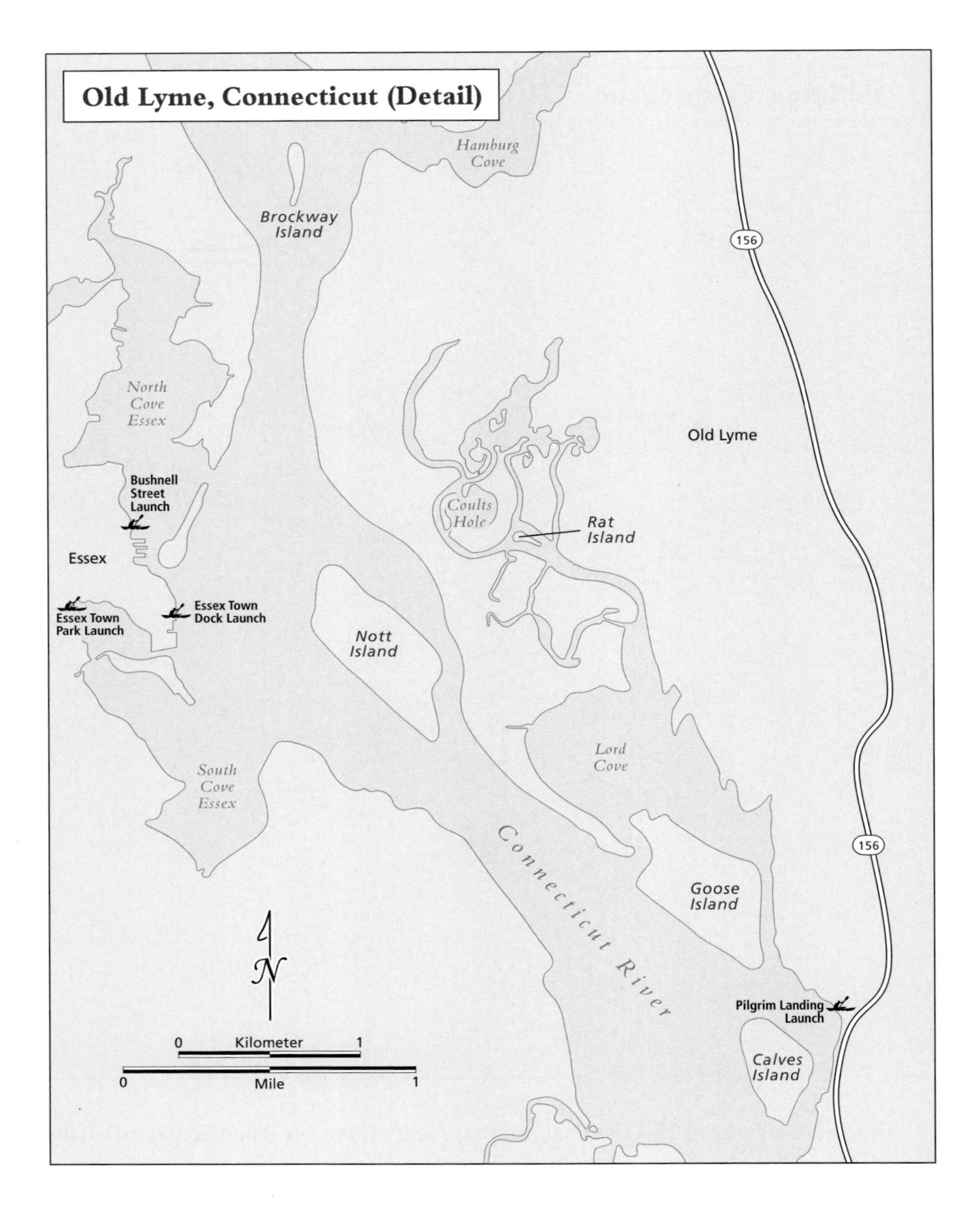

Old Lyme Shore—western end. From the Four Mile River State Boat Launch, head out to the sound and follow the Old Lyme coast, west past Hatchett Reef, for about 2.6 miles. At this point you will encounter the Pavilion Beach Bar. A good turning point

The Great Island State Boat Launch is a favorite launch for touring kayaks, kayak anglers, and SUPs. Griswold Point, where the Black Hall and Back Rivers converge with the Long Island Sound, can provide productive fishing in shallow waters. Mike Kelley and Corey Pelletier are on the search for stripers. PHOTO DAVID FASULO

(unless you want more mileage), but some paddlers land here and explore the area in search of drinks and snacks. Return the same route to the launch (5.2 miles total).

Distance Paddler

From the Great Island State Boat Launch, head south then east along the Old Lyme shore towards White Sands Beach. Paddle past Hatchett Reef, then head towards Rocky Neck State Park (stay out of swimming area). Continue along the coast to Griswold Island (East Lyme). Just to the east of Griswold Island is a small beach/cove to take a break (about 8 miles one way). Return the way you came, or explore some of the island off of Rocky Neck State Park (about 16 miles total).

Rough Water Paddler

The water south of Griswold Point to Bell 8 used to have playful water (known as the "Zipper"), but has gotten shallower over time. In certain conditions it is still fun to play in. The mouth of the Four Mile River, just after the train bridge, can have fun swells to surf during certain conditions.

SUP Friendly

The Black Hall River, from the Great Island State Boat Launch, is a very good tour. You can paddle far upriver, depending on level of interest and conditions. At the mouth of the Black Hall River you can take a break on Griswold Point (some areas are restricted). Another very nice tour is the Lieutenant River. Put in at the Lieutenant River State Boat Launch and head northeast for about 2 miles, then return to the launch. Lord Cove, and its winding waterways, is a cool place to explore from the Pilgrim Landing launch.

Something Fishy

Griswold Point (junction of Black River and Connecticut River) is a popular area for bass and bluefish. In June the Old Lyme coast of the Connecticut River (the woodlot at the northern end of Great Island is a good spot) to the Lieutenant River has schoolie bass. This area is typically fished from high tide to three hours after high tide along the riverbank. Getting out to stretch their legs, kayak anglers have found it a productive exercise to cast large plugs from the shoals along Great Island and Griswold Point when the tide would otherwise prohibit transiting the river. The shallow launch at the Great Island Wildlife Area offers superb access to this lower river fishery, and fluke holes can be found off White Sands Beach. From the Four Mile River launch, Hatchett Reef is productive and holds a variety of fish.

East Lyme, CT

For the coastal cruiser the western end of East Lyme (Rocky Neck State Park, Griswold Island, Watts Island) to Black Point is a great venue. The small islands and varied shore provides interesting contrast and is perfect for late-day cruising. The Four Mile River launch in Old Lyme is a favorite for cartop boaters and provides good access to this shoreline. When the conditions are right, the water just south of the train bridge has nice, easy surf runs to play in.

For more casual paddling and SUPing, the Niantic River is a good spot, but stay clear of the waterway under the Route 156 bridge and train bridge. The current is exceptionally strong, and there is a lot of boat traffic that is barely in control in this section. South of the Niantic River, Niantic Bay offers more-protected paddling, and a nice SUP cruising area is Railroad Beach, which is accessed by walking under the train bridge from Cini Park. Along the western end of Niantic Bay there are many small, private beaches where you can land (up to the high-water mark and not in swimming areas) to take a break.

Bob Ten Eyck exploring Long Ledge, just past Rocky Neck State Park. **PHOTO DAVID FASULO**

Primary Launches: Four Mile River Road State Boat Launch (Old Lyme). While located in Old Lyme, this launch provides good access to the East Lyme/Rocky Neck/Black Point coastline. It is a great launch with ample parking and access to interesting waters. There is good birding right near the launch, and at times fun surfing just after you paddle under the train bridge. Unload boats near the ramp, then park in the main parking lot. Directions: GPS Oakridge Drive, Old Lyme. Follow it to the first right down a road to the ramp.

Cini Memorial Park. This is a nice launch to access the Niantic River; however, *do not* paddle under the bridge—the current and boat traffic is dangerous. There is a floating dock to launch SUPs into the Niantic River on the north side of the bridge, as well as a small sandy beach for kayaks. Directions: GPS 11 Main St. Parking is under the bridge.

Railroad Beach. This beach launch is located on the south side of the train bridge on Niantic Bay. Launching is allowed on the western section of the beach, outside the swim-area buoys. You will need to carry boats under the bridge, and then it is a very long carry to reach the western end of the bridge. More of a landing destination, or SUP surf area if the conditions are right. Directions: GPS 11 Main St. Parking is under the bridge.

Secondary Launch: Grand Street. This is a good launch for the Niantic River, but on-street parking is limited. Nice for SUPs or casual kayaking. Directions: GPS Grand Street and follow it to the end, just before it turns right into the marina.

Cruising Paddler

Rocky Neck and Old Black Point Islands. A popular circuit leaves the Four Mile River launch and explores the shore and rocky islands to Black Point. From the launch, head south to the small rocky island (North Brother) and then past another small rocky island (South Brother). Head east past Long Rock and Long Ledge (2 miles), then north to Watts Island (2.5 miles total). There is a small beach on the south side of Watts Island that is a common stop (public to high-tide mark) as well as a small beach/cove just east of Griswold Island. Paddle around Huntley Island (just west of Watts Island) and continue along the shore, heading west past Seal Rocks (3.4 miles total). Continue past Rocky Neck State Park and back to the launch (4.8 miles total). It is easy to add miles to this circuit by continuing east towards, and around, Black Point (waves can be rough) and into Niantic Bay.

Smith Cove. If the seas are rough, a more protected excursion is into Smith Cove in the Niantic River. From the Cini Memorial Park launch, head north along the eastern shore of the Niantic River. Head west at Keeny Cove (or explore a bit) to the western

Returning to the Four Mile River launch with the Tuesday Night Paddlers. PHOTO DAVID FASULO

shore (2.1 miles). Paddle into the narrow channel into Smith Cove (watch boat traffic) and explore a bit. Head back to the launch (4.45 miles total).

Distance Paddler

The Four Mile River launch to Railroad Beach covers a lot of varied terrain. It is a 12- to 13-mile round-trip. Watch for large waves near Black Point.

Rough Water Paddler

During certain conditions there is fun, short surf just north of the Four Mile River train bridge. The tip of Black Point can also kick up in certain condition, and is generally rough due to boat wakes and ledges.

SUP Friendly

For SUPs the Niantic River is a protected area, but be careful of boat traffic and current near the bridge. Leaving from the Four Mile River launch (Old Lyme) and cruising along

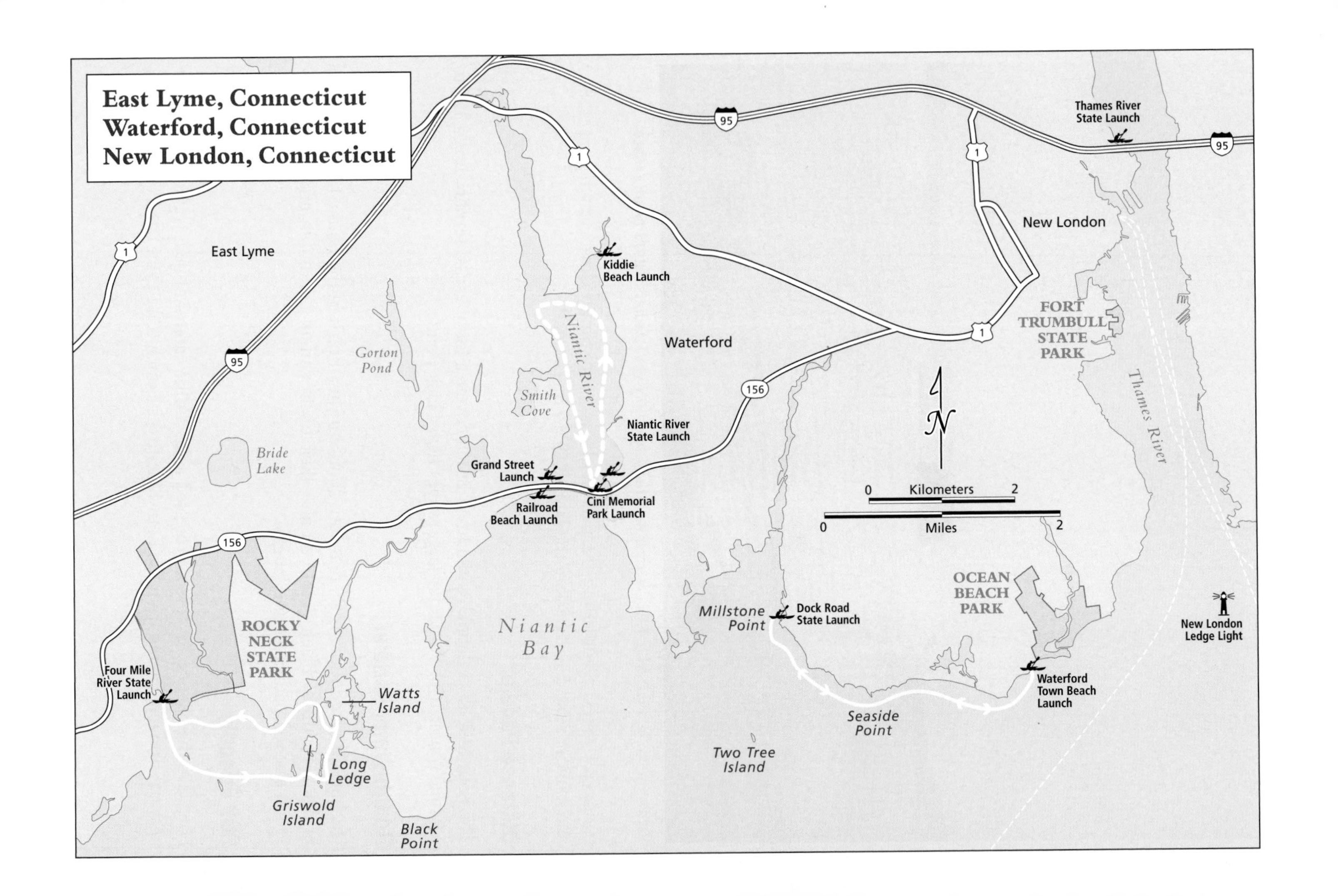
East Lyme, Connecticut
Waterford, Connecticut
New London, Connecticut
East Lyme
Waterford
New London
95
1
156
Thames River State Launch
Kiddie Beach Launch
Niantic River
Niantic River State Launch
Grand Street Launch
Railroad Beach Launch
Cini Memorial Park Launch
Gorton Pond
Smith Cove
Bride Lake
FORT TRUMBULL STATE PARK
Thames River
N
0
Kilometers
2
0
Miles
2
ROCKY NECK STATE PARK
Four Mile River State Launch
Watts Island
Long Ledge
Griswold Island
Black Point
Niantic Bay
Millstone Point
Dock Road State Launch
Two Tree Island
Seaside Point
OCEAN BEACH PARK
Waterford Town Beach Launch
New London Ledge Light

Rocky Neck is hard to beat, but watch for strong current under the bridge on an ebb tide (the return will be very difficult).

Something Fishy

There are lots of good spots in this area. The rocks and small islands off Rocky Neck State Park hold a variety of fish, and the tip of Black Point has bass and blues, as well as large fluke off the tip in depths of 100 feet. Niantic Bay is loaded with fluke, sea bass, and porgy (scup) spots. Niantic Bay also has scallops (permit required). The outflow off the Millstone Nuclear Power Plant, accessed from the Dock Road launch in Waterford, attracts piles of fish until late in the season.

Waterford, CT

Waterford offers pleasant coastal cruising as well as protected waters in the Niantic River. The Waterford Town Beach is a nice destination from the Dock Road State Boat Launch, which provides a 6-mile round-trip cruise along beautiful beaches that are not overly developed. The Niantic River State Boat Launch is well suited for SUPs and recreational kayaks, especially if it is too windy on Long Island Sound. Of special note, the fishing along the Waterford coastline is exceptional. Therefore, the Dock Road State Boat Launch is popular with kayak anglers.

Primary Launches: Niantic River State Boat Launch. This launch is typically crowded in the summer, but it has good access to the Niantic River. The current under the bridge, if trying to access Long Island Sound/Niantic Bay, is very dangerous and should be avoided. Directions: GPS 2nd Street, which brings you to the large parking lot adjacent to the launch.

Dock Road State Boat Launch. This is a good launch, with quick access to fishing spots for the kayak angler. There is ample parking, interesting coastal cruising, and a protected bay for SUPs. Directions: GPS Dock Road and follow it to the end.

Secondary Launches: Waterford Town Beach. This is a beautiful sandy beach open to nonresidents, but the carry is about 1,000 feet from the parking area. The weekday cost is $22 per car, weekends $32, or you may purchase a beach sticker for $107 per vehicle. The town allows the launching of kayaks and paddleboards over by the picnic area as well as the tree line. Paddle craft cannot be launched or brought onto the beach/swim area. There is a shallow lagoon that is also a possible launch next to the bridge on the way in. Directions: GPS 305 Great Neck Rd.

Seaside State Park. There are plans to create a state park on the former Seaside property. Some plans include a cartop launch, some do not. Seaside, originally built as a hospital to treat tuberculosis in the 1930s, was used for a variety of purposes until it was closed in the 1990s. Currently it is a popular stopping point for a break.

Kiddie Beach. This is a nice SUP spot to access Keeny Cove/Niantic River; however, parking is very limited and the water is shallow near the launch. Directions: GPS Fulmore Drive. The launch is located on Niantic River Road, about 900 feet north of Fulmore Drive.

Kailey Malone enjoying the day in the Niantic River. **PHOTO DAVID FASULO**

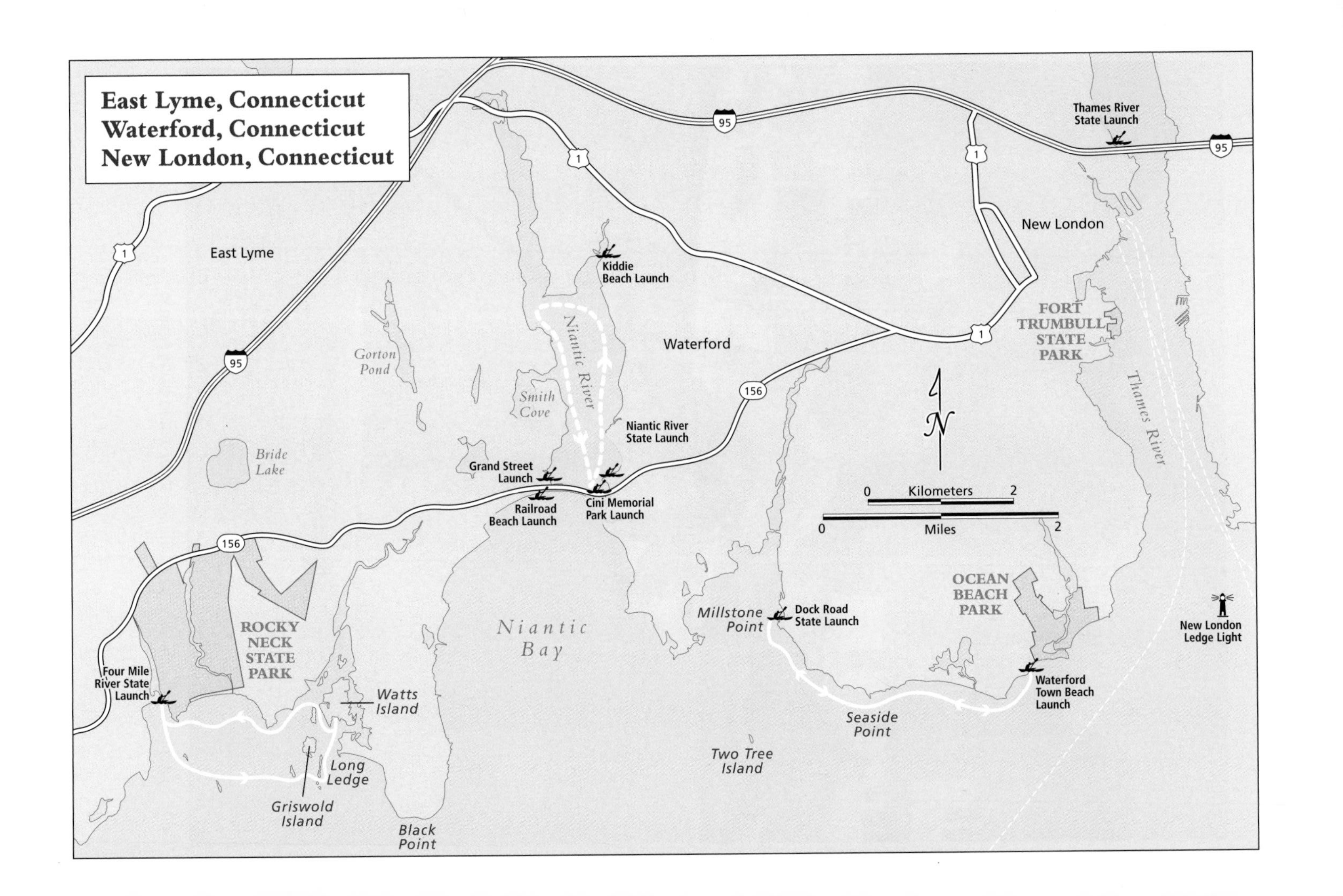
East Lyme, Connecticut
Waterford, Connecticut
New London, Connecticut
East Lyme
Waterford
New London
95
1
156
Thames River State Launch
Kiddie Beach Launch
Niantic River
Niantic River State Launch
Grand Street Launch
Railroad Beach Launch
Cini Memorial Park Launch
Smith Cove
Gorton Pond
Bride Lake
FORT TRUMBULL STATE PARK
Thames River
N
Kilometers
Miles
0
2
ROCKY NECK STATE PARK
OCEAN BEACH PARK
Niantic Bay
Four Mile River State Launch
Watts Island
Long Ledge
Griswold Island
Black Point
Millstone Point
Dock Road State Launch
Two Tree Island
Seaside Point
Waterford Town Beach Launch
New London Ledge Light

Cruising Paddler

The most common route is out of the Dock Road launch, heading east along the shore. A nice place to stop is the west end of the Waterford Town Beach about 3 miles from the launch (6 miles round-trip).

Distance Paddler

Extend the paddle and turnaround point when leaving the Dock Road launch and heading east. One option is paddling to Fort Trumbull and back (12 to 13 miles round-trip).

Rough Water Paddler

Bartlett Reef can kick up, but steer clear of anglers.

SUP Friendly

Niantic River, especially as you go north past the boats, is fun to explore. The hidden Smith Cove on the west is interesting late in the day (watch for boats).

Something Fishy

There are many prime fishing spots from the Dock Road launch. For bluefish, across the bay, anglers fish near the outflow of the power plant at Millstone Point. There are fluke to be found in Niantic Bay, as well as stripers along the rocky shoreline. Many species can be caught in Two Tree Channel, including some very large tautog (blackfish), and the Bartlett Reef area is productive. Additionally, the area around Goshen Reef can be productive for fluke, bluefish, and stripers at certain times of the year.

New London, CT

New London, just south of Fort Trumbull, has some pleasant coastal touring. However, it is not a popular destination for cartop boaters due to the access points. New London Ledge Light is interesting to explore (watch boat traffic), but typically approached from the Bayberry Lane State Boat Launch in Groton. There is good fishing along the mouth of the Thames River, but boat, ferry, and at times nuclear submarine traffic can be daunting. Keep clear of the submarine base on the east side of the river—armed guards patrol the riverfront area and all boaters are required to keep their distance. Vessels are required to stay 100 feet away from the restricted area, and are encouraged to keep to the west side of the channel; loitering in this area is not permitted.

It is not uncommon to see submarines being built or repaired at Electric Boat just south of the I-95 bridge, and the historic *Nautilus* submarine/museum is a memorable site that is north of the bridge (both on the east side of the river). The *Nautilus* submarine, built at Electric Boat in 1954, was the world's first nuclear-powered ship and the first vessel to go to the North Pole. Please remain 100 feet from the *Nautilus* and do not loiter.

New London Ledge Lighthouse. **PHOTO DAVID FASULO**

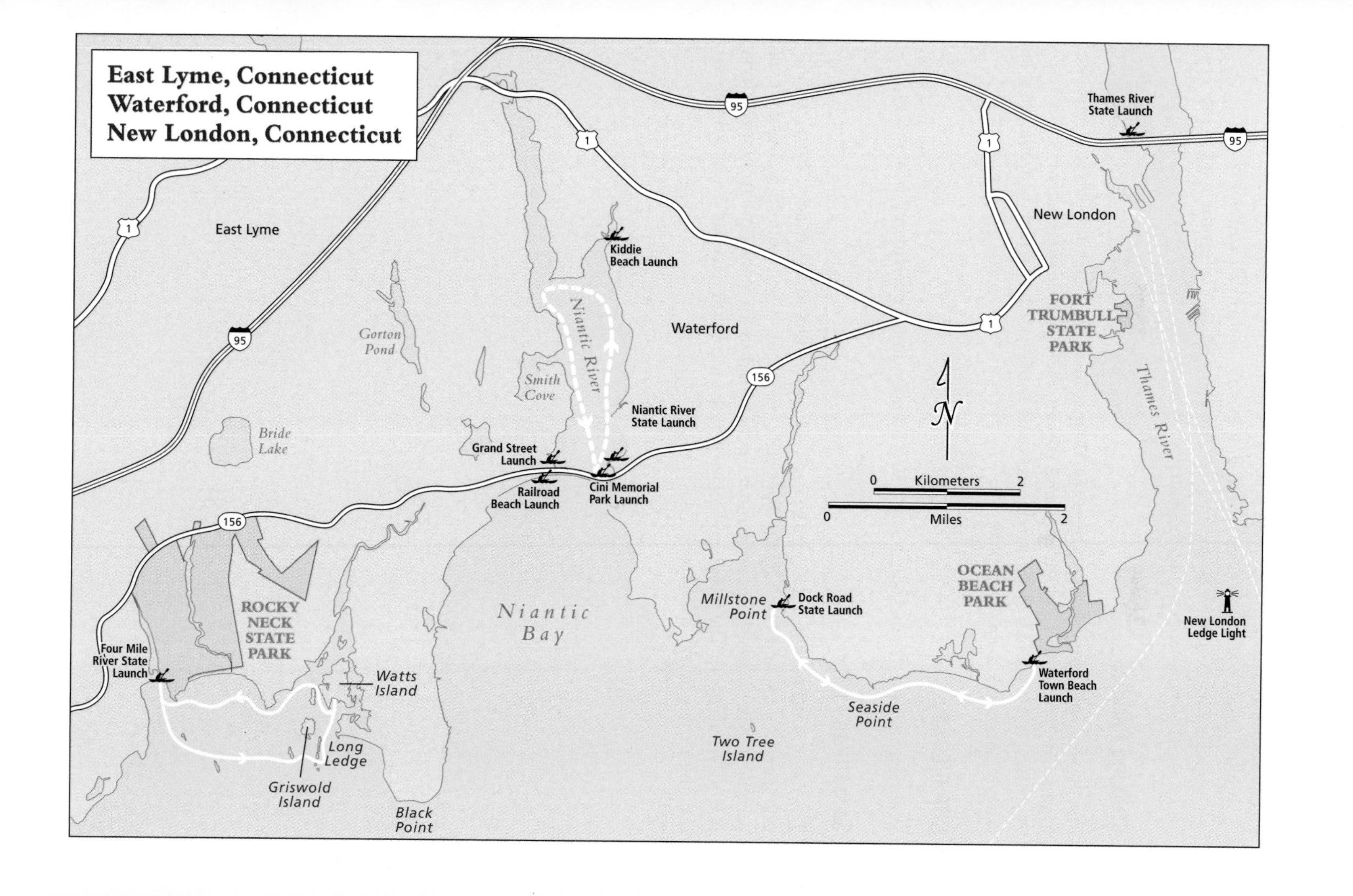

East Lyme, Connecticut
Waterford, Connecticut
New London, Connecticut
95
1
East Lyme
Gorton Pond
Bride Lake
Kiddie Beach Launch
Niantic River
Smith Cove
Waterford
Niantic River State Launch
Grand Street Launch
Railroad Beach Launch
Cini Memorial Park Launch
156
New London
Thames River State Launch
FORT TRUMBULL STATE PARK
Thames River
N
0
Kilometers
2
0
Miles
2
ROCKY NECK STATE PARK
Four Mile River State Launch
Watts Island
Long Ledge
Griswold Island
Black Point
Niantic Bay
Millstone Point
Dock Road State Launch
Two Tree Island
Seaside Point
OCEAN BEACH PARK
Waterford Town Beach Launch
New London Ledge Light

Primary Launch: Thames River State Boat Launch. This is the most convenient public launch, with accessible parking. It is a bit "industrial" and not very popular with paddlers. Directions: GPS State Pier Road. Follow the road to the end to the boat launch (not the State Pier launch).

Cruising Paddler

Just under 2 miles (one way) north of the Thames River State Boat Launch is Mamacoke Island. This is a bit of a hidden gem, and passing the Coast Guard Academy is interesting. South of the launch is industrial, and there is often commercial boat traffic, so it is not a recommended area to explore.

SUP Friendly

Unfortunately, the Thames River is not SUP friendly due to current and boat wakes.

Something Fishy

The rocks at the mouth and along the banks of the Thames River are good spots, including Sarah's Ledge and Black Rock. Black fish, bass, and, if bottom fishing, fluke are all good bets. Near shore, summer flounder can be found south of the Fort Trumbull fishing pier to White Rock. The harbor in Norwich at the top of the Thames is well known for holding stripers in the off-season.

Groton, CT

With an abundance of free public coastal access sites, as well as quick access to prime paddling locations, Groton is one of the finest sea kayak and SUP venues in Connecticut. The Avery Point area is a popular destination for the after-work kayaker or SUPer, with a stop on the small beach on the south side of nearby Pine Island or the nearly mile-long outer beach of Bluff Point State Park. For a well-protected kayak or SUP area suitable for all levels, the Poquonnock River/Bay (be aware of wind and at times current) accessed from Bluff Point State Park is perfect for a short venture, or a longer-distance outing into Long Island Sound. Please note that the Mystic area is half in Groton, half in Stonington, and is given its own chapter.

The favorite launch among locals is the Esker Point town launch, where a well-protected launch with ample parking offers access to Palmer Cove. From this launch, paddlers can head north in the protected cove, or south under the bridge into Long Island Sound between Esker Point and Groton Long Point. From here lies some of the best paddling venues on the East Coast. To the west, Groton Long Point and Groton

Frank Glaser launching out of Esker Point on his way to West Harbor, Fishers Island, during a Tuesday Night Paddle. **PHOTO DAVID FASULO**

Long Point Harbor (recommended destination) are popular. To the east, circumnavigating Mason's and Ram Islands and exploring downtown Mystic (an excursion in itself when launching from the Mystic River) is a great tour along interesting sites.

However, it is when the experienced paddlers (a group of three is considered a safe minimum) venture south into Fishers Island Sound that the excitement and beauty of this area is truly revealed. The area is mapped in the "New York Waters-Fishers Island Sound" section. Highlights include the distinctive "kingdom" of North Dumpling Island (2.5 miles from Esker Point launch), which is a standard first destination (Google the island for its unique history), and Flat Hammock Island (2.6 miles from Esker Point launch) is a good landing spot. West Harbor, about 1.25 miles from Flat Hammock, is also a popular tour. Touring the northern coastline of Fishers Island (care must be taken to time wind and currents), with a rest in the Hungry Point area (7-mile round-trip from Esker Point launch), is a spectacular cruise. Among all of these excursions, the best outing in Connecticut for the experienced distance paddler is the Fishers Island circumnavigation—an 18-mile round-trip requiring a variety of paddling, navigation, and self-reliance skills.

Returning to the Bayberry Lane launch passing Avery Point. **PHOTO DAVID FASULO**

Heading past Morgan Point, towards the Mystic River. **PHOTO DAVID FASULO**

Primary Launches: Bayberry Lane State Boat Launch. This is a prime location for kayaks and SUPs; however, please be courteous when launching (cartop boat launch is next to boat ramp) and parking. The area is also very popular with anglers launching powerboats. Cartop boaters should double-park in the long spaces designed for trailers and keep the ramp clear. Directions: GPS Bayberry Lane to the end and launch.

Bluff Point State Park. According to the Connecticut DEEP website, "Bluff Point is the last remaining significant piece of undeveloped land along the Connecticut coastline. Jutting out into waters of Long Island Sound this wooded peninsula, measuring one and one-half miles long by one mile wide, encompasses over 800 acres." This is a great spot for SUPs and recreational kayaks. There is a launch on the north side of the jetty, but a short walk to a small beach south of the jetty avoids current between the jetties. If you follow the Poquonnock River south, you'll find a cool beach to explore (south side is very nice). Keep in mind there is current, so returning to the launch can be strenuous. Ample parking for groups. Directions: GPS Depot Road and follow it south to the parking area and launch.

Esker Point town boat launch. This is one of the best, and most popular, sea kayak launches in southeast Connecticut. The launch is free and has ample parking and good access to prime paddling destinations. Directions: GPS 937 Groton Long Point Rd. The large parking area is on the north side of the road (across the street from the beach), and the launch is on the southwest section of the parking lot.

Secondary Launch: Eastern Point Beach. This is a very pleasant launch. Cartop boats are restricted to the beach area in front of Zbierski House on the Thames River side of park (small beach in front of house on the water). Parking fee from Memorial Day to Labor Day. Directions: GPS Beach Pond Road and follow it to the end.

Cruising Paddler

Pine Island and Bluff Point. From the Bayberry Lane State Boat Launch, head around the western end of Pine Island. Paddle northeast towards the large, open Bluff Point Outer

Nick Schade at the spindle, Groton Long Point. PHOTO DAVID FASULO

Kayaks and SUPs aren't the only sights in Fishers Island Sound. The Mystic River Mudhead Sailing Association has a Wednesday-night series, typically off the shores of Groton, that can be quite the sight. **PHOTO DAVID FASULO**

The Bluff Point launch has ample parking and protection from waves. Sarah Latham returns after exploring the open beach, where the river meets Long Island Sound. **PHOTO DAVID FASULO**

Beach (nice, small beach on the southeast side of Pine Island to stop on) and cruise the natural shoreline to Mumford Point (2.6 miles). Head around the corner to a beach to take a break (3 miles total). (***Note:*** If you want to extend the paddle from here, checking out the Groton Long Point Harbor is very interesting.) Return along the same path, but cut through at the east end of Pine Island (5.3 miles total).

Groton Long Point and Harbor. From the Esker Point launch, head under the bridge into Long Island Sound and along the eastern shore of Groton Long Point. At the point (1.2 miles; water can be rough at the point during certain conditions), continue west along the shore to the entrance of Groton Long Point Harbor (known by a few other names such as the Lagoon and Venetian Harbor); 2.3 miles total at Green Marker 1. Head into the harbor and east to a bridge (2.9 miles total; during high water you can enter the Upper Lagoon). Return the same route (just under 6 miles total). ***Note:*** There are many areas to explore from Esker Point, including Palmer Cove, the Mystic area, Dumpling Islands, Flat Hammock Island, and Fishers Island.

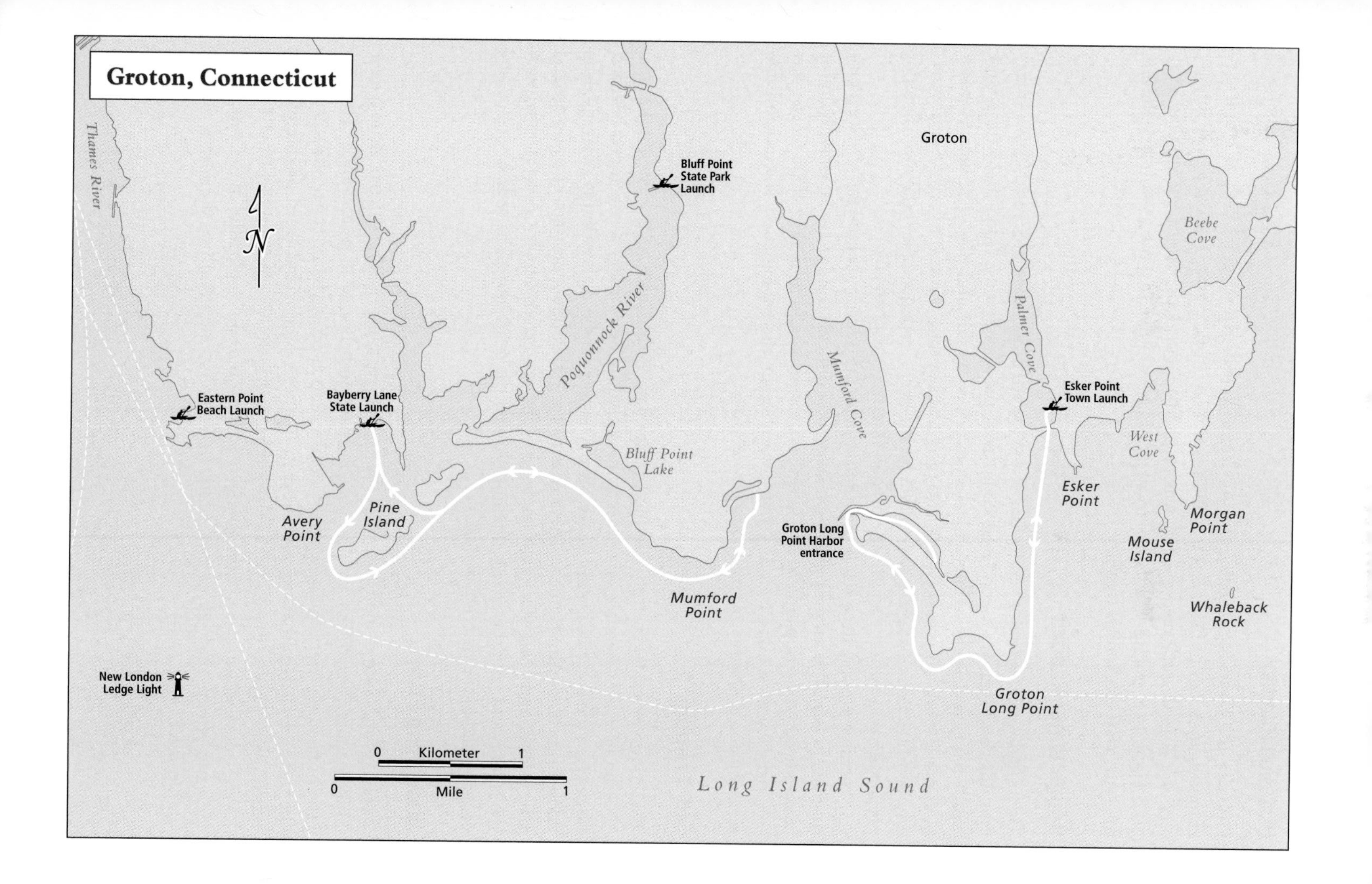
Groton, Connecticut
Thames River
N
Eastern Point
Beach Launch
Bayberry Lane
State Launch
Bluff Point
State Park
Launch
Poquonnock River
Bluff Point
Lake
Groton
Mumford Cove
Palmer Cove
Esker Point
Town Launch
Beebe
Cove
West
Cove
Avery
Point
Pine
Island
Mumford
Point
Groton Long
Point Harbor
entrance
Esker
Point
Morgan
Point
Mouse
Island
Whaleback
Rock
Groton
Long Point
New London
Ledge Light
0
Kilometer
1
0
Mile
1
Long Island Sound

Distance Paddler

Probably the best long-distance trip in Connecticut is the 18-mile Fishers Island circumnavigation out of Esker Point launch (see "New York Waters-Fishers Island Sound" section). A more protected excursion is to paddle west along Groton Long Point, past Bluff Point, and around Pine Island to a rest on the southwest shore (5.4 miles). Return the same way (10.8 miles total).

Rough Water Paddler

The rough water paddling venues out of the Esker Point launch are world-class. At certain tides and winds, Groton Long Point (near the spindle on a flood tide with a west wind) has very large standing and moving waves to surf and play. The area between North and South Dumpling Islands also produces standing waves (prolonged southwesterly wind) to test a paddler's skills. Ram Island Reef is a dependable tidal race (flood or ebb) extending from the south side of Ram Island to the channel buoy.

The area around Race Rock Lighthouse, about 3,000 feet southwest of Race Point on Fishers Island, is an area offering consistently difficult conditions for only the most experienced group of paddlers. The turbulent waters extend from Race Point all the way to Orient Point on Long Island. While always rough, the combination of wind and tide determines the severity of the tide race conditions.

SUP Friendly

The Poquonnock River, from the Bluff Point State Park launch, is a very peasant area. You can head to where the river meets the sound (about 1 mile) for secluded beaches; however, wind and tide should be factored. The area can be shallow but is generally deep enough in the small channels. The Bayberry Lane area offers pleasant cruising around Pine Island, and the Esker Point launch has the protected Palmer Cove (channel near the train tracks, and the cove to the north under the train bridge) as well as nice coastal cruising late in the day (low wind).

Something Fishy

Fishers Island Sound, along much of the Groton coastline, is a productive fishing area. Fluke, tautog (blackfish), sea bass, and bluefish can be found in several areas. The eastern shore along Avery Point, with the nearby launch off Bayberry Lane, offers access to the reefs and ledges that run east–west in line with Pine Island (very productive) and Bushy Point Beach (borders mouth of Poquonnock River). The mouth of the Thames River is also easily accessed from Bayberry Lane. Squid can be plentiful in the Pine Island area and attract a variety of fish. From Esker Point, the mouth of the Mystic River is within reach.

Mystic, CT

The Mystic area is a popular destination and enjoyable experience for all levels of paddlers. To avoid confusion, the visitor should be aware that the portion of Mystic west of the Mystic River is located in Groton, and the portion east of the river is located in Stonington. The Mystic River area provides free, public launching and landing areas, allowing visitors to stroll through downtown and have lunch or dinner at one of the many fine eateries. The jagged Mason's Island and surrounding coastal waters provide interesting paddling and scenery in relatively protected waters (watch for currents and boat traffic).

The well-known Mystic Seaport and Mystic Aquarium attract visitors far and wide, and the area is a popular destination for vacationers with SUPs and kayaks. Paddling along the Mystic Seaport offers rare scenery, such as the whaleship *Charles W. Morgan*. According to the Mystic Seaport website (www.mysticseaport.org), "The *Charles W. Morgan* is the last of an American whaling fleet that numbered more than 2,700 vessels. Built and launched in 1841, the *Morgan* is now America's oldest commercial ship still

The last wooden whaleship in the world, the Charles W. Morgan, *as seen from the water at the Mystic Seaport.* **PHOTO DAVID FASULO**

afloat—only the USS *Constitution* is older." You can also time your paddle to coincide with the annual wooden boat show or the many other events hosted by the Mystic Seaport.

Primary Launches: Mystic River State Boat Launch (Groton). This is a nice site to put in if exploring the northern Mystic River (north of I-95) as well as the Mystic Seaport and downtown Mystic. Directions: Exit 89 off I-95; GPS Bindloss Road, Groton. Follow Bindloss to River Road. Head north on River Road, and just north of the I-95 overpass the launch will be on your right (dirt pull-out with small access area).

Williams Beach (Stonington). This is a "secret" launch for locals, and its continued use requires a low impact and courteous users. While Williams is a public beach, it is run by the Mystic YMCA. The beach is free, and there are no lifeguards on duty. Upon contacting the Mystic YMCA, the author was informed there are no restrictions in regards to launching cartop boats. However, this area should not be used by large groups or private instruction. Swimmers and beachgoers need to be avoided when landing and launching,

Nick Shade enjoying the sunset in Mystic Harbor. **PHOTO DAVID FASULO**

and users must be courteous. Always carpool if possible. Directions: GPS 1 Harry Austin Dr. Parking is behind the Mystic YMCA, and the beach is along Mystic Harbor.

Esker Point town boat launch. This is one of the best, and most popular, sea kayak launches in southeast Connecticut. The launch is free and has ample parking and good access to prime paddling destinations. In terms of access to Mystic, the launch is 4 miles one way to the Mystic River downtown bridge. Directions: GPS 937 Groton Long Point Rd. The large parking area is on the north side of the road (across the street from the beach), and the launch is on the southwest section of the parking lot.

Secondary Launches: Water Street Public Dock and Launch (Groton). A nice little launch if you want to explore Mystic on foot afterwards, and there are several great restaurants in this area. The launch is located between the Main Street bridge and the train bridge, on the western side of the Mystic River. Directions: GPS Burrows Place. Head east on Burrows Place to Water Street. Turn right on Water Street; the launch will be immediately on your left. Limited parking at Burrows Place, or metered parking off Steamboat Wharf.

Isham Street (Stonington). This is a good takeout spot next to (south) of the Mystic Seaport. While technically a launch, there is very limited parking nearby. Directions: GPS Isham Street, Stonington. The launch is at the end of the road, next to the Mystic Seaport property.

Mystic River Dinghy Dock (Stonington): This is another good takeout and a short walk to downtown and good restaurants. You can also launch from this spot, but parking is limited. According to the DEEP Connecticut Coastal Access Guide, "Limited parking on Holmes Street is available. Additional parking is available on Frazier and Forsyth Streets and on 10 Broadway Ave. at the 4th District Voting Hall." Directions: GPS Frazier Street, Stonington. The launch in off Holmes Street (along the water) between Frazier and Forsyth Streets.

Cruising Paddler

Esker Point launch around Mason's and Ram Islands. There are other launches in the Mystic area, but the Esker Point launch from Groton is the most accessible and parking friendly. From the launch, head east past Mouse Island and Morgan Point (1 mile), then northeast towards Mason's Island. Paddle around the north section of the island (Mystic Harbor; can be shallow) towards Williams Beach (possible rest). Head south down the harbor/cove and then under the Mason's Island bridge (4 miles total). Continue south past Enders Island, then west along the southern tip of Mason's Island. Head southwest towards Ram Island (6.2 miles total) and around the southern end of the island (6.9

Ron Gautreau rounding Enders Island. **PHOTO DAVID FASULO**

miles total). Continue west past Whaleback Rock and back to the launch (8.6 miles total).

Note: The 11-acre Enders Island, cared for by Society of St. Edmund ministry, is a interesting rest stop. There is a small beach to land on on the northwest side (near the causeway and parking lot), and the southwest end has interesting features to tour (remain on pathways). The author contacted Enders Island staff and was informed the public is allowed to tour the island. Be respectful of the grounds and other visitors; alcohol is not permitted on the property.

Mystic River State Boat Launch to Isham Street. From the Mystic River State Boat Launch, head south to the Mystic Seaport (just under a mile). Explore the Seaport area to a rest at the Isham Street launch. Meander under the Main Street bridge (be careful of boat traffic and current) to the vicinity of the Water Street launch (just before the train bridge), then back to the launch (3.4 miles total). The trick is to slowly explore the ships around the Seaport and the village. If you choose to extend your tour, land on Williams Beach and then return.

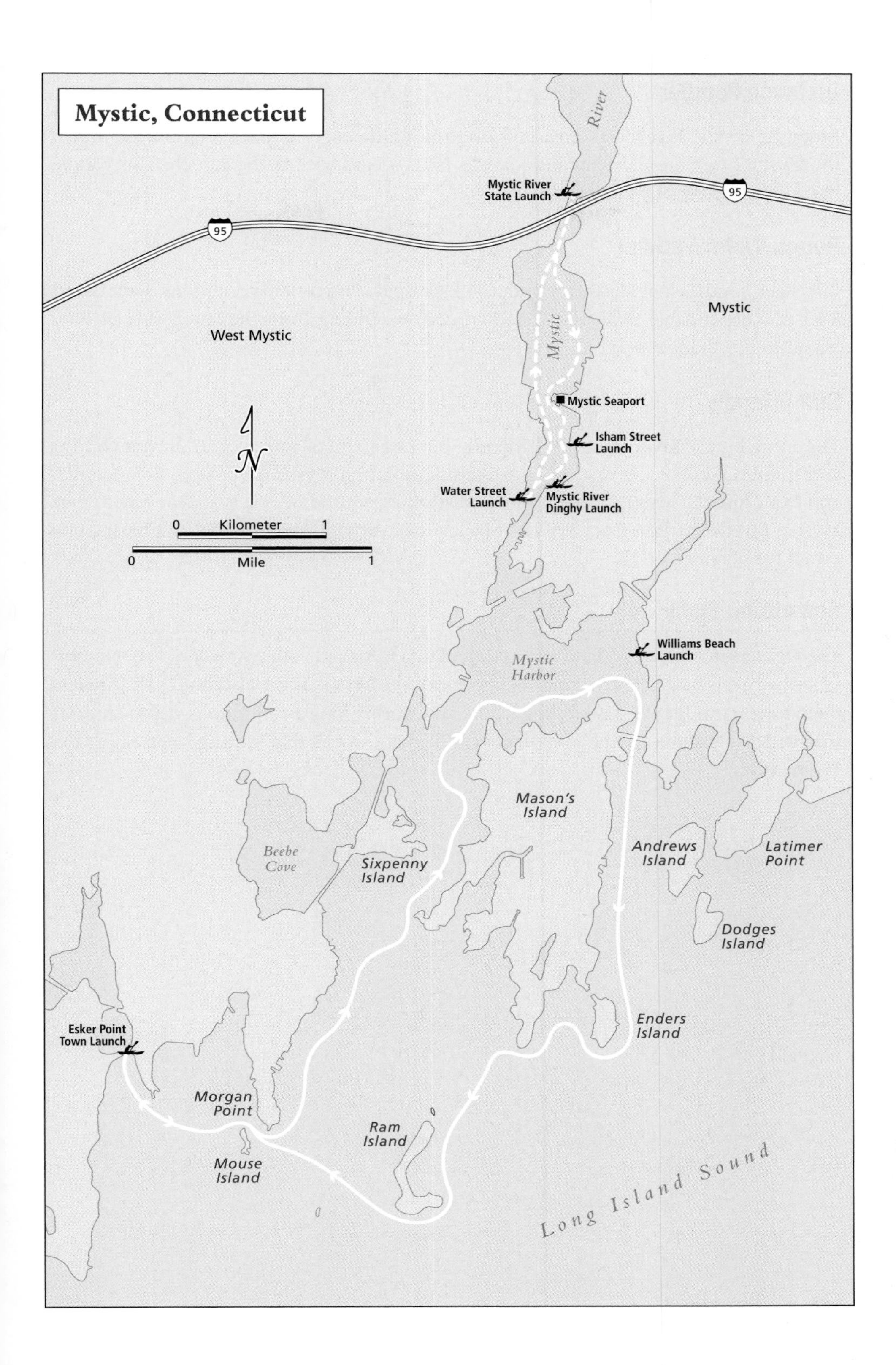
Mystic, Connecticut
River
Mystic River State Launch
95
95
Mystic
West Mystic
Mystic
Mystic Seaport
Isham Street Launch
N
Water Street Launch
Mystic River Dinghy Launch
0
Kilometer
1
0
Mile
1
Williams Beach Launch
Mystic Harbor
Mason's Island
Beebe Cove
Sixpenny Island
Andrews Island
Latimer Point
Dodges Island
Enders Island
Esker Point Town Launch
Morgan Point
Ram Island
Mouse Island
Long Island Sound

Distance Paddler

From the Mystic River State Boat Launch, it is a little over 10 miles total to head down the Mystic River, around Ram and Mason's Islands, and back to the launch. This paddle has a wide variety of pleasant scenery.

Rough Water Paddler

Ellis Reef, southeast of Mason's Island, can kick up during certain conditions. Ram Island Reef is a dependable tidal race (flood or ebb) extending from the south side of Ram Island to the channel buoy.

SUP Friendly

The entire Mystic River area is SUP friendly, but be careful of current near the drawbridge and trainbridge. For the first-timer, launching from the Mystic River State Boat Launch and exploring the Mystic Seaport and then strolling around Mystic is a great way to tour Mystic. Mystic Harbor, from Williams Beach, has very nice scenery but can be shallow out of the channel.

Something Fishy

The area around Mason's Island and Latimer Point is loaded with a variety of fish. Numerous small reefs and islands along the mouth of the Mystic River also hold fish. Anglers often have a productive day trolling a tube and worm along a continuous-depth contour that will likely intersect the abundant boulders and rocks that stud the bottom of the Mystic River.

Stonington, CT

Stonington is a beautiful, and varied, coastal region. Stonington Harbor, with its commercial fishing fleets and large yachts, is a popular area to explore. The nearby Sandy Point provides protected waters and an idyllic setting adjacent to Little Narragansett Bay. Stonington is also a key launch area to reach Watch Hill Cove, as well as the Napatree Point Conservation Area with its open beaches and rough water at the point. Since Mystic is composed of Groton and Stonington, some of Stonington is also covered in the Mystic section.

Stonington is also a strategic launching area for world-class tidal races (rough water/standing waves caused by moving water over structure). For the past several years, it has been home to the Autumn Gales Sea Kayak Symposium. The event is timed for late autumn when the weather systems are fast approaching, and during the spring tides. At this event internationally known BCU coaches and nationally known ACA instructors, along with local paddlers who provide expert regional knowledge, converge in Stonington in the famed waters around Fishers Island Sound. The symposium allows paddlers

Returning to the Barn Island launch after a tour of Watch Hill Cove and Sandy Point. **PHOTO DAVID FASULO**

Large and chaotic waves are not uncommon at Napatree Point (Westerly, Rhode Island) on a big-water day. **PHOTO CARL TJERANDSEN**

to sample advanced conditions, with a solid safety net of guides and coaches, to foster learning experiences.

Primary Launches: Barn Island State Boat Launch. This is a very popular launch in the protected Little Narragansett Bay. The launch also provides quick access (less than 1 mile) to Sandy Point (beach and preserve) and Watch Hill Cove in Rhode Island (1.85 miles). Directions: GPS Palmer Neck Road and follow it to the end.

Saltwater Farm Vineyard launch. An OK launch with a short walk to the water. There is limited parking, but the area is well protected and provides access to the protected Wequetequock River and Cove. The launch can be a bit muddy, and the water is thin at low tide (too low for SUPs at low tide). Directions: GPS 349 Elm St. The small parking area is immediately on the left (before the vineyard).

Landing Area: Sandy Point. Once a popular area to land on and explore, much of the island is now restricted for nesting. However, the beach is still a unique, and beautiful, destination. Cruising around the island is also a great outing.

According to the Avalonia Land Conservancy website (www.avalonialand conservancy.org), "Sandy Point Island is a beautiful 35-acre barrier island in Little Narragansett Bay, about 1.5 miles in length. Only the western tip is in CT and the remainder is Rhode Island. Access is by water only and it is surrounded by shifting sand bars. It is managed as a wildlife refuge and since 2015 is actively monitored by USFWS as part of the National Refuge System. It is a major spawning ground for Horseshoe crabs and it hosts nesting American Oystercatchers, Piping Plovers and Least Terns, all protected species. Areas are roped off and closed to the public during nesting season. It is a significant migratory bird habitat as well. No dogs are allowed on the island. Permits are required during the summer season for usage and are obtained through the Stonington Community Center."

During the summer season, passes are required/checked to land on the island. A day pass is $5 (can be bought online the day you wish to visit) and a yearly pass is $70. Passes are available at www.thecomo.org.

Cruising Paddler

Sandy Point and Stonington Harbor. From the Barn Island State Boat Launch, head to the eastern end of Sandy Point (1 mile). Head west along the northern shore of Sandy Point and then southwest to Stonington Point (2.5 miles total). Paddle into Stonington Harbor to the commercial fishing docks on the right (landing area on the right just before the commercial docks—Stonington Small Boat Association). Continue across the harbor, then follow the coast to the west end of the breakwater/Wamphassuc Point (4.5 miles total). Cruise along the north side of the breakwater and back to the western end of Sandy Point (6.6 miles total), then follow the southern shore of Sandy Point and head back to the launch (about 7.8 miles total).

Sandy Point and Watch Hill Cove. From the Barn Island State Boat Launch, head towards the eastern end of Sandy Point, then cruise along the northern shore of Sandy Point to the western end of the point (2 miles). Continue along the southern shore of Sandy Point and head to Watch Hill Cove to a rest on the beach at the southwest end of the harbor (4.5 miles total). Continue south along the shore of the Napatree Point Conservation Area beach to Napatree Point (6 miles total). (***Warning:*** Napatree Point can be very rough, with large breaking waves. *Stay away* from the pilings and rocks/reef in that area.) Head north back towards the eastern end of Sandy Point (just over 7 miles total) and back to the launch (about 8.5 miles total). A slightly shorter route (5.7 miles) is described and mapped in the Westerly, RI, section.

A late-day return passing the Stonington breakwater. **PHOTO DAVID FASULO**

Distance Paddler

The Tristate Paddle. This paddle hits three states in a day. From Barn Island, paddle to the eastern end of Fishers Island, New York (4.5 miles). (There is a rest stop on the northeast end of Fishers Island; be careful of current and waves at Wicopesset Passage.) Continue to Napatree Point, Rhode Island (6.75 miles total), then head back to the Barn Island State Boat Launch, Connecticut (9 miles total).

Super Distance Paddler

The Stonington Triangle. This circuit was first envisioned by the author, and completed on June 28, 2003, by Nick Schade in a Guillemont Night Heron, Mark Starr in an Impex Montauk, Phil Warner and Kate Powers in a NDK Triton Double, and David Fasulo in a NDK Explorer. The 54-mile circuit was first completed in 14 hours. The paddle goes from Stonington, Connecticut, to Montauk, New York, to Block Island Rhode Island, and back to Stonington in a single day.

Rough Water Paddler

This is a short list of rough water play areas (i.e., tidal races) among the reefs and rocks typically accessed from the Stonington launches. These areas are only for the most

Taking a break at Montauk during the first paddle of the "Stonington Triangle"—54 miles of open water in 14 hours. **PHOTO DAVID FASULO**

experienced and prepared sea kayakers. Without the proper equipment, training, and safety precautions, you can be killed in these waters by the unforgiving waves and currents. Also be aware that these locations can have very powerful and deep standing waves. If you capsize, it is very difficult to recover and for others to rescue you in the turbulent water. There is also no place to "rest" on the ebb tide at Sugar Reef. Nautical charts are required to accurately locate the areas listed below.

- An area locally known as "The Cans": A third of a mile north of the eastern tip of Fishers Island, between green cans #11 and #13 on a flood tide.
- Wicopesset Passage: Between the eastern tip of Fishers Island and Wicopesset Island is best on an ebb tide (between can #1 and the RW buoy) and on the flood just off the tip of Fishers. There are places to get out of the current to rest at this location on the flood tide.
- Catumb Rock: About 1 mile south from Napatree Point (just southwest of Sugar Reef). The ebb race actually sets up around the #2 nun just west of Catumb Rock.
- Sugar Reef: Approximately 0.8 mile southeast of Napatree Point (marked with a stake that looks like an old ship's mast) on the ebb tide. There is no

place to rest out of the current at this location, and the waves/turbulent water can be substantial.

A closer, and more popular, area is Napatree Point. However, although it is tempting to surf in this area, stay away from the wood pilings, as there is shallow water and rocks in that area. The waves on the point are often large and turbulent, so it can be hard to predict waves/surf. A nice surf spot is after (northeast of) the pilings/rocks. There is a secondary wave that is typically long and not too big when the larger waves are crashing at Napatree Point.

(***Note:*** On an early exploration of these reefs, Carl Tjerandsen and I visited Watch Hill Reef [close to Sugar Reef] on a very big wave and current day. During one of my surf runs through the chaos, the bow of my kayak hit a rock and cracked the hull. I was lucky not to have been injured among the large churning waves and swift waters. I recommend staying clear of Watch Hill Reef.)

SUP Friendly

When the conditions allow, the Sandy Point area of Little Narragansett Bay and along the coast of Barn Island are interesting to explore. When the tide is up (too shallow at low tide), paddling out of the Saltwater Farm launch to Wequetequock Cove is pleasant. It is also fun to paddle around Stonington Harbor and venture into Lamberts Cove.

Greg Paquin, organizer of the annual Autumn Gales Sea Kayak Symposium based in Stonington, demonstrating rough water skills at Sugar Reef. **PHOTO JAN BLOCH PHOTOGRAPHY/NEW ENGLAND KAYAK CLUB**

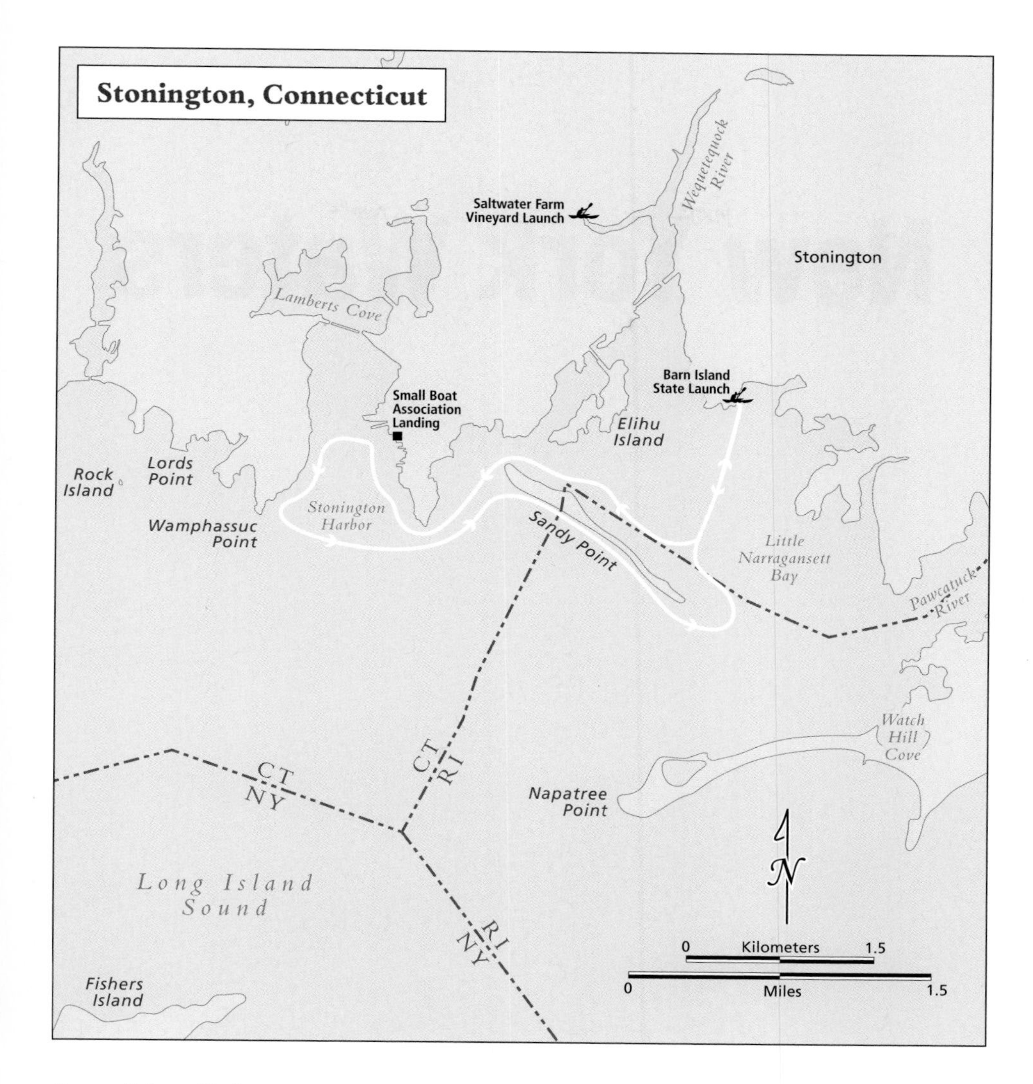

Something Fishy

The Stonington Point area is a good bass spot (more so at night), and the breakwaters hold fish as well. In the fall bluefish swarm around the Sandy Point area, and tautog (blackfish) can be found on the breakwater.

New York Waters

Fishers Island Sound

While the Thimble Islands and Norwalk Islands are always interesting, the author's favorite area in Connecticut is Fishers Island Sound. For the distance paddler and recreational paddler, there are several circuits that leave Groton and are some of the best in Long Island Sound. Aside from the overview described here, some paddlers also take the ferry out of New London to Orient Point, New York. From there they play in the very rough waters around Plum Island and Orient Point.

Primary Launches: Esker Point town boat launch (Groton, CT). This is one of the best, and most popular, sea kayak launches in southeast Connecticut. The launch is free and has ample parking and good access to prime paddling destinations. Directions: GPS 937 Groton Long Point Rd. The large parking area is on the north side of the road (across the street from the beach), and the launch is on the southwest section of the parking lot.

Barn Island State Boat Launch (Stonington, CT). This is a very popular launch in the protected Little Narragansett Bay. Just over 4 miles (one way)

The "kingdom" of North Dumpling, Fishers Island Sound. **PHOTO DAVID FASULO**

Curt Andersen touring West Harbor, Fishers Island. **PHOTO DAVID FASULO**

to Wicopesset Passage on the eastern end of Fishers Island. Directions: GPS Palmer Neck Road and follow it to the end.

Cruising Paddler

Dumplings and West Harbor from Esker Point town launch. Probably the best cruise if new to the area is over to North Dumpling Island (2.6 miles) then past South Dumpling and into West Harbor (4.1 miles total). You can take a break below the mean water line (not in swimming areas), or leave the harbor and head towards Flat Hammock to land and take a break (5.4 miles total, depending on tour of harbor). To return, aim for Groton Long Point, and then back to the Esker Point launch (8.3 miles total). ***Note:*** Boat traffic in high season can be intimidating and can also lead to rough seas (boat wakes). This cruise should be considered a significant crossing, so paddlers should prepare accordingly.

Hungry Point to the east end of Fishers Island. This is a nice route, and offers some open water. If you time the tides and have the wind, it is not too difficult. If you are fighting the wind and tides, you will struggle. Essentially, leave Esker Point and head south towards Fishers Island (just over 3 miles). Paddle east to a break on a small beach near Hungry Point (3.9 miles total). (***Note:*** In the cooler months, Hungry Point is known for

Taking a break on the south side of Fishers Island during a circumnavigation of the island, with Race Rock Lighthouse in the background. **PHOTO DAVID FASULO**

its seal population on the nearby rocks; please keep a respectful distance, at least 100 yards, so as not to disturb them.) Continue east to the east end of Fishers Island (break on beach before Wicopesset Passage), then ride the flood tide/ferry crossing towards Ram Island (8.8 miles total) and then back to the launch (10.5 miles total). This cruise should be considered a significant crossing, so paddlers should prepare accordingly.

Distance Paddler

The classic distance paddle is to circumnavigate Fishers Island. If going counterclockwise, there is a rest stop at Hay Harbor Beach or shortly after Race Point, and then a few spots on the south side of the island. If going clockwise, there is a rest stop at the far eastern end of the island, north side. The trip is about 18 to 20 miles, depending on whether you stay near the island or ferry across to/from the eastern end. Race Point Ledge can be very difficult to get through (exposed rocks, waves, and current); if necessary, it may be safer to land your boat at the point and carry it to the other side. Another area to be careful of is Wicopesset Passage (rough water in narrow passage); carrying a boat around this point is not an option. Planning the trip with the tides and wind is helpful. Also note the south side of Fishers can be exposed, and self-reliance/rescue skills are needed. The

A rough water paddler off to play in the standing waves in the turbulent "Race" near Race Rock Lighthouse. This area is only for expert sea kayakers with proper equipment. PHOTO CARL TJERANDSEN

record for circumnavigating Fishers Island, starting at the Esker Point launch bridge, as of 2017 is 2:44:53 by David Grainger in a surf ski–style kayak.

Rough Water Paddler

The passage between North and South Dumpling Islands can stand up in certain conditions (prolonged southwest wind). Wicopesset Passage is also an area with consistent rough water to play in (flood tide is safer), but stay clear of boats using this passage.

The area around Race Rock Lighthouse is frequented by the strongest, and highest level, paddlers (rescues are very difficult on an ebb tide). The Race Rock Light area has large and turbulent standing waves, but at least the skilled paddler can catch a break in the back eddies near the lighthouse. ***Warning:*** *Stay clear* of anglers and boats in this area.

Looking for some race play on the flood but don't want to paddle all the way to Race Rock Light? Locals and race-paddle tourists alike head for a patch of water a third of a mile north of the eastern tip of Fishers Island. It is referred to as "The Cans" because it sets up between the #11 and #13 green cans that bracket the best water on a flood tide.

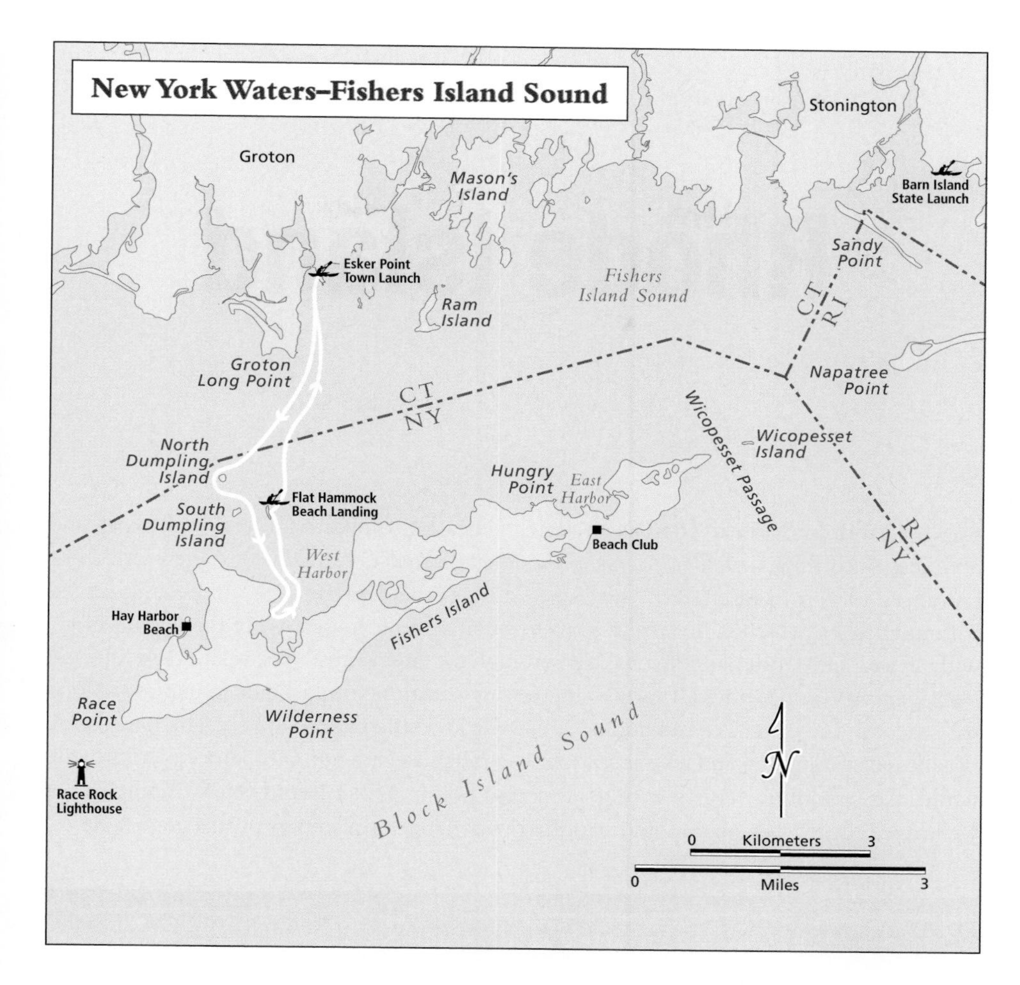

SUP Friendly

Unless you take the ferry over, or are very experienced, it is not wise to SUP over to these islands due to current and waves.

Something Fishy

The Fishers Island area is renowned for all kinds of consistently good fishing. Look for fluke in the channels, as well as bass and blues around the rocks, reefs, and shoreline. Charter boats frequent the Race Rock Lighthouse area and destinations on the south side of Fishers Island.

Rhode Island

Rhode Island, known as "The Ocean State," has a lot to offer paddlers of all types and abilities. According to *Public Access to the Rhode Island Coast* (2004), "There are three entrances to Narragansett Bay: the West Passage, the East Passage, and the so-called Sakonnet River, which is not really a river but an arm of the sea. Only the East Passage, with an average depth of 44 feet, is deep enough for large ships." The relatively protected Narragansett Bay provides all sorts of interesting coastlines and islands to explore. Along the seacoast, the water is clean and ocean swells keep the padding lively. The long sandy beaches, historic forts, and awe-inspiring areas such as Newport and Jamestown provide world-class paddling venues with good access points. Block Island (New Shoreham), a well-loved tourist destination and paddling experience, is also part of this great state.

Elise Walsh enjoying the day at Third Beach, Middletown, Rhode Island. **PHOTO DAVID FASULO**

Rhode Island is famous for its rocky shorelines and coastal mansions. PHOTO DAVID FASULO

The Rhode Island shoreline is vast and varied, and some of the popular locations are listed below. As with Connecticut, stand up paddlers seem to congregate in quieter pockets of water along the shore, in bays, and where group paddles and rental facilities are most common.

Popular tours from western to eastern Rhode Island include:

Napatree Point/Watch Hill Cove, Westerly
Ninigret Pond and Quonochontaug Pond, Charlestown
Point Judith Pond, South Kingstown
Point Judith/Narragansett coast/Dutch Island/Narrow River, Narragansett
Fort Wetherill/Jamestown coast/Jamestown circumnavigation, Jamestown
Bristol Harbor/Hog Island/Colt State Park, Bristol
Newport Harbor/Fort Adams/Kings Beach, Newport
Third Beach/Sakonnet River, Middletown
Sakonnet Point, Little Compton
Block Island coast and Great Salt Pond, New Shoreham/Block Island

In terms of kayak fishing, Rhode Island offers anglers additional species such as cod and black sea bass that are not regularly found to the east and west. The habitat and

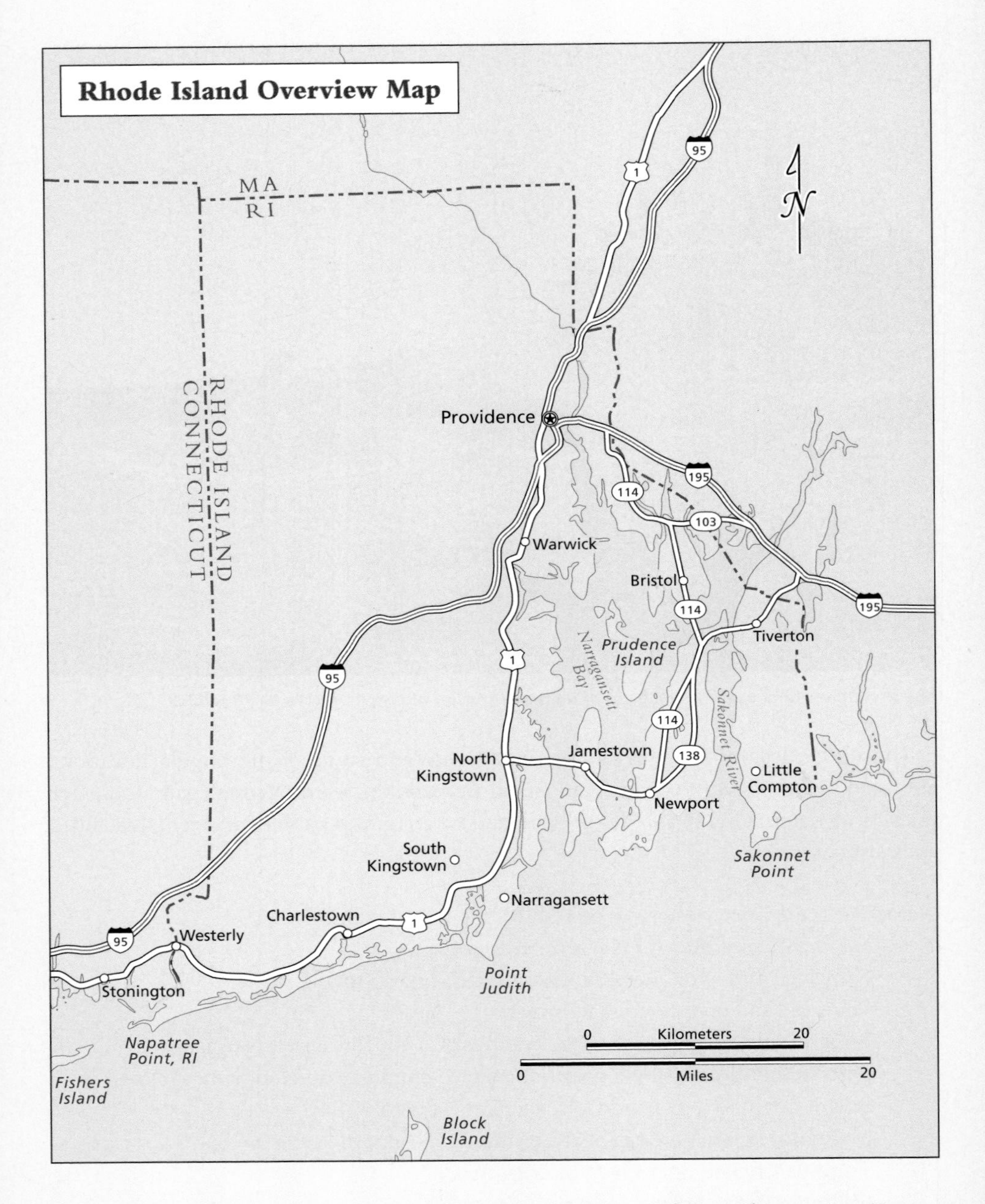

variety of structure also make Rhode Island a desirable kayak fishing destination. Having migrated from Connecticut waters, or having made an entirely offshore migration from Chesapeake Bay directly to Block Island, big bass love Rhode Island. Anglers tend to utilize eels, menhaden, clam bellies, soft plastics, or plugs reeled very slowly.

Westerly, RI

The Westerly area has some of the nicest beaches (8 miles of oceanfront) in the state, but limited public access for cartop boats. For kayakers a favorite destination is the Little Narragansett Bay area, including Sandy Point Island, Watch Hill Cove, and the beautiful Napatree Point. Since access and parking is a problem, many kayakers approach from the Barn Island State Boat Launch in Stonington, Connecticut (1 mile to Sandy Point Island, 1.8 miles to Watch Hill Cove, and 2.37 miles to the tip of Napatree Point).The inner Watch Hill Cove is a fantastic SUP area, but parking is difficult. However, the free two-hour parking (you will get a ticket after two hours) can be just enough time for a good workout. SUP access is quick by launching from the town-owned floating dock near the town green and parking.

Napatree Point is a free, public barrier beach managed by the Watch Hill Conservancy in cooperation with the Watch Hill Fire District. The north side of Napatree Point, closer to Watch Hill Cove, has calm waters and nice beach landings. The actual point, as further described in the rough water paddler section, is typically rough. The southern

Group landing in Watch Hill Cove, after paddling from the Barn Island launch, to search for ice cream in downtown Watch Hill. **PHOTO DAVID FASULO**

Carl Tjerandsen, the grandfather of rough water/reef sea kayak play in the Fishers Island and Block Island Sound areas, taking a break on the ocean side of Napatree Point. PHOTO DAVID FASULO

side of the point offers nice beach cruising, but landing can be difficult due to waves; kayakers typically land on the western end (not the point), just east of the rocks. ***Note:*** You can walk across the dunes to the ocean side of Napatree Point at designated areas (marked by large yellow posts).

Sandy Point Island was once connected to Napatree Point, until the Great New England Hurricane of 1938 cut the peninsula. While mostly located in Rhode Island, Sandy Point Island is also described in the Stonington, Connecticut, section since passes are available from the Stonington Community Center and the closest access is from the Barn Island State Boat Launch. The water can be shallow on the eastern end of the island, but this is a very scenic area to tour. Landing is typically on the north side, but stay out of restricted zones for birds.

A popular area for the most experienced and prepared rough water paddlers is Sugar Reef (see rough water paddler description). The reefs south of Napatree Point and extending to Fishers Island have become a destination for top-level rough water sea kayakers from around the world. For several years the Autumn Gales Sea Kayak Symposium has been attracting world-class sea kayak coaches and instructors from around the world to train others in this area. Be forewarned, without the proper equipment, training, and safety precautions, you can be killed in these waters by the unforgiving waves and currents.

Primary Launches: Barn Island State Boat Launch. This is a large and well-protected free launch in Stonington, Connecticut. Directions: GPS Palmer Neck Road, Stonington (off Route 1) and follow it south to the end. From this launch, it is 1 mile to Sandy Point Island, 1.8 miles to Watch Hill Cove, and 2.37 miles to the tip of Napatree Point.

Westerly Boat Ramp. This is a protected ramp that has access to the Pawcatuck River. The launch is 5.25 miles upriver from Watch Hill Cove. There is parking for four cartop boats; the other parking is for cars with trailers. Additional parking may be possible next to the ramp. Directions: GPS 100 Main St., Westerly; the launch is across the street.

Secondary Launches: Watch Hill Cove/Napatree Beach. This is a really great area to paddle from; however, parking is very difficult. In season there is a nearby lot and on-street parking for a limit of two hours. There are a couple pay lots in town (can fill up in summer), although off-season the nearby lot is free. If paddling from Barn Island, Connecticut, is too far (1.8 miles), figuring out the parking ahead of time and dropping off boats may be worth it since this is such a nice area. The launch is at the end of the road (beach area on the right, Watch Hill Cove southwestern side). You will pass restricted parking areas for the beach cabanas on your left. Directions: GPS Fort Road. The parking lot is adjacent to the waterfront next to a small town green alongside Bay Street (across from the Olympia Tea Room restaurant).

Watch Hill Dinghy Dock. This is a SUP launch in downtown Watch Hill across from the town green. During the summer season, the parking lot and on-street parking close to the launch is limited to two hours—just enough for a nice tour. Off-season the lot is free. There is also parking in pay lots throughout Watch Hill, but they can fill up quickly in the summer. Directions: GPS Fort Road The parking lot is adjacent to the waterfront next to a small town green alongside Bay Street (across from the Olympia Tea Room restaurant); the dock is located on the waterfront between the two-hour parking lot and town green frontage.

Misquamicut State Beach. The state beaches do not allow cartop boat launching when the beach is open for the season. However, launching off-season is possible. This site has access to a nice launch for Winnapaug Pond, but requires dropping off boats and carrying them down a short road. The access is located across the street from the main entrance. Directions: GPS 257 Atlantic Ave., Westerly.

Landing Area: Sandy Point Island. Once a popular area to land on and explore, much of the island is now restricted for nesting. However, the beach is still a unique, and beautiful, destination. Cruising around the island is also a great little outing. According to the Avalonia Land Conservancy website (www.avalonialandconservancy.org), "Sandy Point Island is a beautiful 35-acre barrier island in Little Narragansett Bay, about 1.5 miles in length. Only the western tip is in Connecticut and the remainder is Rhode Island. Access is by water only and it is surrounded by shifting sand bars. It is managed as a wildlife refuge and since 2015 is actively monitored by USFWS as part of the National Refuge System. It is a major spawning ground for Horseshoe crabs and it hosts nesting American Oystercatchers, Piping Plovers and Least Terns, all protected species. Areas are roped off and closed to the public during nesting season. It is a significant migratory bird habitat as well. No dogs are allowed on the island. Permits are required during the summer season for usage and are obtained through the Stonington Community Center."

During the summer season, passes are required/checked to land on the island. A day pass is $5 (can be bought online the day you wish to visit) and a yearly pass is $70. Passes are available at www.thecomo.org.

Jim Manship passing Sandy Point Island late in the day, with Watch Hill in the background.
PHOTO DAVID FASULO

Cruising Paddler

Sandy Point and Watch Hill Cove. From the Barn Island Boat Launch in Connecticut, head southeast towards the eastern end of Sandy Point Island and continue to the beach at the southwestern end of Watch Hill Cove (1.9 miles). Take a break, or cruise along the northwestern side of Napatree Point (2.6 miles total). Head back to the eastern tip of Sandy Point Island (3.4 miles total). Cruise along the north side of Sandy Point Island (or add miles by cruising the southern side then northern side) to a structure near the beach (4.5 miles). Head back to the Barn Island launch (5.7 miles total).

Distance Paddler

From the Barn Island launch in Connecticut, head past the eastern tip of Sandy Point Island to the tip of Napatree Point (2.38 miles). Cruise along the shore of Napatree Point to Watch Hill Point (4.3 miles total). Go around the point (beware of rough water) to East Beach and a view of the Ocean House and as of 2017 the pop star Taylor Swift's house (4.9 miles total). Return to Napatree Point the way you came, but then cruise along the north shore of the point to the entrance of Watch Hill Cove for a break on the

Tanya Sandberg-Diment playing in the waves off Napatree Point. **PHOTO DAVID FASULO**

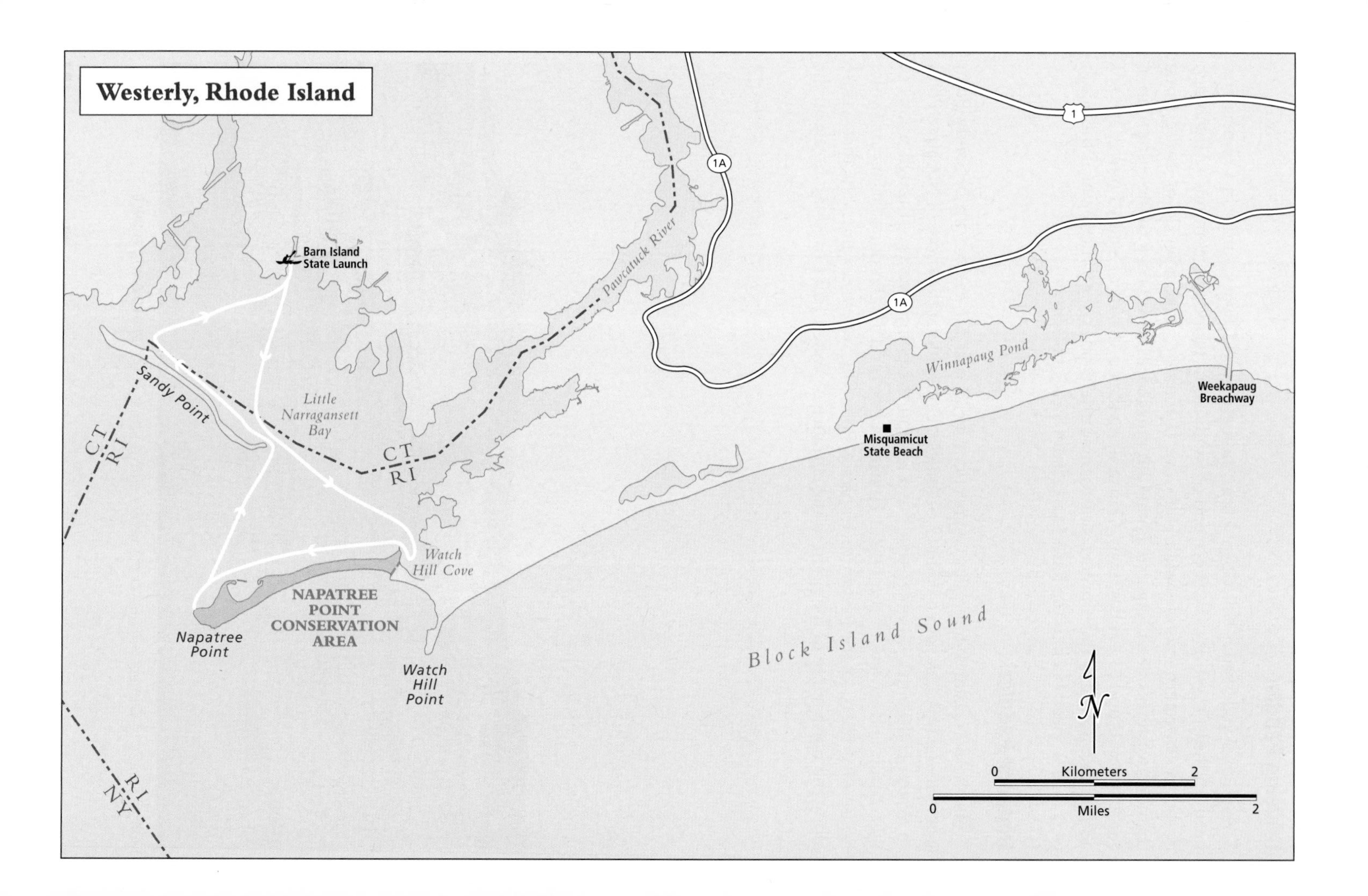
Westerly, Rhode Island
Barn Island State Launch
Pawcatuck River
1
1A
1A
Winnapaug Pond
Weekapaug Breachway
Misquamicut State Beach
Little Narragansett Bay
Sandy Point
CT
RI
CT
RI
RI
NY
Watch Hill Cove
NAPATREE POINT CONSERVATION AREA
Napatree Point
Watch Hill Point
Block Island Sound
N
0
Kilometers
2
0
Miles
2

beach (9.07 miles total). Head to the eastern end of Sandy Point Island (10.1 miles total). Continue along the northern end to a structure near the beach (11.2 miles total), or add distance by going around the south side of the island. Head back to the Barn Island launch (12.4 miles total). (***Note:*** "Distance" is relative to the conditions and paddler's experience. The author typically does this loop on a Tuesday night in the summer with Connecticut locals.)

Rough Water Paddler

Sugar Reef is located about 1 mile offshore southeast of Napatree Point, and is marked by a metal pole on the northern section of the reef. Use a nautical chart to locate the reef. The rough water on this reef is "world-class" and only for the most experienced groups with training in rough water skills and rough water rescue. The standing waves at the head of the reef (outgoing tide) can be significant. On an outgoing tide, paddlers do not get a break because they are pulled back in the turbulent water and waves by the current if they cannot continually overtake the current. The reefs extending from Watch Hill Point to Fishers Island have become destinations for top-level rough water sea kayakers.

The southwestern tip of Napatree Point used to be a favorite spot among rough water paddlers, but many now feel the rocks and piling are too significant of a hazard. These hazards are present close to the most tempting surf zones. Be forewarned that large breaking waves tend to occur at Napatree Point (tip) and are difficult to predict due to their chaotic nature. However, there is often enjoyable surf (long rides on smaller predicable waves) just northeast of the rocky zone and pilings.

SUP Friendly

If you can find parking, Watch Hill Cove and the beach along Napatree Point are great places to paddle, especially late in the day in the summer.

Something Fishy

The Napatree Point area (tip of point) holds fish, but beware of rough seas in this area. The eastern end of Sandy Point, where it gets deeper, sees action from bass and blues in the fall. Fluke can be found all along the shoreline from Napatree Point to Point Judith in the summer. The reefs and rocks (Sugar Reef, Watch Hill Reef) are productive but too rough for kayak fishing. Many kayak anglers, with the proper early-season protective clothing, can be found fishing Watch Hill Cove in early April, awaiting the first schoolie striped bass on their eastern migration. This area only gets larger striped bass as April turns to May.

Charlestown, RI

The Charlestown coastline offers miles of open beach cruising, but the access points listed (breachways) are treacherous for kayaks and SUPs if trying to access Block Island Sound. The town of Charlestown does not allow launching of cartop boats from town beaches. From Memorial Day to Labor Day, East Beach (state beach) does not allow cartop launching on the ocean side of the beach, but allows access to Ninigret Pond. With such difficult access to Block Island Sound, it is difficult to recommend ocean paddling routes.

Rhode Island's largest coastal salt pond, Ninigret Pond, offers well-protected and scenic water for the casual kayaker and protected SUP cruising. According to *Public Access to the Rhode Island Coast* (2004), "Also known as Charlestown Pond, this 1,711-acre coastal lagoon is totally located within the town of Charlestown. A small channel under Creek Bridge connects Ninigret with Green Hill Pond in South Kingstown. The pond is bounded on the south by barrier beaches, to the west by the village of Quonochontaug, and on the east by Charlestown Beach. The ocean breachway in the southeastern end connects with Block Island Sound, and fresh water flows into the pond from numerous small brooks and springs."

Exploring the wildlife in Ninigret Pond. **PHOTO DAVID FASULO**

Block Island Sound Launches: The breachways provide access to several miles of sandy beach in each direction. However, they are dangerous access points due to strong current and boat traffic.

Quonochontaug Breachway. This is a state launch ramp—please give anglers a wide berth. The launch provides access to Block Island Sound, but is dangerous due to swift currents and powerboats. Parking fee when park is open. Directions: GPS West Beach Road and follow it to its end.

Charlestown Breachway. This is a state launch ramp with an entrance fee in the summer; please give anglers a wide berth. The launch provides access to Block Island Sound, but is dangerous due to swift currents and powerboats. Parking is somewhat restrictive, as it is for vehicles with trailers, so you may need to drop off your boat and park in the main lot. Directions: GPS Charlestown Beach Road and follow it to its end.

Quonochontaug Pond Access: Use the Quonochontaug Breachway access, and paddle northeast away from the current and sandbar (can be dangerous on an outgoing tide).

Launch area at Quonochontaug Breachway. **PHOTO DAVID FASULO**

Ninigret Pond Launches: Ninigret National Wildlife Refuge. This is a nice beach launch with ample parking (overflow parking a short walk from the launch). However, during the summer months the protected area can be filled with seaweed and at times be unpleasant. Directions: GPS Park Lane (off Route 1A, across from the police department at 4901 Old Post Rd.). Follow it for 1 mile to the parking area (follow signs for fishing access). Follow the dirt road to the launch (a kayak sign marks the road). Check out the launch as you leave for the markers, to prevent getting lost on the return.

Access point at Ninigret National Wildlife Refuge. PHOTO DAVID FASULO

East Beach State Beach. This area provides a pleasant access point for Ninigret Pond, but per state park regulations, launching is not allowed on the ocean side of the beach during the summer season. Directions: GPS East Beach Road (off Route 1, Westerly). Follow East Beach Road past Blue Shutters Town Beach. Once you enter East Beach State Park, the parking and launch (short trail to the pond) will be on your left (parking can fill up quickly). This is also a well-known site for windsurfers.

Perry Creek Access. This town-owned area is open to the public and is a good access for Ninigret Pond or Green Hill Pond. Best to paddle at the top of the tide so you can explore outside the channel, and be careful of very strong current near the bridge. GPS 557 Charlestown Beach Rd. You will go over a bridge and follow signs to Charlestown Town Beach. Take the dirt road on the right before entering Charlestown Town Beach to a small parking area and launch.

Charlestown Breachway. This is a state launch ramp, with an entrance fee in the summer. The launch provides access to Ninigret Pond (best at top of the tide), but current can be very swift if using this site. Directions: GPS Charlestown Beach Road and follow it to its end.

Watchaug Pond Launch: Baron C. Hurley Landing. While not a coastal cruising area, Watchaug is a very large (573 acres) pond that is a good second choice if the winds are too much for the ocean or coastal ponds. Directions: GPS Sanctuary Road. The launch is located on a dirt road north of Sanctuary Road, between Seneca Trail and Montauk Road.

Cruising Paddler

Northeastern Ninigret Pond Loop. This loop has varied terrain, but currents and low water can affect the route so it is best on a rising and higher tide. From the Ninigret National Wildlife Area launch, head north 1.5 miles along the coast to Fort Neck Park. (***Note:*** When leaving the launch, note any markers to find it again when returning.) Paddle back down the cove along the east side to Marsh Point (2.3 miles total). Follow the coastline (channel with deeper water) to the Perry Creek launch for a break (3.5 miles total). (***Note:*** At this point you can go under the bridge and explore Green Hill Pond, but current under the bridge can be swift.) Head back towards the launch, but then dip south towards Governors Island and continue to Hall Point (5.7 miles total). Follow the coastline back to the launch (6.6 miles total).

Western Ninigret Pond Loop (best at higher tides). From the East Beach launch, paddle along the western shore of Ninigret Pond to the northern shore and Foster Cove entrance (1.84 miles). Do a loop on Foster Cove, back to the entrance (3.08 miles total). (***Note:*** The water in the cove can be shallow—best at higher tides.) Continue west to Hall Point (3.9 miles total), then head back east to the launch (5.6 miles total).

Quonochontaug Pond Loop (best at higher tides). Once the current near the launch is negotiated, this is a pleasant cruise of a coastal lagoon. Head north from the Quonochontaug Breachway launch (out of current and shallow water) and then west. Paddle into the western "cove" (1 mile), then continue towards the western end and Weekapaug Inn (1.8 miles total). Pleasant cruising follows along the northern shore past Shady Harbor and Picnic Rock (3.8 miles total). Continue to explore the coastline before heading back to the launch (5.8 miles total).

Distance Paddler

From the Perry Creek access, or any other access point, paddling along the entire coastline of Ninigret Pond is just over 10 miles (excluding Foster Cove).

Rough Water Paddler

While rough water can be found at the entrances to the breachways, these areas should be avoided because it interferes with boaters and anglers.

SUP Friendly

Ninigret Pond is well protected from every launch, but currents may be too strong at the eastern end near the Perry Creek access. Because SUPs need deeper water, best to plan for higher tides in the ponds. Green Hill Pond is accessible from the Perry Creek launch, but current under the bridge can be strong.

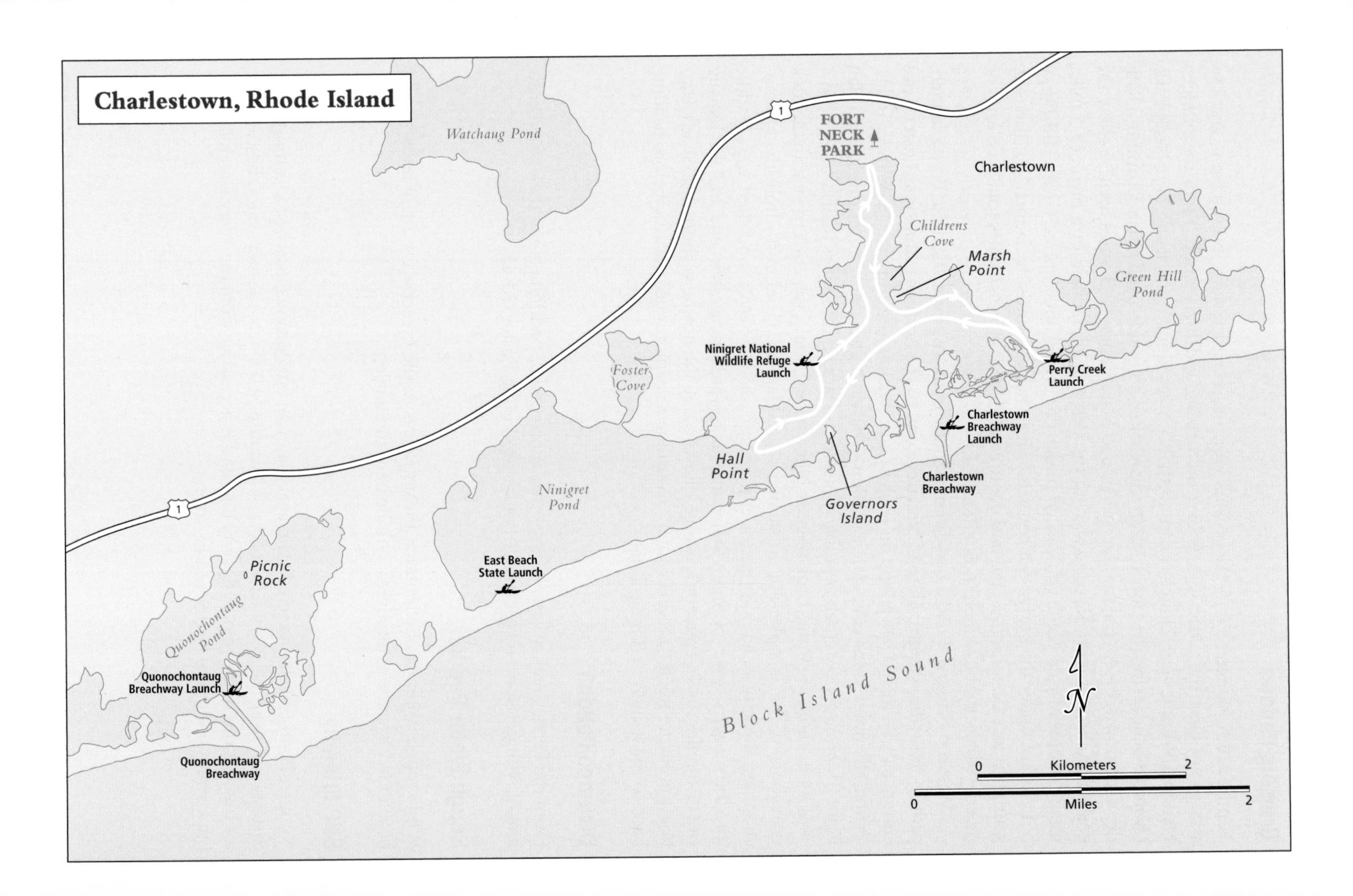

Charlestown, Rhode Island
Watchaug Pond
1
FORT NECK PARK
Charlestown
Childrens Cove
Marsh Point
Green Hill Pond
Ninigret National Wildlife Refuge Launch
Perry Creek Launch
Foster Cove
Charlestown Breachway Launch
Hall Point
Charlestown Breachway
Governors Island
Ninigret Pond
1
East Beach State Launch
Picnic Rock
Quonochontaug Pond
Quonochontaug Breachway Launch
Quonochontaug Breachway
Block Island Sound
N
0
Kilometers
2
0
Miles
2

Something Fishy

Southern Rhode Island beaches and lagoons are areas where a significant number of fluke are caught each day in the summer. While many fishermen flock to the breachways, very few kayak anglers transit the breachways. The breachways are treacherous and require a complete understanding of the currents and wind direction, as standing waves may form at the mouth where a southern wind intersects an ebbing tide. The breachways are popular fishing spots, but please keep clear of anglers fishing from land as well as boat traffic. The real gem lies not in the offshore waters, but instead in the coastal lagoons that hold schoolie stripers and the occasional large striper for a period of time after the initial spring migration occurs and throughout the cinder worm emergence (locally referred to as "the hatch"). The date of the emergence is somewhere between late April and early May. The largest bass can be seen sipping cinder worms right at the surface. This style of fishing lends itself to an approach with more finesse, using a fly rod and cinder worm flies.

South Kingstown, RI

South Kingstown has miles of open beach, but similar to Westerly and Charlestown, ocean access is restricted Memorial Day to Labor Day. The beach cruising can be enjoyable, but at times monotonous. However, for the more-casual kayaker and SUP enthusiast, Green Hill Pond and Point Judith Pond (Saugatuck River estuary) offer varied and protected waters. Potter Pond is pleasant, but access can be difficult due to strong current entering or exiting the pond and limited access/parking at the Succotash Marsh Wildlife Management Area.

There are also pleasant, and protected, waters off the Narrow River. Pettaquamscutt Cove, 1.1 miles south of the Narrow River State Boat Ramp, borders the John H. Chafee National Wildlife Refuge. According to refuge website (www.fws.gov/refuge/John_H_Chafee), "This refuge is one of five national wildlife refuges in Rhode Island. Established in 1973, the John H. Chafee National Wildlife Refuge at Pettaquamscutt Cove can be elusive to many human visitors. However, it is well-known to the migratory waterfowl

Brian Dlhoposky finding fish in Point Judith Pond. **PHOTO DAVID FASULO**

that rely on it, including the largest population of black ducks in Rhode Island. In fact, the 550-acre refuge was established specifically to protect the population of black ducks that winter there. The refuge's tidal salt marshes and forests attract many types of birds, including great egrets, herons, and several species of plovers and other shorebirds. It is also one of the few places in Rhode Island that is home to the salt marsh sharp-tailed sparrow."

While the author has chosen to cover mostly quiet water for South Kingstown, the surfing in the Matunuck area in Block Island Sound is very popular. The surfing season typically picks up after Labor Day, when beach access is open and opposing north winds help build the seas. Surfing requires specific skills and surf etiquette for all to have a safe and enjoyable experience. If choosing to surf in this area (kayak, SUP, or board), it is best to take a lesson from a qualified professional.

Primary Launches: Perry Creek Access (Charlestown): This town-owned area is open to the public and is a good access for Ninigret Pond or Green Hill Pond; however, the current can be strong near the bridge. It is also best to launch at the top of the tide to explore outside the channel. GPS 557 Charlestown Beach Rd., Charlestown. You will go over a bridge and follow signs to Charlestown Town Beach. Take the dirt road on the right before entering Charlestown Town Beach to a small parking area and launch.

Marina Park. This is a town-owned ramp site that has free parking (across the street) and no ramp fees. With the exception of boat traffic, it is a very nice launch. Once south of the Upper Pond/narrow channel, it is a pleasant area to explore. The launch is located on the north end of Point Judith Pond. Directions: GPS 210 Salt Pond Rd. (address of the restaurant between the two ramps).

Succotash Marsh Wildlife Management Area. This is a great launch site to access the southern end of Point Judith Pond or Potter Pond (if the current is safe under the bridge to Potter Pond). Located on the west side of the Point Judith breachway, this is a beach launch. It is *not* a place for groups, as parking is very limited—please carpool. Directions: It is easiest to GPS 1175 Succotash Rd., South Kingstown (restaurant south of the launch), then continue north on Succotash Road to the wildlife management area.

Narrow River State Boat Ramp. This is a nice launch for the Narrow River. Be aware that the current can be swift, and give anglers a wide berth. Directions: GPS Pollock Avenue (off of Middlebridge Road) and follow it to the river.

Narrow River at Route 1A (Sprague Bridge, Narragansett). This launch provides quick access to Pettaquamscutt Cove (1,400 feet) or the rough water where the Narrow River meets Narragansett Bay (less than 1 mile). It is also a pleasant paddle to the Narragansett Town Beach and sandbars, followed by

In certain conditions, the surf in the South Kingstown area can be substantial. John Tobiassen entering serious water. **PHOTO CARL TJERANDSEN**

hanging out on the beach. There are two launch areas, both part of the John H. Chafee National Wildlife Refuge. On the south side of the road, west side of the bridge, a path across the street leads to a beach launch. On the north side of the bridge, east of the bridge, there is a parking lot with better access. Directions: GPS Boston Neck Road, Narragansett, to bring you to the northeast side of the bridge (located near the intersections of Bridge Point Drive and Old Boston Neck Road).

Secondary Launches: East Matunuck State Beach (off-season). Rhode Island state beaches do not allow cartop boat access Memorial Day to Labor Day, so it is only an off-season launch. Directions: GPS 950 Succotash Rd.

Deep Hole state parking lot. This access point is generally used by surfers. It is a rocky beach with surf that is typically not a good launch or landing for kayaks. Proper surf etiquette is required, and always give anglers a wide berth.

Directions: GPS Matunuck Beach Road and follow it almost to the end to a small parking area.

Cruising Paddler

Point Judith Pond. This is a very pleasant area to tour. From Marina Park, leave the upper pond (through the Narrows—watch for boat traffic) and head west around Cummock Island (1.2 miles). Head south down the western shore past Gardner and Plato Islands (2.25 miles total). Continue south past the waterway to Potter Pond (3.6 miles total) and a rest stop on the Succotash Marsh Wildlife Management Area beach (3.75 miles total). Return to the launch by the eastern shore, exploring islands (Jonathan, Ram, etc.) and points (7.5 miles total). ***Note:*** The waterway north of the Succotash Wildlife Management Area will take you past the Matunuck Oyster Bar and into Potter Pond. However, for better or worse, the current under the bridge and just before the pond is very strong at certain tides.

Green Hill Pond. From the Perry Creek access (Charlestown), head east into Green Hill Pond (be careful of current under the bridge). Once in the pond, there are several coves and islands to explore, but it is best at high tide. A coastal route heads along the east shore past Ram Island (under 1 mile), then jogs west past Gooseberry Island (1 mile total) and up and around Cedar Island (1.6 miles total). Head back along the western shore down and around Jacob Island (2.7 miles total). Continue west back to the ramp (about 4 miles total). You can add distance by exploring the many coves.

Narrow River. From the Narrow River State Boat Ramp, head south past the Middlebridge Road bridge to the entrance of Pettaquamscutt Cove (shallow entrance—follow channel markers from south side of sandbar) on the west (1.08 miles). Explore the cove and the John H. Chafee National Wildlife Refuge, which borders much of the cove, and Gooseberry Island. From the cove entrance to the end and back is 3.79 miles (total from launch). Return to the launch (about 5 miles total). If you continue downriver to where the river meets the ocean, the water is typically rough—just over 2 miles from the ramp. You can also head north up the Narrow River about 3.5 miles (one way), which is a nice early-season paddle.

Distance Paddler

You can cruise along the oceanfront for miles off-season. Cruising the entire length of Point Judith Pond is about a 9-mile round-trip from Marina Park, and the many islands and small inlets make for an interesting day.

Rough Water Paddler

The East Matunuck State Beach area is a very popular surf spot (beach launching off-season). Best to use shorter surf boats, as out-of-control broached or flipped long boats

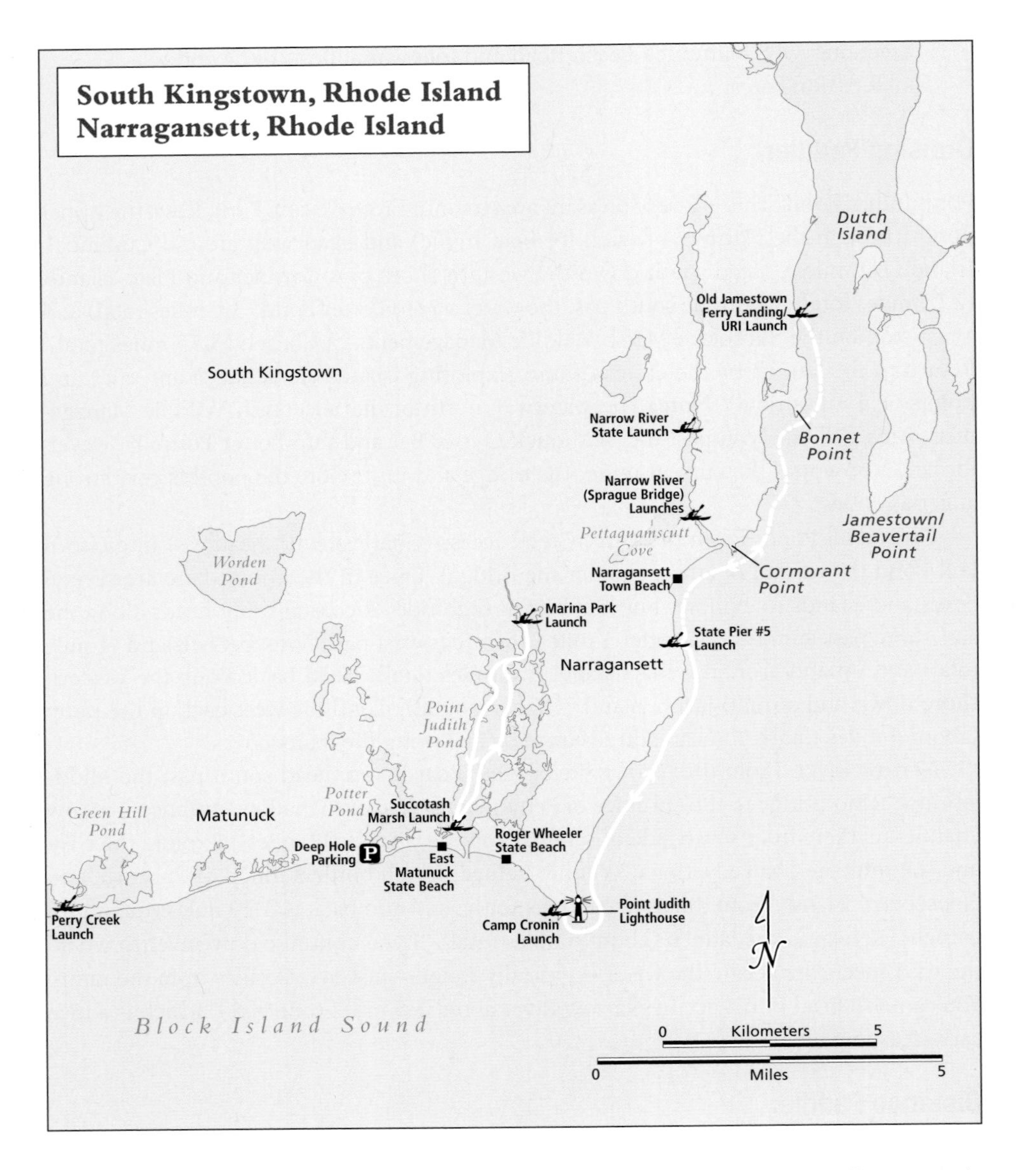

can be dangerous to board surfers (causing serious disagreements on and off the water). Most kayakers stay in the Deep Hole area. Another well-known area is the mouth of the Narrow River/Pettaquamscutt River where it meets Narragansett Bay. The mouth is just over 2 miles from the Narrow River State Boat Launch, or under a mile from the Narrow River at Route 1A (Sprague Bridge) launch, Narragansett.

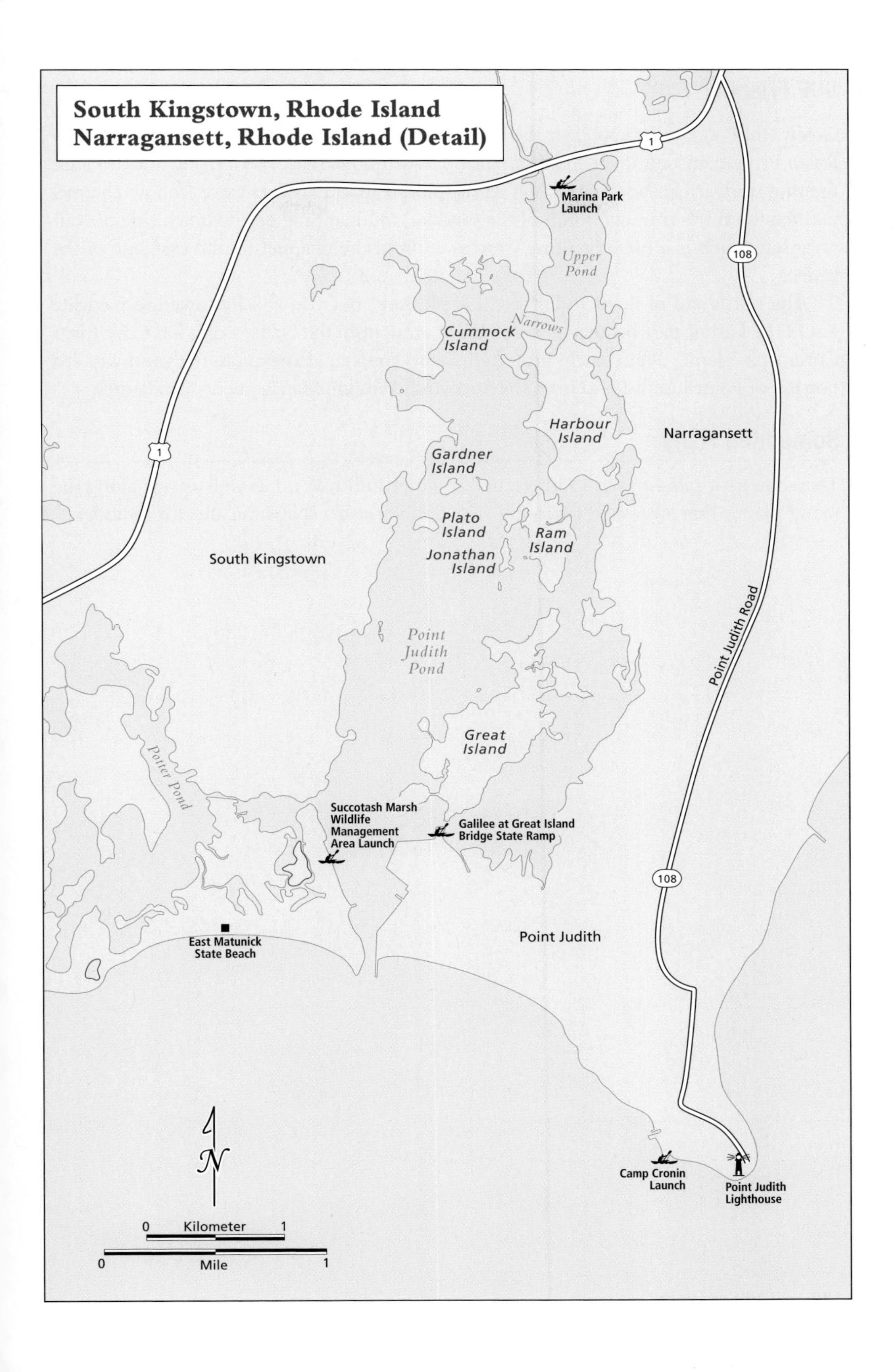
South Kingstown, Rhode Island
Narragansett, Rhode Island (Detail)
1
Marina Park Launch
108
Upper Pond
Narrows
Cummock Island
Harbour Island
Narragansett
Gardner Island
Plato Island
Ram Island
Jonathan Island
South Kingstown
Point Judith Pond
Point Judith Road
Great Island
Potter Pond
Succotash Marsh Wildlife Management Area Launch
Galilee at Great Island Bridge State Ramp
East Matunick State Beach
Point Judith
N
Camp Cronin Launch
Point Judith Lighthouse
0
Kilometer
1
0
Mile
1

SUP Friendly

Green Hill Pond, once you clear the bridge, is pleasant and typically calm. The Narrow River/ Pettaquamscutt River area from the Sprague Bridge is nice on a rising tide (because fighting upriver can be a pain). You can explore Pettaquamscutt Cove (follow channel markers from the entrance south of the sandbar), and landing on the north side of Narragansett Beach is a fun adventure (stay away from the channel on the east side of the beach).

The north end of Point Judith Pond is pleasant, but you will first need to navigate out of the harbor past boaters (1 mile). Once away from the boats, Congdon Cove (near Cummock Island) offers nicely protected water. You can also explore the southwestern portion of Point Judith Pond from the Succotash Wildlife Management Area launch.

Something Fishy

There are rock piles on the southern end of Point Judith Pond as well as rips along the many islands that are worth exploring. The pond is also a spawning area for flounder.

Narragansett, RI

The town of Narragansett and its coastal waters, including the stunning western Narragansett Bay (West Passage), provide access to some of the most dramatic moving waters and waves in Rhode Island. Where the Narrow River meets Narragansett Bay, small to medium-size waves are common in this turbulent area, and it is a popular location for kayak surfers and rough water enthusiasts year-round. Off-season the Point Judith and Narragansett area is popular with surfers because the access points open up, and the north wind helps to form rideable waves. The Narragansett area has some nice SUP areas and is also a jumping-off point for some serious distance circuits.

Primary Launches: Succotash Marsh Wildlife Management Area. This is a great launch site to access the southern end of Point Judith Pond or Potter Pond (if the current is safe under the bridge to Potter Pond). Located on the west side of the Point Judith breachway, this is a beach launch. It is *not* a place for groups, as parking is limited—please carpool. Directions: It is easiest to GPS

Huge breaking waves, from an offshore storm, at the Point Judith Lighthouse. **PHOTO DAVID FASULO**

1175 Succotash Rd., South Kingstown (restaurant south of the launch), then continue north on Succotash Road to the wildlife management area.

Camp Cronin DEM Fishing Access, Point Judith. This site provides protected access (beach west of breakwater) to Point Judith Harbor of Refuge and the stunning Point Judith Lighthouse area. Directions: GPS 1470 Ocean Rd. (Point Judith Lighthouse); the access road is located on the right, just before reaching the lighthouse. Follow the road to the end.

State Pier #5 (Monahan's Clam Shack—classic seafood stand). This is a well-protected launch, but parking is very limited and not appropriate for groups. There is nearby on-street parking, which fills up quickly in the summer. The launch is 1.6 miles from the mouth of the Narrow River outlet, and 4.8 miles north of the Point Judith Lighthouse. Directions: GPS 190 Ocean Rd.

Narrow River at Route 1A (Sprague Bridge, Narragansett). This launch provides quick access to Pettaquamscutt Cove (shallow entrance—follow channel markers from south side of sandbar) and the rough water where the Narrow River meets the ocean (less than 1 mile). It is also a pleasant paddle to the Narragansett Town Beach and sandbars, followed by hanging out on the beach. There are two launch areas, both part of the John H. Chafee National Wildlife Refuge. On the south side of the road, west side of the bridge, a path across the street leads to a beach launch. On the north side of the bridge, east of the bridge, there is a parking lot with better access. Directions: GPS Boston Neck Road, Narragansett, to bring you to the northeast side of the bridge

Cruising along the classic "West Passage" from the Old Jamestown Ferry Landing/URI launch to Narragansett. **PHOTO ERIK BAUMGARTNER**

(located near the intersections of Bridge Point Drive and Old Boston Neck Road).

Old Jamestown Ferry Landing/URI Bay Campus. A popular launch for western Narragansett Bay, and less than a mile (open water) to Dutch Island (4,424 feet). Directions: GPS 200 South Ferry Rd. Continue past the University of Rhode Island Bay Campus to the end. Small parking lot and beach launch.

Secondary Launches: Middletown Bridge. There is a concession, Narrow River Kayaks (www.narrowriverkayaks.com), at this bridge that rents kayaks and SUPs. They also allow launching off a nice sandy beach ($5 per vessel). It is a good launch if you want to bring newcomers and rent boats. Directions: GPS 94 Middletown Rd.

Galilee at Great Island Bridge State Ramp. Current can be strong under the bridge, and boat traffic is heavy west of the bridge. According to signs, parking in the main lot is for vehicles with trailers; nearby on-street parking

Bob Foltz passing Bonnet Point during a distance cruise from Pier #5, Narragansett, to Warwick Harbor. **PHOTO DAVID FASULO**

may be available off-season, and there are pay lots in the vicinity. Directions: GPS Galilee Escape Road. The ramp is at the intersection with Great Island Road.

Roger W. Wheeler State Beach. This is a relatively well-protected beach (due to breakwaters) off-season. Launching is not allowed Memorial Day to Labor Day. Directions: GPS 100 Sand Hill Cove Rd.

Narragansett Town Beach. This is a common surf area off-season. Launching is not allowed Memorial Day to Labor Day. Kayakers also approach this area from the Sprague Bridge launch. Directions: GPS 39 Boston Neck Rd.

Cruising Paddler

"West Passage" from Old Jamestown Ferry Landing/URI to Pier #5. From the Old Jamestown Ferry Landing/URI launch, head south along the shore past the Bonnet Cliffs to Bonnet Point (1.8 miles). Continue south to Cormorant Point and the mouth of the Narrow River/Pettaquamscutt River (4.3 miles total). Play in the waves and rocks if you dare, or continue south past Narragansett Town Beach to a break at State Pier #5 and Monahan's Clam Shack (5.8 miles total). Return the same route (11.6 miles total).

"Southwest Passage" from State Pier #5 to Camp Cronin. From the Pier #5 launch (very limited parking), head south along the coast to the Point Judith Lighthouse (beware of large waves near the point; 4.7 miles). Paddle around the breakwater to a break at a protected beach on the northwest side of the breakwater, away from swimmers (6 miles total). Return the same route (12 miles total). ***Note:*** The best launch site for the West Passage area (Camp Cronin or State Pier #5) depends on the direction of the afternoon winds and tide. The parking at Camp Cronin is much better, and you can get a snack during the summer at Pier #5 (Monahan's Clam Shack) during a lunch break. However, on the occasions the author has explored the area, the afternoon wind, from the south, was very strong.

Dutch Island and Jamestown. A popular cruise is to go around Dutch Island, which is located about 1 mile from the Old Jamestown Ferry Landing/URI launch. You can then take a break near Fox Hill Pond, Jamestown (2.8 miles), and then return to the launch (5.6 miles total).

Distance Paddler

For big distance, very experienced paddlers will paddle to Block Island from a launch in the vicinity of the Block Island Ferry. Distance kayakers also launch out of the Charlestown or Quonochontaug Breachway to reach Block Island. The author has done this journey round-trip in the summer, as well as a one-way trip in January with a return trip to the mainland on the Block Island Ferry.

Another distance run is to combine the above-mentioned West Passage and Southwest Passage. If doing this, it is more fun to spot cars at the launch and takeout point

Tim Motte playing in the waves where the Narrow River/Pettaquamscutt River meets Narragansett Bay. **PHOTO DAVID FASULO**

for a one-way paddle (check wind and tides). The author has paddled from Pier #5 to Warwick Harbor in a day by shuttling cars in this manner.

Rough Water Paddler

A well-known area is the mouth of the Narrow River/Pettaquamscutt River where it meets Narragansett Bay. Even highly experienced kayakers have destroyed boats near the mouth of the Narrow River. It is just over 2 miles from the Narrow River State Boat Ramp, South Kingstown, or under 1 mile from the Narrow River at Route 1A (Sprague Bridge) launch, Narragansett.

SUP Friendly

The Point Judith Harbor of Refuge, with access from the Camp Cronin launch, is a pleasant venue except for boat wakes on weekends. The Narrow River/Pettaquamscutt River, from the Sprague Bridge, is popular and gives you a few options (upriver, downriver to the beach, or exploring Pettaquamscutt Cove). You can also rent kayaks and SUPs

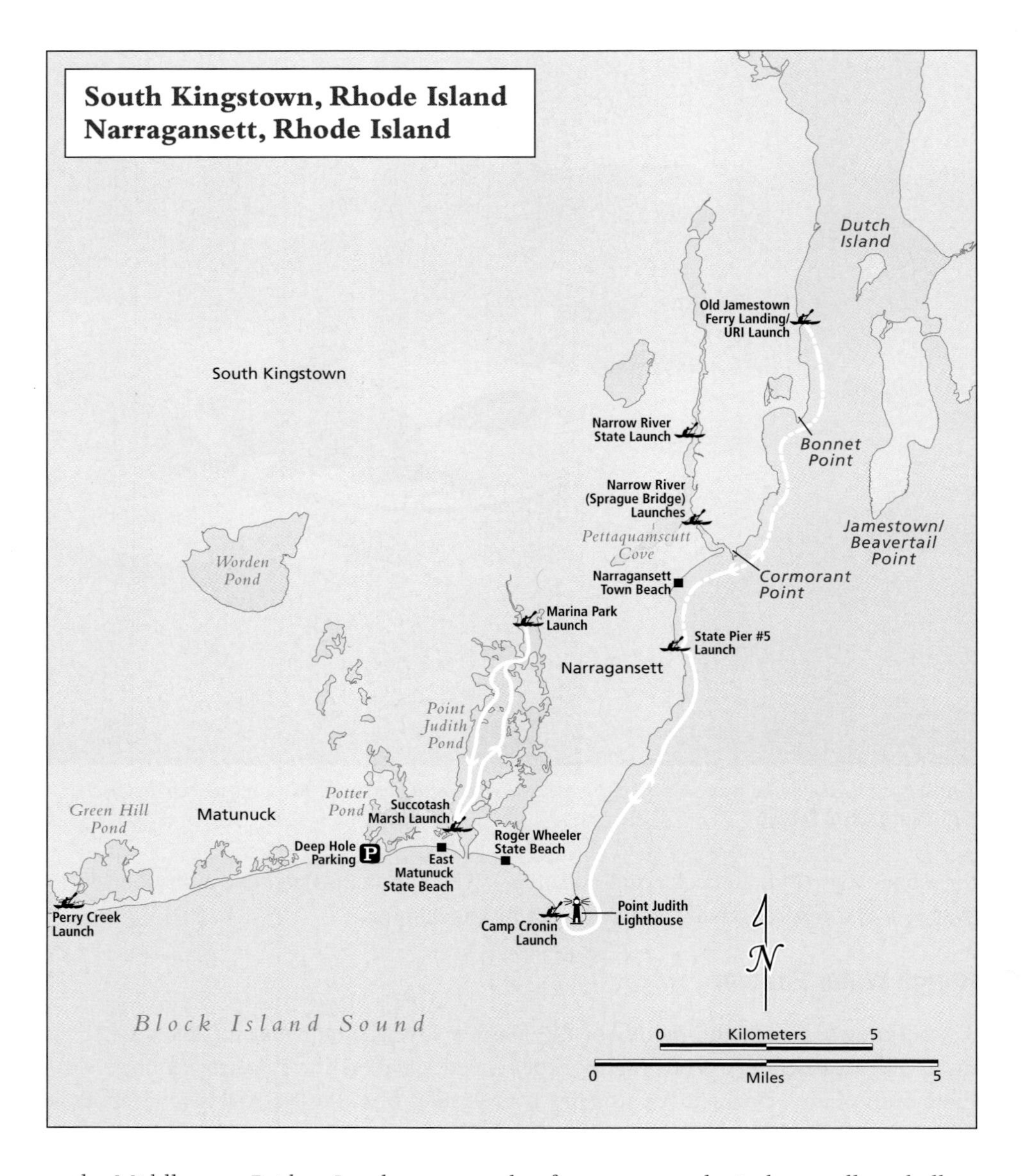

at the Middletown Bridge. Just be sure to plan for current and wind, as well as shallow areas. Landing at the Narragansett Town Beach, or the sandbar just before the beach, is a popular outing.

Something Fishy

Narragansett Bay holds a variety of fish, including striped bass, fluke, scup, and black sea bass, along the entire coast. The rocky area along State Pier #5 and the breakwaters at

The Middletown Bridge launch is a popular location to rent kayaks or SUPs, and then explore the Pettaquamscutt River and Cove. A good outing is to land on the sandbars and the beach north of the entrance channel (very strong current) to Narragansett Bay. **PHOTO DAVID FASULO**

Point Judith can be productive. Trolling a tube and worm rig very slowly (1 to 1.2 knots) and only a foot or two above the bottom will result in a variety of species. Long drifts reward the angler with the opportunity to fish a varied bottom, while also avoiding the numerous lobster pots that will gobble up fishing tackle.

North Kingstown, RI

The North Kingstown shoreline is a mix of quaint coves and the vast industrial Quonset Point area. Although located in an industrialized area, Compass Rose Beach and especially Spinks Neck Beach are pleasant launch sites with a variety of paddling opportunities. The more-popular kayak tours tend to follow the open shore, while SUPs stick closer to the charming village of Wickford. Rome Point, and Calf Pasture Point (just north of the Spinks Neck launch), provide secluded beaches bordered by nature preserves.

Primary Launches: Wilson Town Park, Wickford Village. This is a nice launch for SUPs and recreational kayaks to cruise around Mill and Fishing Coves. There is a ramp, but also a small beach for cartop boats and parking north of the launch (on the right on your way out on the one-way road). There is no fee, and it is less than 1 mile from the breakwaters protecting Wickford Harbor (beware of boat traffic) to the entrance of Narragansett Bay. Directions: GPS Intrepid Drive and follow it east to the Wilson Park fishing area launch.

Taking a break on Blue Beach, located just west of the start of the industrial area at Quonset Point and northeast Wickford Harbor. **PHOTO DAVID FASULO**

Compass Rose Beach. An old seaplane beach in the Quonset Point area that provides a nice beach launch and typically ample parking. The downside is that it is surrounded by industry. Directions: GPS Roger Williams Way and follow it east. Take a right just before the Martha's Vineyard Ferry Terminal.

Spinks Neck Beach. This area has a nice beach and quick access to the beach at Calf Pasture Point, but it is located in an industrial area. Directions: GPS Patrol Road, which is off Allen Harbor Road, and follow it to the parking lot at the end of the road.

Secondary Launches: North Kingstown Town Beach. Off-season (Labor Day to Memorial Day) launch only. A bit of a carry to the beach, but generally gentle surf for landing and launching. Directions: GPS Beach Street and follow it east to the end.

Wickford Municipal Town Dock. This launch has a floating dock for SUPs, but it is not a good launch for kayaks. No fees, but the area is busy with boat traffic, and parking can fill up. Directions: GPS Brown Street (next to Kayak Center, just north).

Landing Area: Blue Beach. This is an out-of-the way beach located at Sauga Point (Wickford Harbor area) and the start of the industrialized area. There is a parking area off of Circuit Drive, but it is a very long carry.

Cruising Paddler

Spinks Neck Beach to Sandy Point. Launch from Spinks Neck Beach and head north past Calf Pasture Point to the Potowomut River (2.3 miles). Continue to Sandy Point for a break (3.1 miles total) just before Greenwich Bay. Return the same route (6.2 miles total).

Wilson Town Park to Rome Point. From the launch, head east past the island and out of Wickford Harbor (be careful of boat traffic at breakwater). Head south to a sandy peninsula (3.4 miles) just past Bissel Cove (Rome Point). Paddle along the pleasant beach until you find a spot to take a break. Return the same route (6.8 miles total).

Distance Paddler

From the Compass Rose Beach launch, head south along the coast to the Old Jamestown Ferry Landing/URI launch (7.5 miles). Return the same route (15 miles total). You can add miles with a side tour of Dutch Island.

Rough Water Paddler

Outside Wickford Harbor, the late-day wind can produce some fun surf runs.

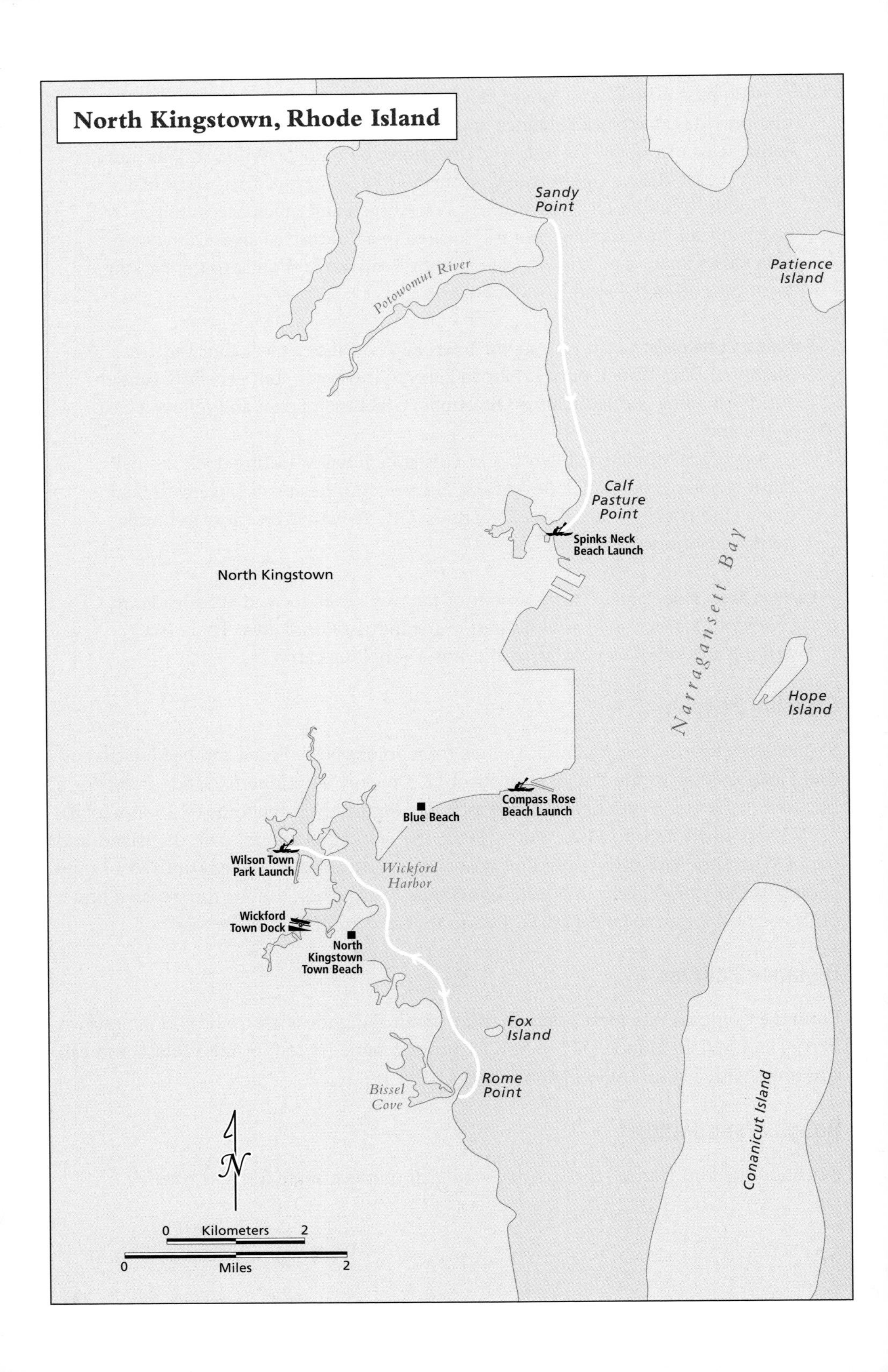
North Kingstown, Rhode Island
Sandy Point
Patience Island
Potowomut River
Calf Pasture Point
Spinks Neck Beach Launch
North Kingstown
Narragansett Bay
Hope Island
Compass Rose Beach Launch
Blue Beach
Wilson Town Park Launch
Wickford Harbor
Wickford Town Dock
North Kingstown Town Beach
Fox Island
Rome Point
Bissel Cove
Conanicut Island
N
0 Kilometers 2
0 Miles 2

SUP Friendly

From the Wilson Town Park launch, you can explore the protected Mill and Fishing Cove area. For a nice cruise, launching from Spinks Neck Beach and exploring Calf Pasture Point is a good outing when conditions permit.

Something Fishy

The area around Poplar Point, just outside of Wickford Harbor, probably has the easiest access and most structure combined with current. This area serves up some of the most abundant scup and fluke in the vicinity. The lighthouse and bridge pilings are also a worthwhile trek; however, vessel traffic and open water will keep the West Passage very choppy throughout the day after the sea breeze picks up.

Warwick, RI

According to the Warwick Department of Tourism (www.visitwarwickri.com), "Founded by Samuel Gorton in 1642, Warwick has witnessed the major events of American history. Warwick was decimated during King Philip's War (1675–76) and was the site of the first shot fired of the American Revolution against the British schooner *Gaspee*." Warwick is unique due to its access-friendly policies regarding nonresidents. Unlike other coastal towns, Warwick does not charge for parking or entrance to either residents or nonresidents. The only restriction is that kayak and SUP launching is not permitted at Oakland Beach from June through August. Greenwich Bay and Warwick Point are nice areas to explore, but boat traffic/wakes can be heavy. Patience Island, and the coves between Patience and Prudence Islands, are beautiful destinations that have a remote feel. Greenwich Bay, when the wind and boat traffic is light, is a pleasant area to explore. Landing on the eastern end of the beach, at Goddard Memorial State Park, allows for a nice place to stretch and catch some sun.

Warwick Point Lighthouse. **PHOTO DAVID FASULO**

Primary Launches: Conimicut Point Park. This launch is a little off the beaten path, but it is a good spot to head north up the Providence River to Gaspee Point. However, parking is very limited. It is a town park that offers more parking than the Conimicut Point State Ramp. You can beach-launch next to the dirt ramp on the north side of the parking lot. Directions: GPS Point Avenue and follow it to the end.

Conimicut Point State Ramp. This ramp is located next to (north) of Conimicut Point Park. It is a nice ramp/beach launch, but parking is limited. Directions: GPS Shawomet Avenue and follow it to the end.

Passeonkquis Cove State Ramp. This is a pleasant and protected launch, but parking is limited (not for groups). It is a nice launch to SUP or kayak over to Gaspee Point beach, or cruise north along Rock Island. Directions: GPS Gaspee Point Drive and follow it to the end.

Oakland Beach town ramp. This is mainly a powerboaters' ramp (so show good ramp etiquette), but provides good access to Patience Island (2.6 miles). ***Note:*** According to signs, parking is permitted for ramp use only, so you may

Heading out of the Oakland Beach town ramp launch to circumnavigate Prudence Island (approximately 23 miles). Timing the wind and tides is a key factor when distance paddling. **PHOTO DAVID FASULO**

Bob Foltz in Greenwich Bay, heading towards the Goddard launch, after paddling from State Pier #5, Narragansett (spotting cars). **PHOTO DAVID FASULO**

want to leave a note on the windshield stating you are a cartop boater (since you will not have a trailer). Directions: GPS Bay Avenue and follow it south to the large ramp area.

Oakland Beach. This is a busy town beach located next to (south) of the Oakland Beach town ramp. Cartop boats are not allowed to launch June through August. If launching, it is best to use the east end. Directions: GPS Oakland Beach Avenue and follow it south to the end.

Goddard Memorial State Park. This is a very nice access point for Greenwich Cove, and is just under a mile to Greenwich Bay. The only downside is the boat traffic. Off-season the beach (eastern end) makes for an even nicer launch. Directions: GPS 1095 Ives Rd., Warwick. Use the main entrance in the summer; off-season there is an entrance at the west end through two stone pillars. The launch ramp is located on the northwest side of the park.

Secondary Launches: Salter Grove State Park. This is a well-protected beach/mud access to the Providence River. May be a bit too calm/stagnant in the summer, but a nice site for beginners. Parking fills up quickly. Directions: GPS Landon Road. The entrance is at the intersection of Narragansett Parkway and Landon Road.

Longmeadow State Ramp. A beach/rocky launch with limited parking. Not a prime spot, but a nice area to launch and cruise up to Conimicut Point. Directions: GPS Samuel Gorton Avenue and follow it to the river.

East Greenwich Boat Launch and Dock. This access is located across the cove from the Goddard Park launch. No real advantage over Goddard Park; listed for access information. No fee, but can be crowded with large boats. Directions: GPS Crompton Avenue (East Greenwich). Entrance to the launch is 900 feet north of the intersection with Rocky Hollow Road.

Cruising Paddler

Oakland Beach to Patience Island. Patience Island, and especially the protected area between Patience and Prudence Islands, is a beautiful area. However, be careful of rough water and boat traffic between Warwick Point and Patience Island, as well as strong current. From the Oakland Beach town launch, head south along the shore to Warwick

Curt Anderson exploring Patience Island. **PHOTO DAVID FASULO**

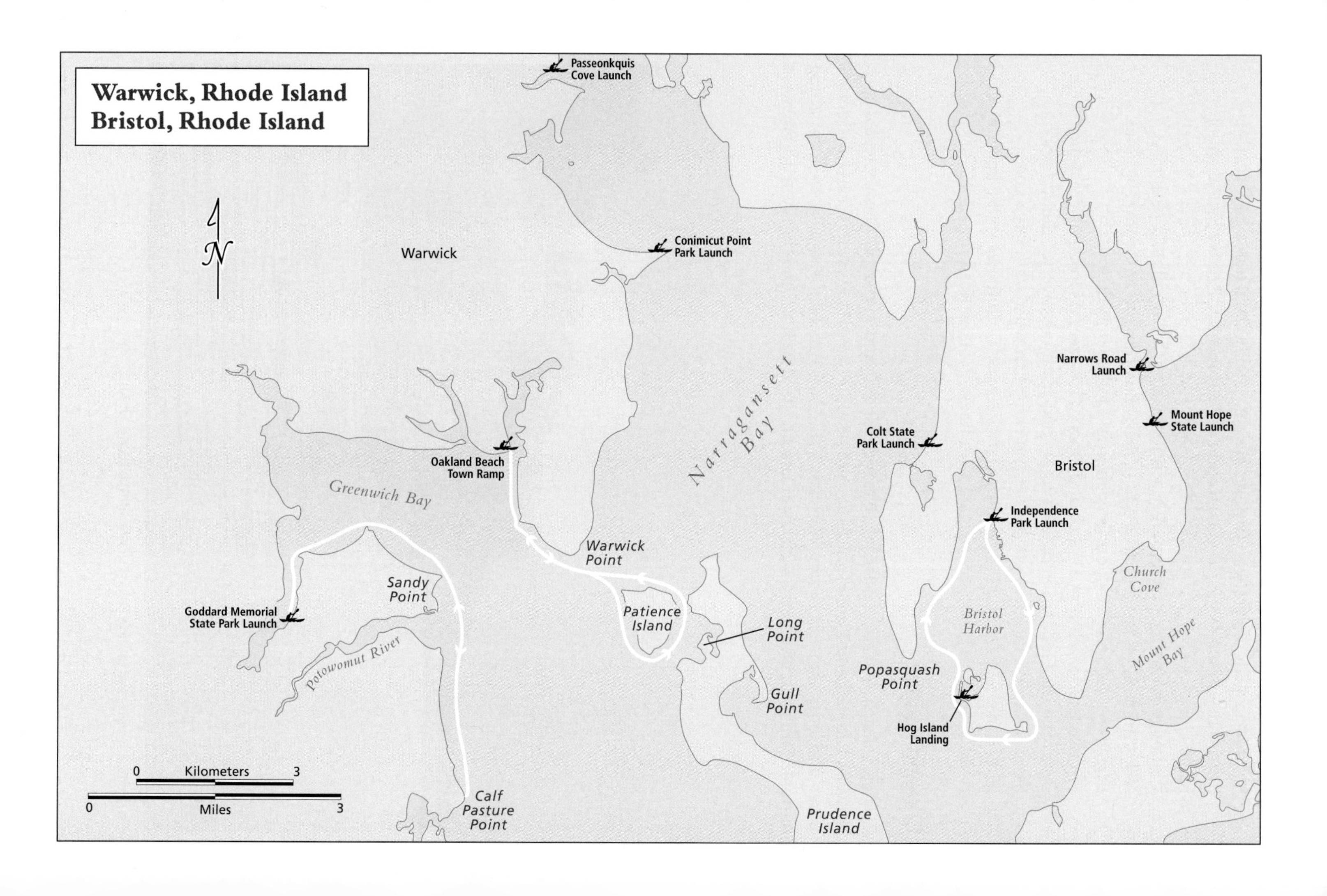
Warwick, Rhode Island
Bristol, Rhode Island
N
Passeonkquis Cove Launch
Conimicut Point Park Launch
Warwick
Narragansett Bay
Narrows Road Launch
Mount Hope State Launch
Colt State Park Launch
Bristol
Oakland Beach Town Ramp
Greenwich Bay
Independence Park Launch
Warwick Point
Church Cove
Sandy Point
Goddard Memorial State Park Launch
Patience Island
Long Point
Bristol Harbor
Mount Hope Bay
Potowomut River
Popasquash Point
Gull Point
Hog Island Landing
0
Kilometers
3
0
Miles
3
Calf Pasture Point
Prudence Island

Point/Lighthouse (1.68 miles). Cross over to Patience Island (2.4 miles total), then head along the western shore. Paddle past the southern tip, then east across the harbor to a break at Long Point (4 miles total). Return to the launch, passing the eastern shore of Patience Island (7.9 miles total).

Goddard State Park to Calf Pasture Point. From the Goddard Memorial State Park launch, head towards Greenwich Bay past the Goddard Park beach (1.8 miles). Head east around Sandy Point and then south past the Potowomut River (3.8 miles total). Continue south to a rest on secluded beach on Calf Pasture Point (5.5 miles total), then return to the launch (11 miles total).

Distance Paddler

Prudence Island circumnavigation. Depending on how much you explore, it is about a 23-mile circuit out of the Oakland Beach town ramp launch. A more common launch for the circumnavigation seems to be the Weaver Cove Boat Ramp in Portsmouth, since the distance is only 1.5 miles to Prudence Island versus just over 3 miles from the Oakland Beach launch. However, with a falling tide in the morning, and a rising tide and south wind in the afternoon, the Oakland launch is a reasonable starting point.

Rough Water Paddler

The water kicks up around the Warwick Point/Warwick Lighthouse area due to currents, boat traffic, and reefs.

SUP Friendly

Launching from Conimicut Point Park and cruising north along the Providence River to Gaspee Point is protected, but can be shallow. The area in front of Goddard Memorial State Beach is nice for cruising, although there is boat traffic (creating wakes) on busy weekends.

Something Fishy

Warwick offers the southern limit of spring striped bass fishing that extends north to the Providence River during the late spring. Conimicut Point offers the beginner kayak angler the opportunity for a short paddle to abundant fishing below the lighthouse. This area is immediately adjacent to a somewhat busy shipping channel, and the mariner must be aware of his or her surroundings. Atlantic menhaden can remain in the area through mid to late June, offering the opportunity to chunk striped bass along the shore. Charted rock piles, wrecks, and obstructions should not be ignored either, as they hold enormous schools of scup throughout the fair-weather fishing season. There are rocks, ledges (Gould and Southeast), and moving water along Warwick Point. Anglers also cruise along the coastline of Patience Island.

Bristol, RI

Bristol County is a wonderful area for the mariner. The downtown area, on Bristol Harbor, has several restaurants within walking distance. If visiting downtown Bristol, or Colt State Park, it is worth packing bicycles as well. The East Bay Bike Path starts (southern end) in Independence Park on Bristol Harbor and passes through Colt State Park (both locations offer nice cartop boat launches), then continues north to East Providence. Hog Island is a fun destination, and by spotting cars much of the coastline can be explored in a single day. It is worth noting that Bristol hosts the oldest continuously celebrated Fourth of July event, starting in 1785, in the nation.

Primary Launches: Independence Park. This is a very nice launch with convenient access to Bristol Harbor and nearby restaurants. Directions: GPS Oliver Street and follow it to the intersection with Thames Street. Follow the concrete access to the launch and parking. This is also a parking area for the 14.5-mile East Bay Bike Path (southern end); therefore, parking can fill up.

John Sharlin heading along the Bristol coast to the Mount Hope Bridge. **PHOTO DAVID FASULO**

Taking a break on Hog Island (Portsmouth) with John Sharlin during a tour of the Bristol coast.
PHOTO DAVID FASULO

Colt State Park. This is a beautiful park, and visitors should also check out the bike paths and 2-mile promenade along the seawall. Directions: GPS Asylum Road (off Route 114). Follow this to Colt State Park Road and the launch (on the right) on Colt Drive.

Mount Hope State Boat Launch. This is a key launch for Mount Hope Bay, with access to the Kickemuit River Shellfish Management Area and the small Spar Island (1.2 miles). Good ramp etiquette is required. Directions: GPS Annawamscutt Drive. Just after Lafayette Drive (on the left), take a right on the access road.

Narrows Road Launch. This area has a protected sand launch and is good place to SUP into the Kickemuit River (watch for strong current at the "narrows"). More relaxed than the state boat launch just south on Annawamscutt Drive. Directions: GPS Narrows Road and follow it east to the end.

Cruising Paddler

Bristol Harbor to Hog Island. From the Independence Park launch, head south along the shore, past Walker Island, and then across the harbor to the northern end of Hog Island (2.3 miles). Paddle along the eastern shore, then southern shore, of Hog Island and then head north along the western shore to a narrow beach protecting a cove (4.3 miles total) for a break. Continue northwest towards Popasquash Point (if conditions allow) and follow the eastern shore, then cross back to the launch (7.1 miles total).

Distance Paddler

Bristol Coast Tour. This is a good tour, but you need to spot a car at the Colt State Park launch and then launch boats from the Mount Hope State Boat Launch or Narrows Road launch (about 3 miles apart). The tour is described from the Narrows Road launch, but the start and end points depends on tides and wind. From the Narrows Road launch, head down the coastline to Mount Hope Point (2.4 miles) and then along Church Cove past Seal Island. Continue down the coast to the tip (Bristol Point) and the Mount Hope Bridge, just past Roger Williams University (4.8 miles total). Cross the bay and paddle past the southern end of Hog Island, then head north up the island to a break on a beach adjoining a shallow cove (6.6 miles total). (***Note:*** You can extend the miles by exploring Bristol Harbor if conditions permit.) Head across the harbor to Popasquash Point (7.3 miles total), then follow the coastline to the launch at Colt State Park (10.4 miles total).

Rough Water Paddler

The water tends to kick up between Bristol Point and Hog Island. When the conditions are right (strong southerly), there are small surf runs going into Bristol Harbor.

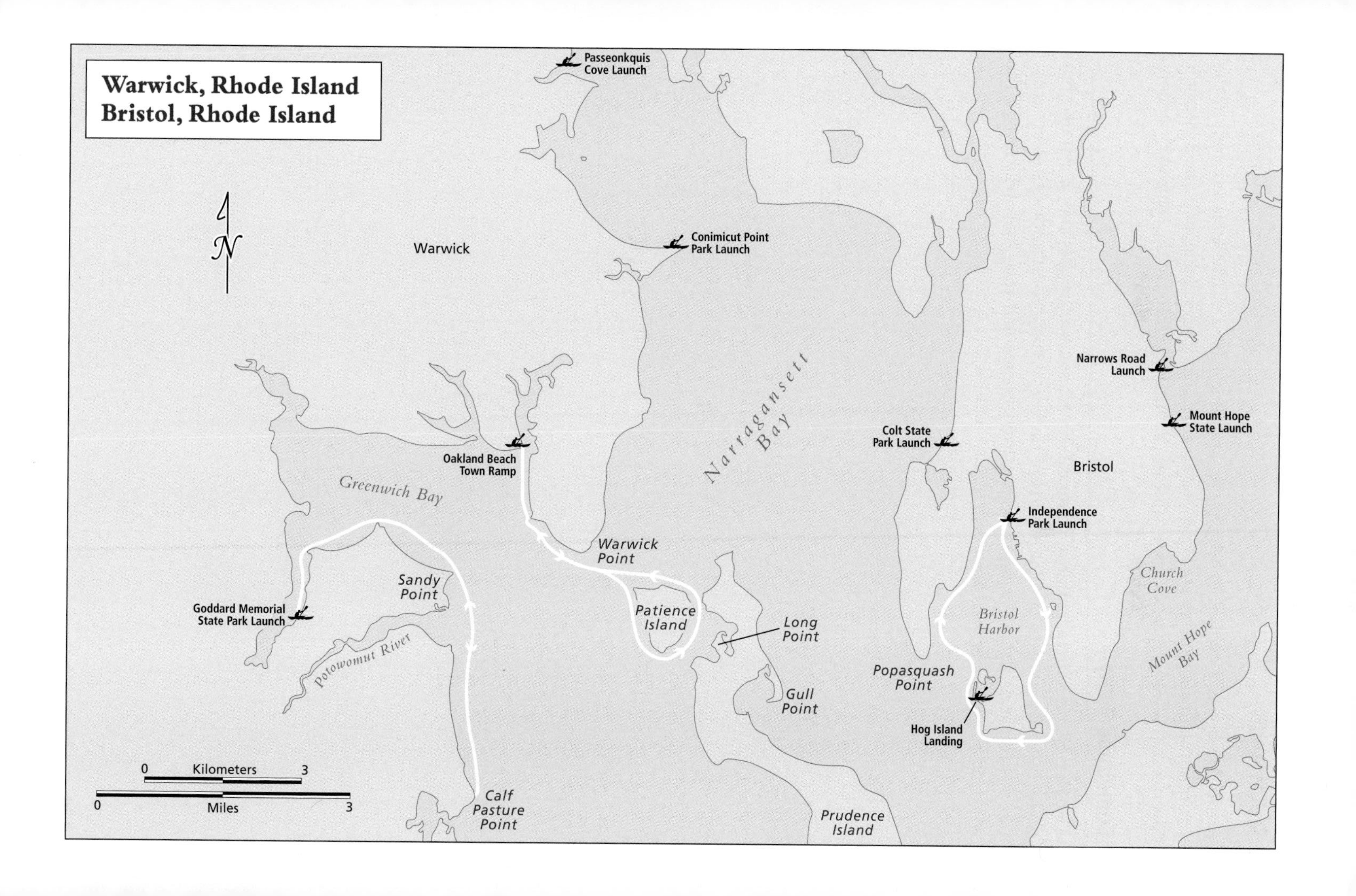
Warwick, Rhode Island
Bristol, Rhode Island
N
Warwick
Passeonkquis Cove Launch
Conimicut Point Park Launch
Oakland Beach Town Ramp
Greenwich Bay
Narragansett Bay
Warwick Point
Goddard Memorial State Park Launch
Sandy Point
Potowomut River
Patience Island
Long Point
Gull Point
Calf Pasture Point
Prudence Island
Colt State Park Launch
Popasquash Point
Narrows Road Launch
Mount Hope State Launch
Bristol
Independence Park Launch
Church Cove
Bristol Harbor
Mount Hope Bay
Hog Island Landing
0 Kilometers 3
0 Miles 3

SUP Friendly

Bristol Harbor is a cool place to explore, and Hog Island is reachable but only if the returning wind and current are favorable. From the Narrows Road launch, the Kickemuit River/cove is a well-protected spot—just be careful going through the "narrows" section.

Something Fishy

The Hog Island Shoal Light area, about 1,800 feet south of Hog Island, is popular but tricky in a kayak due to current. In Bristol Harbor, Walker Island provides some structure for fish. Eels drifted at night over charted humps and rock piles will reward the kayak angler with trophy striped bass in June and July.

Portsmouth, RI

Portsmouth is located on a series of large islands. The major island, Aquidneck (which is also home to Middletown and Newport), is bordered by Narragansett Bay on the western shore and the Sakonnet River on the eastern shore. The islands of Hog Island and Prudence Island are also located in the town of Portsmouth. One of the nicer tours is from the Weaver Cove Boat Ramp to Prudence Island. The crossing to Prudence gives the paddle a "big water" feel but in relatively safe waters (only 1 mile from a shoreline—Dyer Island). Since Prudence Island is far from crowded, exploring Prudence to Sandy Point gives the feel of being in a remote location. The only downside is that the boat traffic and wakes can be heavy at times.

Primary Launches: Sandy Point Town Beach. A rocky beach, and boats are not allowed on the north end of the beach. Nonresident fee is $10 weekdays and $15 on weekends Memorial Day to Labor Day. Directions: GPS Sandy Point Avenue and follow it east to the end.

Cruising along the southern end of Prudence Island. **PHOTO DAVID FASULO**

Weaver Cove Boat Ramp. A good launch for Dyer Island (less than 1 mile) and Prudence Island (1.6 miles). Directions: GPS Burma Road. The entrance is about 0.5 mile south from Stringham Road.

Secondary Launch: Gull Cove State Ramp. Not the most aesthetic area, due to its proximity to the road, but flat water for beginners. Island Park Cove and the islands inside the cove are nice to tour, but the water can be shallow and the current can be strong, especially near the bridge. Directions: A bit tricky to initially find, hence the directions are set up for the first-time visit. GPS 314 Boyds Lane (commuter lot on Route 138 south of Route 24). Head south on Boyds Lane a couple hundred feet, then take a left onto the Route 138/Fall River Expressway entrance. Just under a mile from the entrance, there is a dirt road on the right (state fishing access).

Landings: Hog Island. If you choose to explore Hog Island, the easiest approach is from Bristol Harbor (see Bristol section for launches). There is a pleasant beach landing on the northwestern side of the island. According to

Hog Island, located in Portsmouth, is a common rest stop when launching from Bristol Harbor. **PHOTO DAVID FASULO**

Amenities on Prudence Island. **PHOTO DAVID FASULO**

lighthousefriends.com, "The early settlers of Newport found the island, and others nearby, convenient for livestock, as the animals could not wander afar, no fences were necessary, and natural predators like wolves and foxes could not reach the island. Hogs were regularly kept on the small island, giving rise to the island's now common name."

Prudence Island. This is an enjoyable destination, and a big day on the water for distance kayakers who choose to circumnavigate the island. Timing the wind and tide will make the journey much easier. Potter Cove is a serene area, and much of the coastline has beach landings. The southern tip has a rocky landing with steamers buried under the rocks. The Weaver Cove ramp is a good access point, but kayakers also use Bristol Harbor and Warwick launches to tour Prudence Island. You can also take a ferry out of Bristol (www.prudencebayislandtrasport.com).

Cruising Paddler

Weaver Cove Boat Ramp to Prudence Island. From the launch, it is about 1.8 miles to Prudence Island, and just under a mile to Dyer Island. There is a nice beach (with picnic tables) just north of the large pier/dock on the southeastern tip of Prudence Island. A

John Lathrop passing Gould Island (Portsmouth). **PHOTO DAVID FASULO**

nice circuit is to cross to Prudence Island (1.8 miles), then head north up the coast to Sandy Point (lighthouse on the point; 3.8 miles total). Take a break, then return the same route, but passing Dyer Island on the north side (7.6 miles total).

Sandy Point to Sapowet to Fogland. From the Sandy Point launch, head north along the shore to McCorrie Point (2 miles). Paddle across the Sakonnet River (watch current and wind) to Sapowet Point and Sapowet Cove (2.7 miles total). Head down the coast to Fogland Beach (5 miles total), then across the river to the launch (just under 6 miles total).

Sandy Point to Third Beach. It is just under a 5-mile paddle from Sandy Point to Third Beach (Middletown). The shoreline, especially just before Third Beach, has many interesting geological features. This paddle needs to be timed according to wind and tide, because fighting both back to the launch would be very difficult (10 miles total).

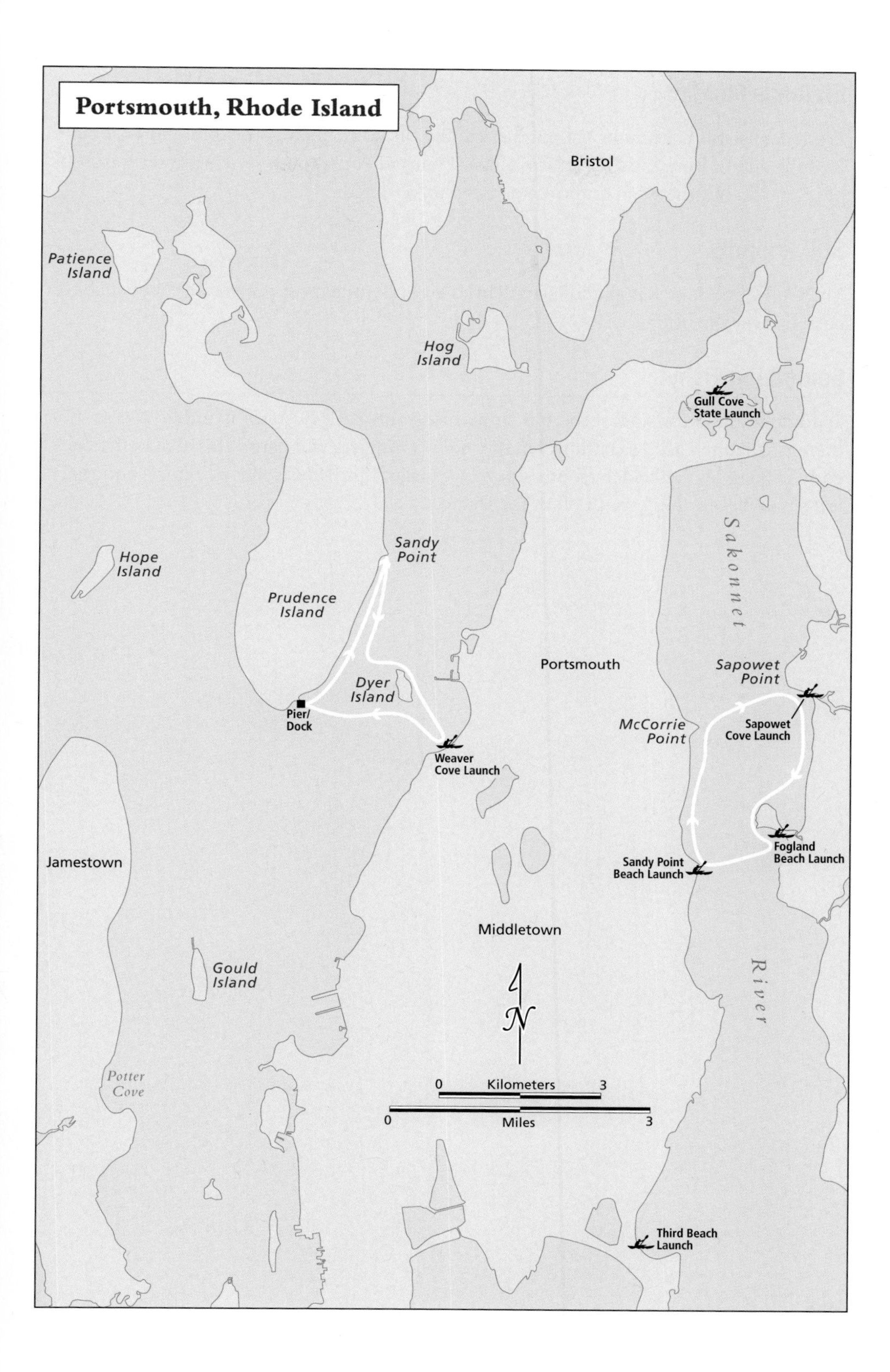
Portsmouth, Rhode Island
Bristol
Patience Island
Hog Island
Gull Cove State Launch
Sandy Point
Hope Island
Prudence Island
Sakonnet
Portsmouth
Sapowet Point
Dyer Island
Pier/ Dock
McCorrie Point
Sapowet Cove Launch
Weaver Cove Launch
Jamestown
Sandy Point Beach Launch
Fogland Beach Launch
Middletown
Gould Island
River
N
Potter Cove
0
Kilometers
3
0
Miles
3
Third Beach Launch

Distance Paddler

Prudence Island circumnavigation. Depending on how much you explore, it is about a 21-mile circuit from the Weaver Cove Boat Ramp in Portsmouth. There are several stopping points, but the wind and the tide need to be timed.

SUP Friendly

The Gull Cove State Ramp and Island Park Cove offer the most protection, but watch for current near the bridge.

Something Fishy

Teddy's Beach (west side of the old stone bridge on Park Avenue) is public access, but there isn't launch access (parking) in the vicinity. Anglers will patrol this area in the back eddy formed by the bridge (south side). Dyer Island provides some structure, and there is a small reef running south off of the island.

Middletown, RI

Middletown has a nice variety of areas, with the Sachuest Point National Wildlife Refuge being the focal point. Middletown is also SUP friendly, and a good place to avoid heavy boat traffic and wakes that are common in the Newport Harbor area. SUPs can utilize Sachuest (Second) Beach for cruising and surfing (kayaks are not allowed to land/launch in season), and the well-protected Third Beach is perfect for beginners and advanced paddlers alike. Third Beach also has a great launch for kayaks, allowing quick access to the interesting western shore of the Sakonnet River or the more-exposed Sachuest Point. If you are a family preferring to play on paddle craft, versus playing in the ocean waves and swells, Third Beach is a good choice.

Primary Launches: Third Beach Ramp. This is a great launch. Third Beach is typically protected and offers a pleasant cruise upriver along a rocky coastline, or a very scenic (but potentially rough) tour south along Sachuest Point. Parking

Locals Tuckerman and Ryder at Third Beach. **PHOTO DAVID FASULO**

Surfers playing at the designated Surfer's End, Sachuest (Second) Beach. **PHOTO DAVID FASULO**

fee when the beach is open. In-season fee is $10 weekdays and $20 weekends and holidays. Kayaks and SUPs can be rented at the beach in season. Directions: GPS Third Beach Road and follow it south to the end.

Sachuest (Second) Beach. Paddleboards are allowed to launch in season; kayaks are allowed to launch off-season. In-season fee is $10 weekdays and $20 weekends and holidays. There is also a nice spot on the far western end of Sachuest Beach designated the Surfer's End. Surf etiquette is required if using this area. Parking is more restrictive on the Surfer's End section of the beach. Directions: GPS Sachuest Road. The entrance to the main beach is on Sachuest Road, just after the intersection with Hanging Rock Road. The designated Surfer's End of the beach is at the intersection of Hanging Rock Road and Paradise Avenue.

Cruising Paddler

Third Beach to Sachuest Point to Easton's (First) Beach. This is a nice circuit, but be aware of typically rough conditions at Sachuest and Easton Points. Also be aware that once you depart the launch, there may not be an opportunity to land until you return to the launch. From the Third Beach ramp, head south around to the tip of Sachuest Point (1.92 miles). Cruise past Second Beach (check out Purgatory Chasm in the cliff

The jagged coast of the Sachuest Point area. **PHOTO DAVID FASULO**

not far from the western end of the beach) and around Easton Point (rough water; 4.48 miles total). Head north along the point to a landing (waves and conditions permitting) at Atlantic Beach (the far right end of Easton's Beach) near a large boulder—be careful of swimmers and surfers (5.3 miles total). Return the way you came (10.6 miles total).

Sakonnet River rocky shore. This is an underrated circuit that is generally protected and passes a pleasant, rocky, Maine-like coastline. Similar to Maine, there are few rest stops. From the Third Beach launch, head north along the rocky coast. There are potential landings after 2.2, 2.6, and 3.5 miles (total). Black Point (3.5 miles total) is a good turnaround, as the coast is not too interesting beyond this point (7 miles total).

Distance Paddler

Third Beach to Sachuest Point to Easton's (First) Beach, plus the Newport mansions. Follow the cruising route from Third Beach to the east end of Easton's Beach, but add 7.2 miles total to the trip by exploring the mansions out to Lands End (from the eastern end of Easton's Beach, Lands End is about 3.6 miles one way). It is 17.8 miles round-trip, but that is if you stay near shore and don't cut across the bays at Second Beach and Easton's Beach. Lots of coastline, with potential rough water and possibly no stops due to conditions.

The rocky shore of the Sakonnet River, just north of Third Beach, has unique scenery in a pleasant setting. **PHOTO DAVID FASULO**

Rough Water Paddler

The Easton's (Second) Beach area can have good off-season surfing, and SUPs are allowed to surf in season. Sachuest Point has some bumpy water, but beware of rocks and ledges. Sometimes advanced paddlers will leave from the Third Beach launch and cross the Sakonnet River and land on Sakonnet Point. From there they will paddle in the typically rough water outside the point. The crossing (3.6 miles one-way), which can be difficult due to current and wind, avoids a rather remote drive to the Sakonnet Point.

SUP Friendly

There are a couple really interesting circuits for SUPs. From Third Beach, follow the western shoreline past the "pudding stone"–type rock formations along the shoreline and other interesting features along the way. From Easton's (Second) Beach, follow the western shoreline starting at the designated Surfer's End. Cruise along interesting cliffs and past Purgatory Chasm, then past large boulders and a bay at the southern point. For the beginner, Third Beach is typically the most manageable area in the vicinity.

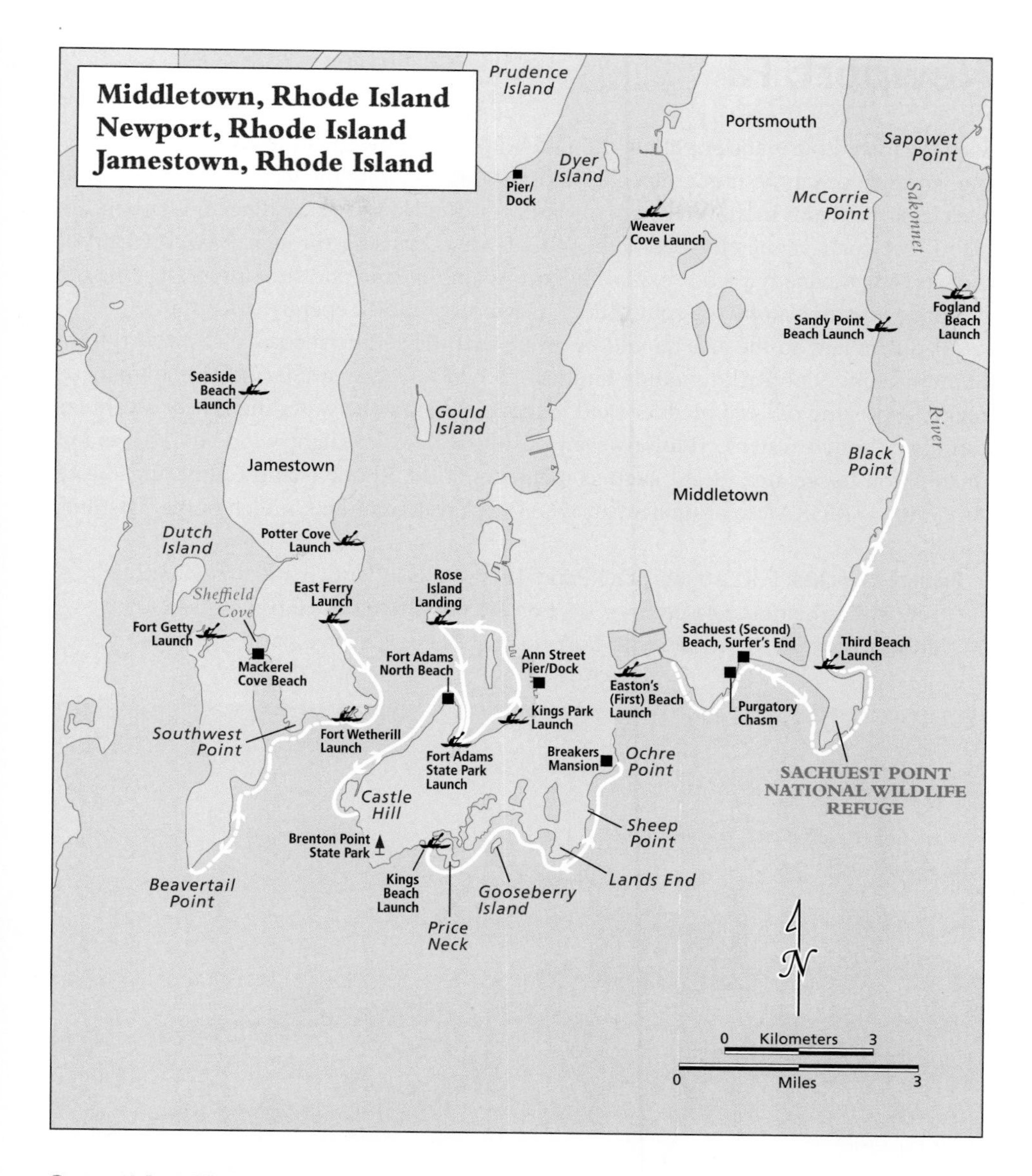

Something Fishy

The Sachuest Point area has currents and structure, and Flint Point Ledge is less than a mile from the Third Beach launch. This area is best approached while using a tube and worm rig trolled slowly near the bottom. The steep drop-off allows the kayak angler to navigate along a constant depth to find fish.

Newport, RI

Viewing incredible mansions along the Cliff Walk, attending music festivals, sailing, surfing, and exploring the numerous bars and restaurants along the waterfront are some of the classic activities in the lively city of Newport. The Newport coastline and harbors are also spectacular venues for paddlers. Whether it is cruising through Newport Harbor and viewing the many yachts, exploring Fort Adams by land and sea, or investigating the dramatic coastline along the south shore, Newport seems to energize its visitors.

Paddlers new to the area should be aware that the southern coast of Newport, from Brenton Point State Park to Lands End, is exposed to ocean swells and the shoreline is rocky; consisting of large boulders and ledges just below the waterline. These attributes can create rough water conditions even on relatively calm (light wind) days. It is not uncommon to see area locals, such as members of the Rhode Island Canoe and Kayak Association (RICKA), wearing helmets when sea kayaking in this stretch of the coastline.

Primary Launches: Fort Adams State Park. This is a great launch and a fascinating tourist destination. Directions: GPS Fort Adams Drive (off Harrison Avenue) and follow it to the entrance to Fort Adams. There is a large parking lot on

Rough Point, adjacent to the famous Newport Cliff Walk, as seen by kayak. **PHOTO DAVID FASULO**

Members of the Rhode Island Canoe/Kayak Association heading out from the Kings Beach launch in the early season. **PHOTO DAVID FASULO**

the left near the entrance. Take the road across from the parking lot to a fork, then head north to another fork. Take a right to the ramp and parking. Please note that this is one of the only launches in the vicinity with ample parking. However, parking at the actual ramp is somewhat limited. If possible, shuttle cars and people to the main parking area near the entrance to allow room for other visitors.

Kings Park. This is a good launch site to access Newport Harbor and Brenton Cove. A ramp is available as well as a wide sandy beach. Limited on-street parking for nonresidents near the boat ramp. Directions: GPS 125 Wellington Ave.

Kings Beach. This is a state-maintained fishing area in a protected cove. It also happens to be one of the only access points for the stunning Price Neck and Gooseberry Island area of Newport. However, conditions (strong south wind or large ocean swells) may allow only experienced sea kayakers to launch from this site due to breaking waves. Parking is somewhat limited, and it is crowded in season. If possible, drop off extra cars up the road at the free parking areas (there is a dirt parking area within walking distance along the beach) on Ocean Avenue. Directions: GPS Prices Neck Road. The entrance is a dirt road 365 feet west of Prices Neck Road off of Ocean Avenue.

Secondary Launches: Easton's (First) Beach. This has the quickest access to the famous Cliff Walk area, but roadside parking is metered and has time limits. This is a beach launch, and can be tricky due to waves and seaweed; therefore it is not a popular launch site. It is a popular beach with surfers. No boating or surfboarding is allowed within the guarded area between blue flags. For the parking lot, fee is $10 weekdays, $20 weekends and holidays. Directions: GPS 175 Memorial Blvd.

Battery Park. This is a very nice launch and is under a mile to Rose Island. However, parking is extremely limited, especially May through October for nonresidents. Directions: GPS Battery Street. The park is located on Washington Street, between Battery and Pine Streets. Park along Washington Street.

Elm Street/Storer Park. At the end of Elm Street is a small boat launch. Parking is limited, especially May through October for nonresidents. (***Note:*** The streets north of Elm [Poplar and Willow] also have access ramps.) Directions: GPS Elm Street and follow it to the water.

Taking a break on, and a tour of, Rose Island is a great outing. **PHOTO DAVID FASULO**

View of Ann Street Pier from the water—a good spot to stop for a drink or snack on Thames Street.
PHOTO DAVID FASULO

Landing Areas: Rose Island. This is a great destination to land on and explore. The landing admission is $5 June through September. The lighthouse museum and picnic area is open to the public July 1 to Labor Day from 10 a.m. to 4 p.m. daily. You can also stay overnight at the lighthouse; contact www.roseisland lighthouse.org for details.

Ann Street Pier/City of Newport Public Harbor Walk. This is a public dinghy dock with a protected beach adjacent to it. It's a good spot to land while exploring Newport Harbor to walk around Thames Street for a drink or snack. Launching from here is possible, but there is very limited parking. Directions: GPS Ann Street. The landing/launch is on Thames Street (across from Ann Street).

Fort Adams North Beach. On the northwestern tip of Fort Adams is a small beach. This is a nice spot to land and walk over to the Fort Adams area to purchase fresh lemonade in the summer.

Cruising Paddler

Kings Beach to Newport mansions. This is one of the most dramatic paddles in Newport. It is also the most dangerous due to ocean swells, rocks and ledges, and stretches of coastline with no easy way off the water. Many paddlers who follow this circuit wear helmets. Of course, in mild conditions, and if you only go to Lands End, the paddle can be benign. From the Kings Beach (fishing area) launch, head east along the shoreline past Price Neck (be careful of breaking waves). Paddle along the north side of Gooseberry Island and continue east past "Reject's Beach" to Lands End (2.1 miles). If conditions allow, continue around the corner and north up the coast, passing the famous Newport mansions and tourists along the Cliff Walk. A good turnaround point is Ochre Point, next to the Breakers Mansion (4.1 miles total). Return towards Lands End (possible rest stop at 4.5 miles total in Sheep Point Cove just south of Ochre Point), minding the rocks and waves (6 miles total). Head along the southern end of Gooseberry Island to the launch (8 miles total). (***Note:*** You can add some miles by exploring the very interesting coves, but be careful of breaking waves and current at the entrances to these coves.)

Fort Adams State Park launch to Castle Hill. This is a great tour, but be forewarned the water at the north end of Fort Adams State Park, as well as the northwestern side

Brenda Rashleigh exploring the Price Neck area. PHOTO DAVID FASULO

Exploring Fort Adams by water. If time permits, the land-based tour is also worth the time. **PHOTO DAVID FASULO**

(along the fort wall), is typically rough due to boat wakes and wind waves. From the Fort Adams State Launch (drop off boats and park in the main lot if the small lot is full), head north along the Fort Adams coast to the northern point (rough water; 1 mile). Paddle along the western shore to the Castle Hill Lighthouse (good photo opportunity; 3 miles total). Continue around the point to the eastern end of a private beach (public to high-water mark) for a break (3.5 miles total). Return the same route (7 miles total).

Fort Adams State Park launch to Rose Island landing. This is another great Newport tour, and more protected than Castle Hill. From the Fort Adams launch, cruise along Newport Harbor (admiring the yachts) then under the Goat Island bridge to a rest (if needed) at the Elm Street launch, just north of Storer Park (2.2 miles). From the Elm Street launch, paddle over to the Rose Island landing area (3.2 miles total). Take a tour of the lighthouse and grounds, then return to the launch passing the west side of Goat Island and the eastern shoreline of Fort Adams (5 miles total). (***Note:*** Rose Island is also approached by experienced sea kayakers from launching out of Fort Wetherill State Park in Jamestown.)

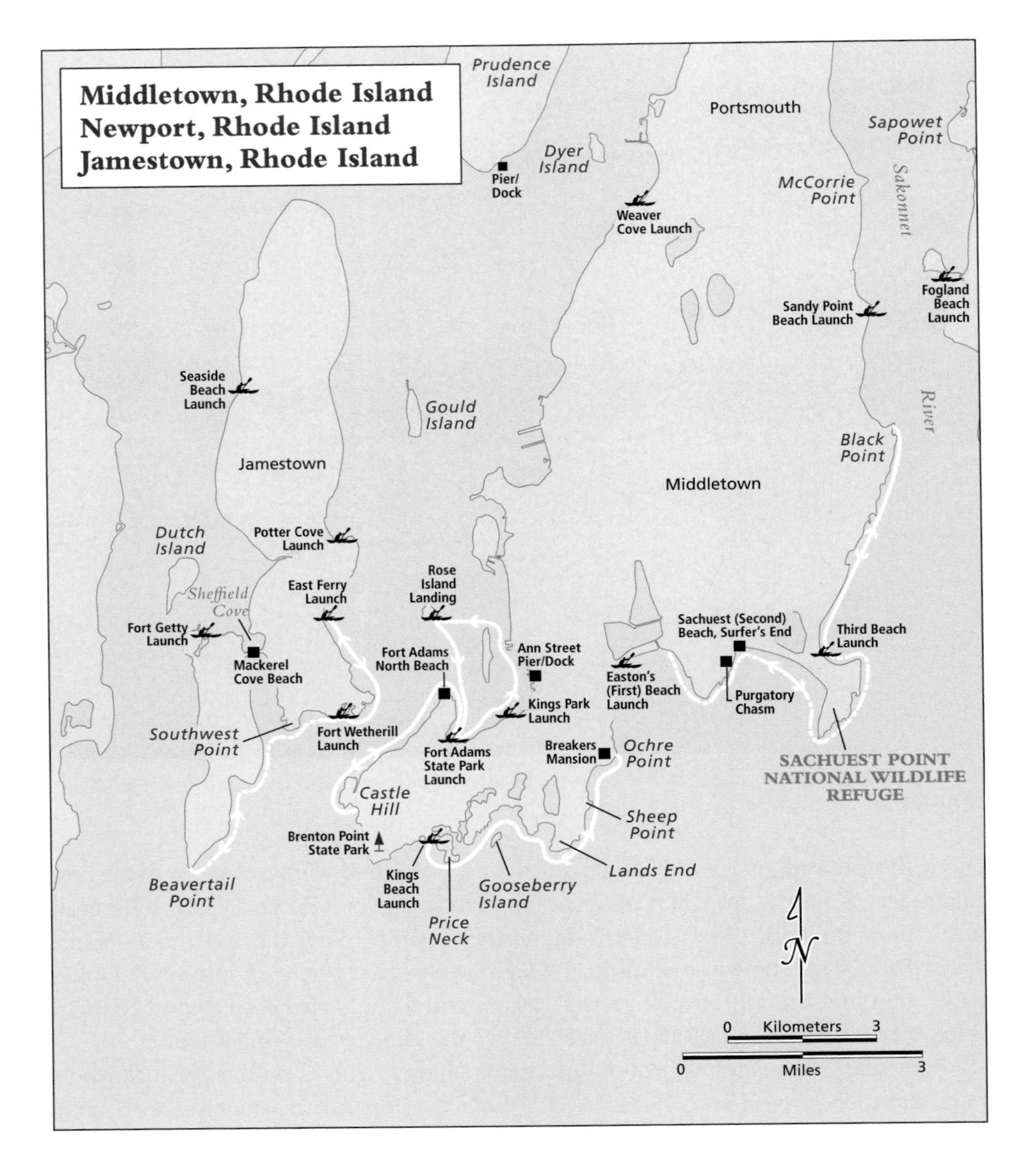

Distance Paddler

Fort Adams State Park launch to Lands End. For a combination of distance, rough water, and dramatic scenery, Fort Adams to Lands End and back (14 miles total) is hard to beat. The best rest stop is at the Kings Beach (fishing access) launch. However, be forwarded that several areas, such as Brenton Reef off of Brenton Point, Price Neck, and Lands End,

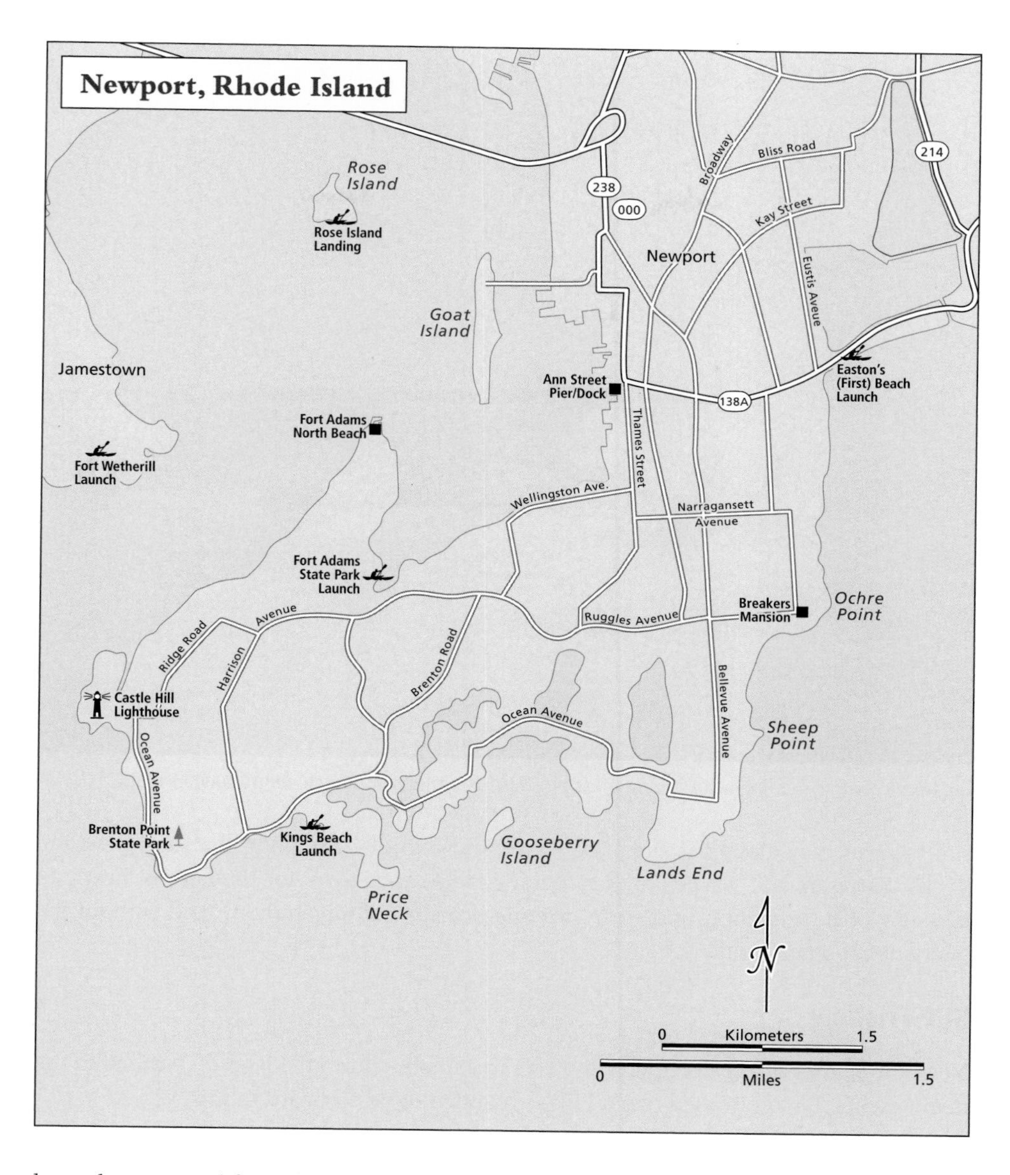

have the potential for very rough water, breaking waves, and exposed rocks/ledges. It is not a journey to be taken lightly in certain conditions.

Rough Water Paddler

The locals seem to enjoy "rock gardening" between the Kings Beach (fishing access) launch and Lands End. While wearing helmets and possessing solid paddling and rescue

Jonathan Alvarez holding his morning prize off of the Kings Beach launch. **PHOTO DAVID FASULO**

skills, locals play along the breaking waves and rocks/ledges along the shore—timing swells, currents, and waves. Rock gardening is not an activity for the faint of heart, or in a new boat (scratching and even breaking boats is not uncommon), and without the safety net of other paddlers.

SUP Friendly

Newport Harbor is a really interesting area to explore—from the jagged coastline to the many yachts. Be forewarned that a PFD is required to be on board in this area.

Something Fishy

Kings Beach (fishing access) has many rocks and some reefs just offshore and is a popular area for fishing. This area is the most exposed and treacherous launch in Rhode Island and requires a north wind to be able to fish in the lee. Any southern wind in the forecast will have offshore waves breaking on submerged reefs and spilling an unknowing kayaker. The fall run of false albacore will have numerous anglers (in boats) competing with kayakers to get on the school first.

Jamestown, RI

Jamestown, and especially the Fort Wetherill area, is a very popular destination for sea kayakers and deservedly so. The Fort Wetherill launch has quick access to some of the best ocean kayak areas in Rhode Island, with stunning cliffs lining the scenic coastline right from the launch. Nearby Fort Getty offers camping, along with paddling from the campground and a quick trip to Dutch Island. However, access beyond the high-water mark on the beaches at Dutch Island is restricted at this time. According to the Rhode Island Department of Environmental Management (2016), "Until such time as concerns created by abandoned military installations are remediated by the Army Corps of Engineers (who are presently working on the island) it is a No Trespass policy. Public access and invitation will be determined once the Public Safety liability is addressed." As the author understands it, improvements are currently being made with the hopes of public access in the near future.

For advanced paddlers, Fort Wetherill also serves as a launch point for Rose Island (passing the Clingstone house on the rocks), Newport Harbor, Castle Hill, and the typically rough Beavertail Point. Unlike downtown Newport, which is great fun, downtown

Kate Powers following the rocky shoreline back to the Fort Wetherill launch. **PHOTO DAVID FASULO**

Jamestown is less congested and worth a visit. There is a decent variety of restaurants and a charming downtown to extend your day after getting off the water.

Primary Launches: Fort Wetherill State Park. This is a favorite launch site for sea kayakers. It is a popular scuba diving site, and the parking lot, while large, can fill up—best to carpool. There are other lots nearby if full. This site has great access to rocky shorelines, along with protected coves nearby for SUPs. Directions: GPS Fort Wetherill Road and follow it almost to the end (follow signs for scuba launch).

Fort Getty. This is a nice spot that offers camping and a boat launch, and is a good launch for Dutch Island. Entrance fee in season (May 15 through October 15) is $20 per day or $100 for the season for nonresidents. Ramp and parking is at the north end. Directions: GPS Fort Getty Road and follow it to the north end (kayak launch across the street from boat launch).

Secondary Launches: Seaside Beach. A town multiuse area with a beach ramp and parking for fifteen cars. Parking permit required May 15 through October 15. Directions: GPS Frigate Street. At the intersection of Frigate Street and Seaside Drive, head north on Seaside Drive for 150 feet and the launch is on the west side of the road.

Potter Cove. A nice SUP launch, and also a good area to spot a car for a down-island run to Fort Wetherill. There is a parking area with a staircase down to the beach. A little tricky to find the first time, it is located near the toll station. Directions: GPS Freebody Drive. At the intersection of East Shore Road and Freebody Drive, head east on Freebody Drive for 400 feet to the parking area on the north side of the road.

East Ferry. A nice spot in downtown Jamestown, but parking fills up quickly (not for groups). Parking from 6 a.m. to 6 p.m., limited to eight hours. Directions: GPS Knowles Court. The parking is across the street from Conanicus Avenue.

Mackerel Cove Beach. A nice beach launch, but launching is not allowed until after 5 p.m. in season (no such restriction in the off-season). This is a key spot if doing the Jamestown "1/2 circumnavigation," shortening the route by portaging boats across the narrow divide between Sheffield Cove and Mackerel Cove. Parking for residents only May 15 through October 15, 8 a.m. to 5 p.m. Directions: GPS Hamilton Avenue, then follow this to Beavertail Road. The beach is about 100 feet west of the intersection.

Cruising Paddler

Fort Wetherill to Beavertail Point. This may be the most popular sea kayak tour in Rhode Island. From the launch, head west along the shore to Southwest Point and the entrance to Mackerel Cove (1.1 miles). Paddle across the cove entrance, then continue along the shore to Hull Cove (2 miles total). Check out Hull Cove, then continue along the coast to Beavertail Point (3.6 miles total). (***Note:*** The Beavertail Point area can be *very* rough. Experienced sea kayakers have flipped over and even broken boats in this area, so explore with caution.) Return the same route (7.2 miles total). You can extend the journey with a tour through Mackerel Cove. Also, if you can round Beavertail safely to extend the tour, the coastline just northwest of the point has interesting scenery.

Fort Wetherill to Newport. From the Fort Wetherill launch, it is 1.6 miles to the northern end of Fort Adams/Newport Harbor entrance. When the sea conditions are mild (light wind, small waves), sea kayakers often start at Fort Wetherill and then explore Newport, depending on their preferences (Rose Island, Newport Harbor, or Castle Hill).

Fort Wetherill to Jamestown. A nice tour with a landing to stretch your legs and explore downtown Jamestown a bit. From the Fort Wetherill launch, head north along the shore and around Bull Point (can be rough near the island) to a break on East Ferry Beach, just north of the piers (2 miles one way). Return the same route (4 miles total). ***Note:*** If conditions allow, some paddlers like to explore Rose Island (1.3 miles offshore from Jamestown) combined with this tour.

Dutch Island, typically approached from the Fort Getty or Old Jamestown Ferry Landing/URI Bay Campus launch, is a popular tour. **PHOTO ERIK BAUMGARTNER**

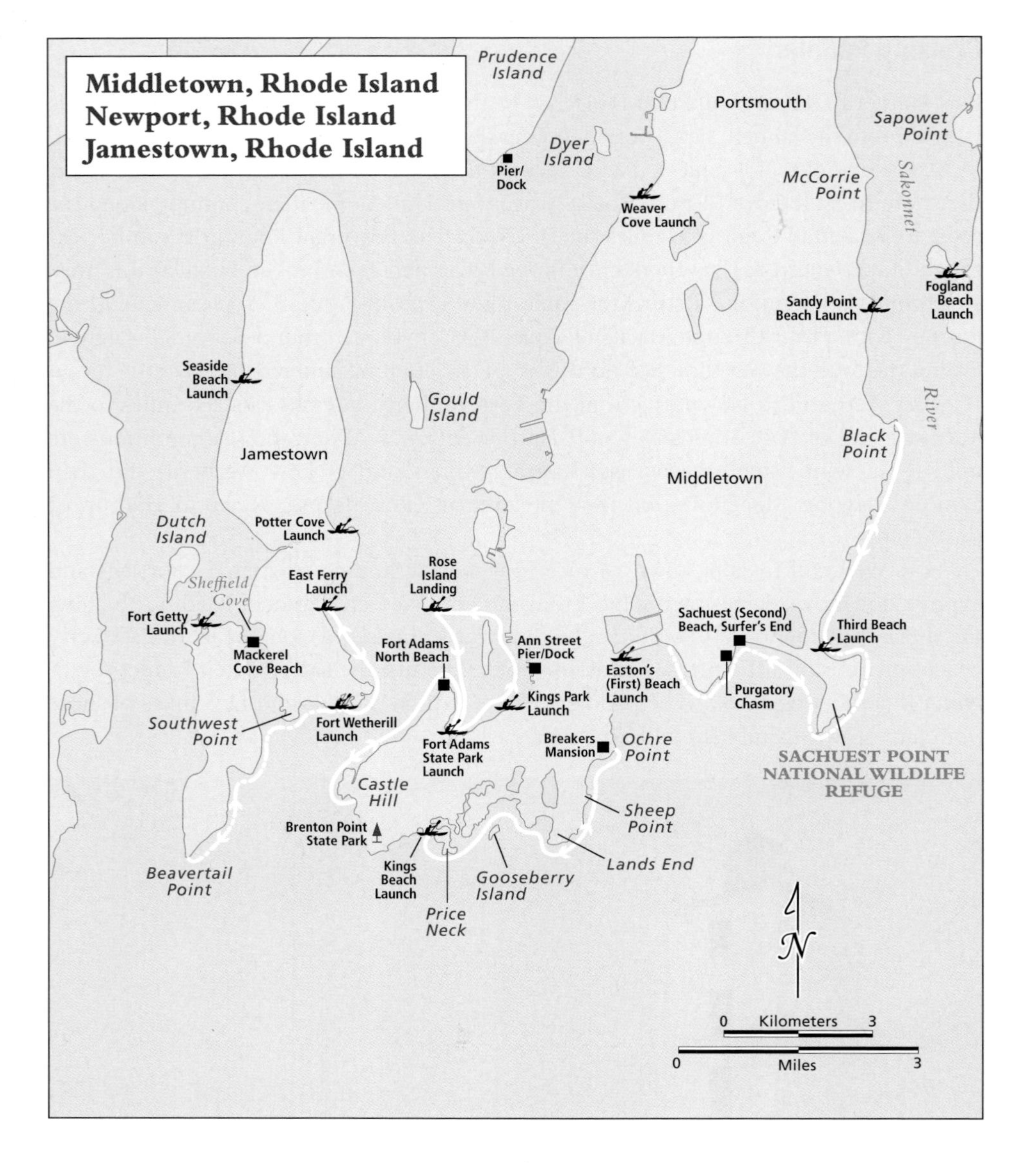

Jamestown 1/2 Circumnavigation. One of the top three paddles in Rhode Island, but should be done in the off-season (if Beavertail Point is not too rough) because Mackerel Cove Beach (used to shorten the trip) is typically off-limits to small boats during the summer months before 5 p.m. From the Fort Wetherill launch, head southwest along the coast, around Beavertail Point, and up to Fort Getty (6.8 miles), then head east and then south into Sheffield Cove and Mackerel Cove Beach (7.7 miles total). Carry boats

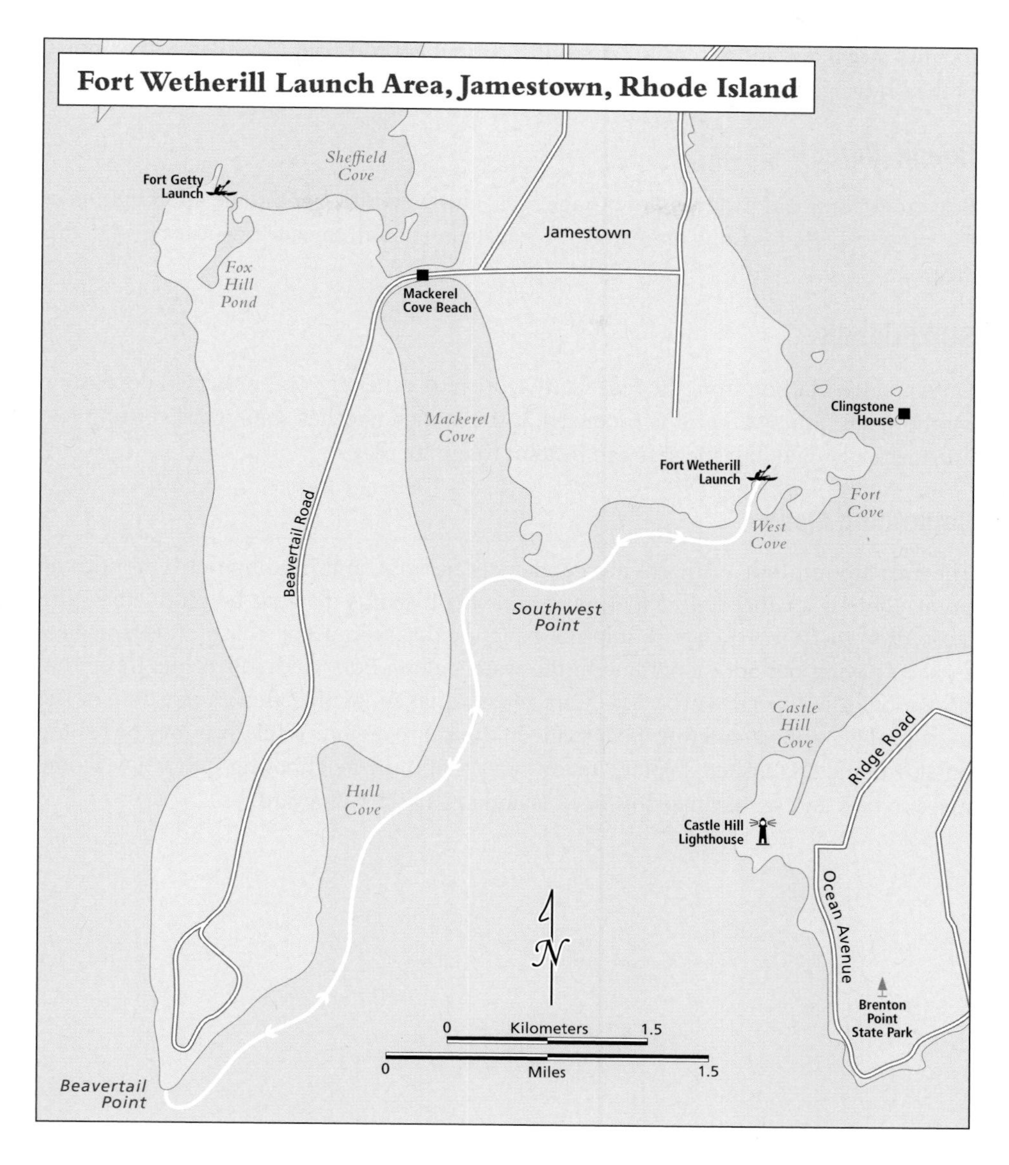

over the road, and launch from Mackerel Cove Beach. Head down Mackerel Cove to Southwest Point, then back to the launch (10 miles total).

Distance Paddler

Jamestown Circumnavigation. This is a popular tour for experienced sea kayakers. From the Fort Wetherill launch, it is about a 22-mile circumnavigation. Be sure to pay attention to wind and tides, and be careful around Beavertail Point. Potter Cove Beach (just north of the bridge going to Newport) is a good resting spot.

Rough Water Paddler

Beavertail Point can produce very rough seas, and when the conditions are rough, only the most experienced and prepared sea kayakers should consider venturing into this area.

SUP Friendly

Dutch Island Harbor, from the Fort Getty launch, is generally well protected depending on the wind. Fort Wetherill is protected at the launch and has some great touring just outside the launch, but the seas can be a bit rough for SUPs.

Something Fishy

The area around Fort Wetherill has good spots for bass, and heading north around the point, there is a collection of rock piles and small islands that can be productive. The steep drop to 70 to 100 feet should not be ignored as "too deep." Many anglers neglect to keep paying out additional line in the waters along Fort Wetherill, while those that do are often rewarded with a fish. Care must be taken, as this area offers some of the most prolific sailboat and tour-boat traffic in the entire region. While you may be fishing outside of the established channel, many boaters find the neighboring waters a welcome place to tack and set a course for Block Island or Martha's Vineyard.

Tiverton, RI

Tiverton is located on the East Bay section of Rhode Island and has some very good access points. The Tiverton/Sakonnet River waters are generally protected from the ocean swells, but you need to keep an eye on current (tidal and river) and an ever-present wind. One of the more interesting adventures is to spot a car and put in from an access point north of that car (or south if on a flood tide with a southerly wind). By timing the ebbing current, you can get an assist to your takeout point and drive back to the original put-in. Sapowet Cove to Fogland is 2.5 miles one way, and the Nannaquaket Bridge to Fogland is 5.5 miles one way. .

Primary Launches: Nannaquaket Bridge. There is a small parking lot to access Nannaquaket Pond, mostly used by anglers, on the west side of the bridge. You will need to carry over some boulders to access the water. Be careful of boat traffic and strong current under the bridge. Directions: GPS Nannaquaket Road until you reach the bridge.

Sapowet Cove. A great beach launch for kayaks or SUPs near the bridge off Seapowet Avenue. Directions: GPS Driftwood Drive (for a landmark). The launch is off of Seapowet Avenue 1,077 feet north of Driftwood Drive, just northwest of the bridge on Seapowet.

Fogland Beach/Boat Ramp. This is a really nice spot, but be careful of getting pulled too far south due to current and wind. This is a town beach that has kayak and paddleboard rentals. Nonresident fee in the summer. The shallow bay on the north side of the beach is also pleasant (cut through halfway down-beach). Directions: GPS Fogland Point Road or 3 Rod Way (they seem to be the same road). There is a free boat ramp at the end of Fogland Road, with a sandy parking area at Fogland Beach.

Secondary Launch: Grinnell's Beach/Stone Bridge. Due to strong current, launch on the south side of the bridge and plan your trip accordingly. Off-season parking is available at Grinnell's Town Beach. There is a nonresident fee and no launching allowed in season. Directions: GPS 1800 Main Rd., then head west on Stone Bridge Road.

Cruising Paddler

If you pay attention to the tides, launch from Sapowet Cove and head to the northern point on Fogland (1.6 miles). Continue past Fogland Beach and along the shore to High Hill Point (house/lighthouse) and the rocky point (3 miles one way). Head back up to Fogland for a break, then back to Sapowet Cove (6 miles total).

John Lathrop passing the unique rock formations on High Hill Point. **PHOTO DAVID FASULO**

Distance Paddler

To go for distance, spot a car downriver and then put in north of that location. The author paddled from the Grinnell's Beach/Stone Bridge to Sakonnet Point, 12.6 miles one way, with relative ease in the early season with the ebb current.

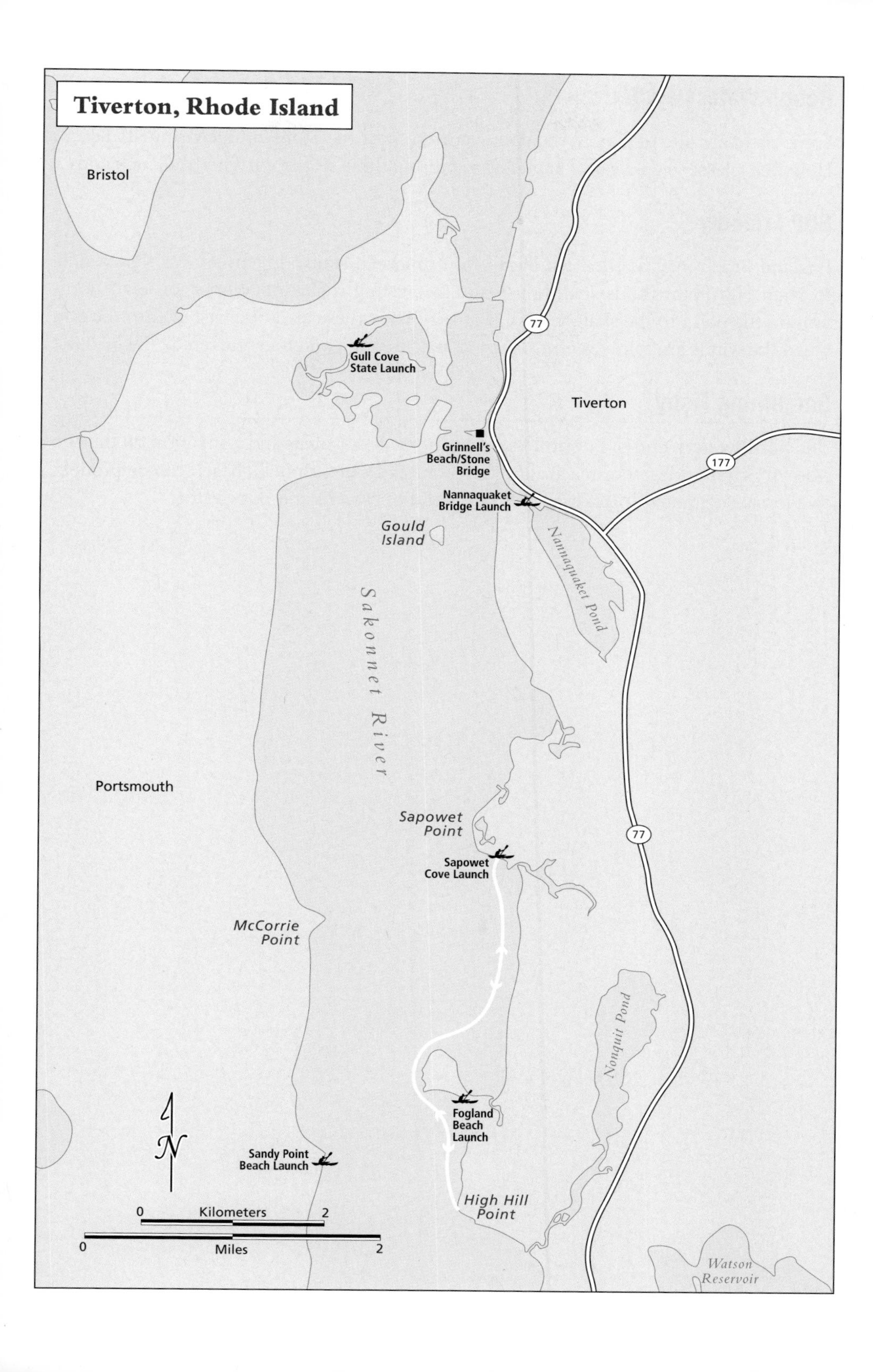
Tiverton, Rhode Island
Bristol
Gull Cove
State Launch
77
Tiverton
Grinnell's
Beach/Stone
Bridge
177
Nannaquaket
Bridge Launch
Gould
Island
Nannaquaket Pond
Sakonnet River
Portsmouth
Sapowet
Point
77
Sapowet
Cove Launch
McCorrie
Point
Nonquit Pond
Fogland
Beach
Launch
N
Sandy Point
Beach Launch
High Hill
Point
0
Kilometers
2
0
Miles
2
Watson
Reservoir

Rough Water Paddler

Some paddlers like to play in the strong current near the Stone Bridge/Grinnell's Beach. However, please keep clear of anglers if exploring these strong currents and back eddy.

SUP Friendly

Fogland Beach may be the friendliest—you can head south downriver less than a mile to High Hill Point (house/lighthouse and interesting rock formations), or head north around the point to the shallow cove. For the SUPer these areas are best later in the day, when the winds are calm, or cruise Nannaquaket Pond (watch for current at the bridge).

Something Fishy

The northwestern end of Fogland Beach has some rocky areas and a small rip on the ebb tide. At certain tides, the area around the Stone Bride at Grinnell's Beach can be productive for spring tautog (blackfish), but be careful of current and boat traffic.

Little Compton, RI

The south shore of Sakonnet Point, as well as the south shore of Newport and Jamestown, are probably the best scenic open-ocean paddling areas in Rhode Island. Because it is more secluded, Sakonnet Point is less popular than the Jamestown or Newport areas. While beautiful, keep in mind that the southern coast is exposed to large ocean waves, so check conditions beforehand and plan accordingly.

Sakonnet Point has several small rocky islands to explore, with West Island being a favorite. West Island is off-limits due to bird nesting. However, at high tide experienced kayakers, with the proper safety equipment, sometimes pass through an opening on the south side into a small lagoon on West Island, requiring some "rock gardening" skills. In the distance the iconic Sakonnet Lighthouse overlooks the point, and there is a nice beach on the end of the point to take a break and enjoy the scenery. A common turnaround is Warren Point (1.5 miles from the beach on Sakonnet Point), or you can tour all the way to South Shore Beach (4.8 miles from the beach on Sakonnet Point), with the Massachusetts border less than a mile east from South Shore Beach.

John Sharlin cruising past the rocks and lighthouse at Sakonnet Point. **PHOTO DAVID FASULO**

Taking a break on the Sakonnet Point beach, with the iconic Sakonnet Lighthouse in the background.
PHOTO DAVID FASULO

Primary Launch: Sakonnet Harbor Access. A nicely protected area and a key location for paddling along Sakonnet Point. No fees. Directions: GPS 163 Sakonnet Point Rd. and continue down the road about 500 feet (Haffenreffer Wildlife Refuge). There is a small parking lot across from the lot for trailered boats. Since the parking lot is small, please carpool and double-park if you are with a small group.

Point of Interest: South Shore Beach. This is a nice location, but the beach launch can be rough depending on conditions (as well as the rocks). There is a parking fee for nonresidents in season. The launching of cartop boats as an activity that is allowed, or not allowed, was not confirmed. Directions: GPS 125 South Shore Rd.

Cruising Paddler

The most popular, when the conditions allow, is to leave from the Sakonnet Harbor access and explore West Island (hidden lagoon with a narrow access) and then East Island. It is also fun to check out the iconic Sakonnet Lighthouse if conditions allow. Work your way back to shore (be careful of hidden wave-producing ledges) and along the coast to Warren Point (3.8 miles one way). Follow the shore back to the Sakonnet Point beach for a break, then head back to the launch (7.6 miles total). There is a nice beach between Warren and Briggs Points, but offshore waves can make landing difficult.

Distance Paddler

From the harbor access, it is 6.7 miles to the Massachusetts border (past South Shore Beach and just before Quicksand Point). If the waves are not too bad, you can land

John Sharlin entering the lagoon on West Island. **PHOTO DAVID FASULO**

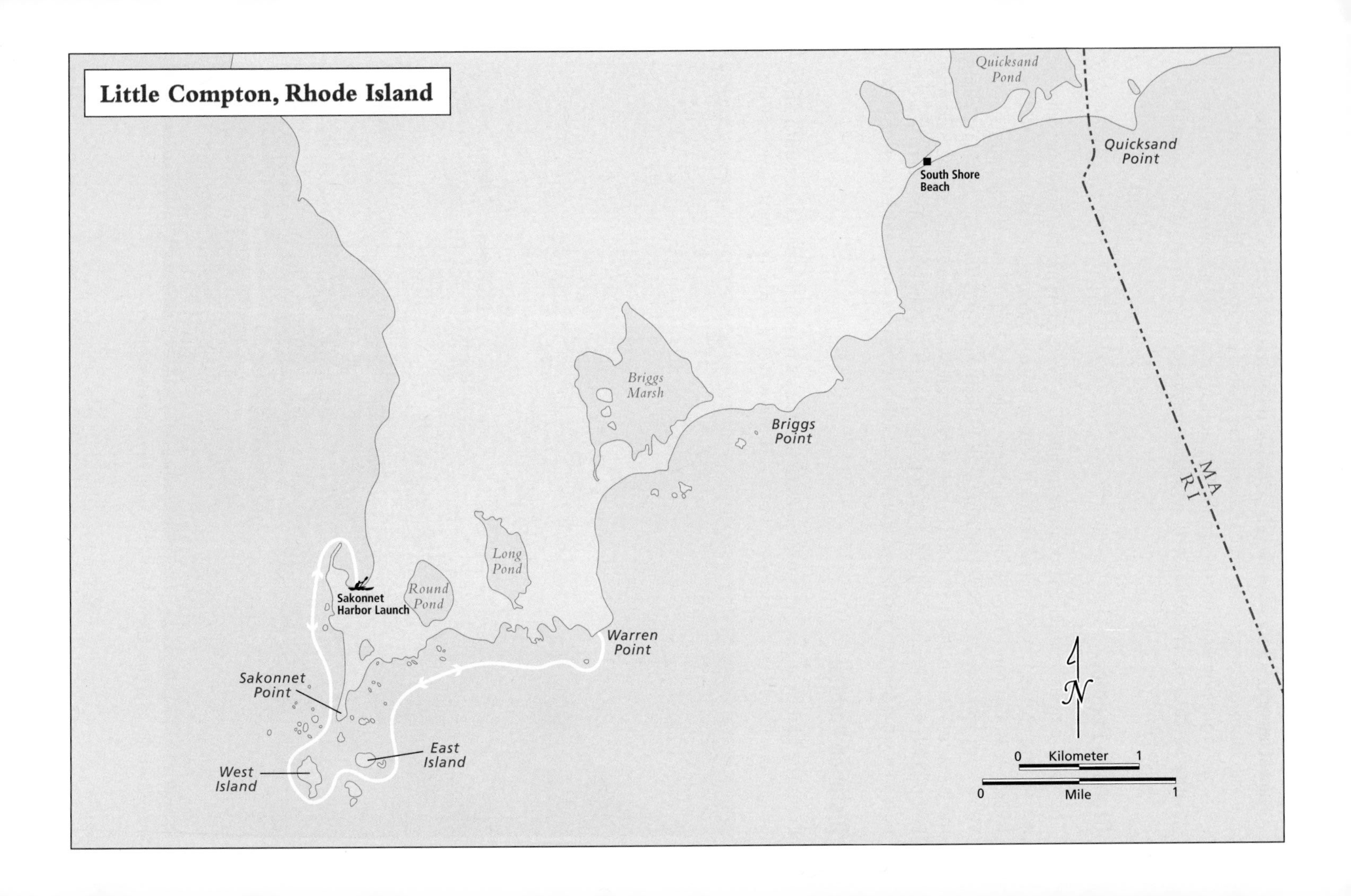
Little Compton, Rhode Island
Quicksand Pond
Quicksand Point
South Shore Beach
MA
RI
Briggs Marsh
Briggs Point
Long Pond
Round Pond
Sakonnet Harbor Launch
Warren Point
Sakonnet Point
East Island
West Island
N
0 Kilometer 1
0 Mile 1

on the rocky beach east of South Shore Beach for a break and then return (13.4 miles total).

Rough Water Paddler

When there are ocean swells, or wind waves, Sakonnet Point can kick up. In these conditions, plenty of rough water spots along the coast are churned up by the rocks and ledges.

SUP Friendly

It is 1.19 miles to the end of the Sakonnet Point beach from the harbor launch access. This can be causal, or unreasonable, depending on the current (best on flood tides so you can get back) and sea conditions. You can also head upriver and catch a ride back down if the tide is ebbing.

Something Fishy

There are remains of an elite fishing club on West Island that existed from 1862 to 1906. Fishermen would fish from "bass stands" (wooden platforms) with guides—the island's southeast corner apparently being one of the more productive spots. "Fishy" ledges and rocky areas can be found throughout the area; however, as with Kings Beach, Newport, it is best to fish on a light north wind, as the area is exposed to large ocean swells and breaking waves.

Block Island (New Shoreham), RI

Sometimes called "the Bermuda of the Northeast," Block Island is a spectacular playground for boaters and beach-goers. Many people, typically boaters who hang out in the vicinity of the Oar, seem to find their happy place on Block. The island can be quite fun at night, but staying on Block is not inexpensive. However, Block Island also makes for an enjoyable day trip using the ferry service.

The majority of paddlers will stay inshore and explore the edges of New Harbor/Great Salt Pond (watch for boat traffic), as well as Trims Pond and Harbor Pond. For the more experienced sea kayaker, the ocean side of Block Island has great cruising. However, the reef on the northern end of the island produces very rough water combined with strong current. The southern end can have large refracting waves, and it can be difficult to land on much of the island due to the rocky shore and breaking waves—so plan accordingly.

Kayak and SUP rentals are available at the Indian Head Neck Road access point. If day tripping Block Island, unless you need a performance sea kayak for the shoreline, it may be easier to rent from this location. You can also bring cartop boats aboard the ferry services. Lastly, on occasion, very experienced sea kayakers paddle from the mainland to Block Island, either a one-way trip or both ways. The author has done this a few times

Lisa Risebrow going for a morning paddle in the Great Salt Pond. **PHOTO DAVID FASULO**

(once in January), but be advised that conditions can dramatically change with little warning on this exposed crossing.

Ferry Rates: Block Island Express, New London, Connecticut. The rate is $25 per person one way and $15 one way for a kayak or paddleboard. From New London the ferry is passenger only to Block Island (no cars).

Block Island Ferry, Point Judith, Rhode Island. Vehicles ($79.20 car round-trip; $97.40 SUV round-trip); kayak $14.75 one way/$29.50 round-trip; paddleboard $9.55 one way/$19.10 round-trip.

Primary Launches/Accesses: According to the town, "All of the Block Island beaches are public, so all of the locations mentioned do not have any access restrictions. Parking is restricted only by posted signs and availability." However, the town does discourage/restrict long-term storage of kayaks and paddleboards on the beaches: "We have some locations where kayaks are left on the beach for the summer and then abandoned in the fall. It then becomes the town's responsibility to remove and dispose of them. Therefore, we ask kayakers and paddleboarders to not store their equipment on the beach long term."

New Harbor/Great Salt Pond Access: Indian Head Neck Road. This is the best access point to reach New Harbor/Great Salt Pond (north), Trims Pond (west), and Harbor Pond (south). The launch is located on Ocean Avenue, across from the junction of West Side Avenue (next to Dead Eye Dick's restaurant). Limited parking is located along the west side of Ocean Avenue. Kayak and paddleboard rentals are available in the summer.

Andy's Way. A right-of-way leading to a nice beach at the northern end of the Great Salt Pond, with limited parking and a 160-foot carry to the beach. This is a very nice SUP and casual kayak area, and good clamming too. Directions: GPS Andy's Way (off Corn Neck Road).

Dinghy/Mosquito Beach. Access to the southeast end of the Great Salt Pond. Kind of a muddy beach, and requires walking down a boardwalk. Directions: Follow Beach Avenue to the intersection with Corn Neck Road. Head north on Corn Neck Road for 3,600 feet to a small parking area on the west side of the road.

Northern/Eastern Ocean Accesses: Grove Point/Settler's Rock. Ocean access to the northern end of Block Island, or the protected Sachem Pond. A launch for calm conditions only due to strong current, rocky shore, and breaking waves. Directions: Follow Corn Neck Road to the northern end, where it ends at a small parking lot (fills up quickly).

Mansion Beach. An open beach on the northeast section of Block Island. It is a nice sandy and secluded beach, but breaking waves can make launching difficult. Directions: GPS Mansion Road and take it to the end and a primitive parking area. It is about a 400-foot carry to the beach.

Frederick Benson Town Beach. The swimming areas must be avoided, and can have breaking waves. There are no parking fees. Directions: GPS 7 Corn Neck Rd.

Western Ocean Access: West Beach Road. This area has limited parking and difficult access to the ocean. Not an attractive access point and not recommended. Directions: GPS West Beach Road and follow it to the shore (parking on the side of the road).

Old Harbor Accesses: Old Harbor Dock. This is one of the few areas that restrict kayak and SUP access due to the high concentration of commercial traffic. However, it is a destination for distance kayakers paddling from Rhode Island who wish to return via ferry. Kayakers are advised to use Surf Beach (see below).

Surf Beach. If you can find parking (it is a reasonable carry from the ferry with beach wheels), this may be the best beach, depending on wind conditions, to launch directly into the ocean. Surf Beach is located just north of the breakwater (in front of the Surf Hotel) at the intersection of Dodge and Water Streets.

Cruising Paddler

Block Island ocean paddling is very conditions dependent. To experience the ocean, probably the best area (depending on conditions) is the coastline between Mansion Beach (bit of a carry to the parking lot) and Surf Beach (next to the Old Harbor breakwater). With a prevailing west wind, this seems to be the gentlest coastline along the island. Popular interior areas are the Great Salt Pond and the more protected Trims and Harbor Ponds.

Distance Paddler

A Block Island circumnavigation (about 18 miles) is a beautiful, but potentially dangerous, tour for experienced sea kayakers. The north reef can be very rough, and there can be limited area to land depending on conditions. Kayakers typically take the ferry over and use Surf Beach. Experienced sea kayakers also paddle from the Point Judith Harbor area, 11 miles to the northern tip of Block Island, and then to Surf Beach near the Old Harbor breakwater (just over 15 miles total).

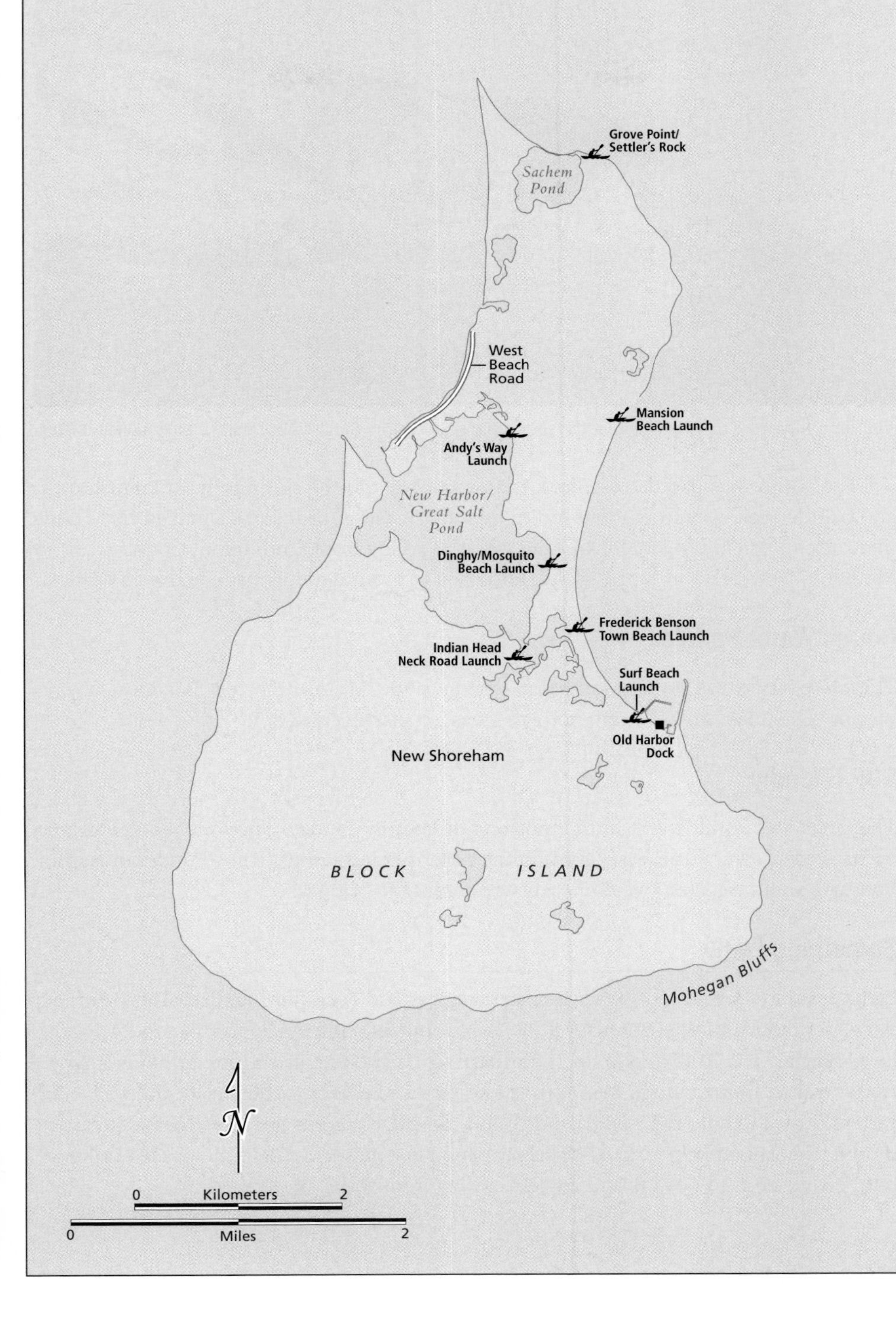

Block Island, Rhode Island
Grove Point/
Settler's Rock
Sachem
Pond
West
Beach
Road
Mansion
Beach Launch
Andy's Way
Launch
New Harbor/
Great Salt
Pond
Dinghy/Mosquito
Beach Launch
Frederick Benson
Town Beach Launch
Indian Head
Neck Road Launch
Surf Beach
Launch
Old Harbor
Dock
New Shoreham
BLOCK ISLAND
Mohegan Bluffs
N
0 Kilometers 2
0 Miles 2

Jim Zagryn passing the southeast bluffs while circumnavigating Block Island. **PHOTO ERIK BAUMGARTNER**

The author has paddled to Block Island and back in the summer from Point Judith, and paddled one-way from Point Judith in January. The author and a small group of paddlers also took a break on Block Island when paddling from Stonington, Connecticut; to Montauk, New York; to Block Island; and back to Stonington in a single day (54 miles).

Rough Water Paddler

There are surf areas on the southeast section, and the northern reef is almost always bumpy. The tides can be strong in these areas, so plan accordingly.

SUP Friendly

The Great Salt Pond is best in the morning or later in the day, when the wind and boat traffic settle down. Otherwise, skirting the edge is entertaining. Trims Pond and Harbor Pond are well protected (watch for current under the bridges).

Something Fishy

Block Island is renowned for its monster stripers and plentiful bluefish. There are lots of keeper fluke and sea bass just off the island, but the best spots may be too far for the kayak angler. The Sandy Point area (northern tip) is productive starting in June for stripers, and then fluke and sea bass, but the water can be very turbulent for a kayak. Surf casters do well along the island, and if you can safely access the rocky coast, it can be productive. The most protected bet is probably the entrance area to the Great Salt Pond, but be courteous to boaters and anglers casting from shore.

Sources

Connecticut:

ConnYak Connecticut Sea Kayakers, www.connyak.org
Connecticut Coastal Access Guide, www.lisrc.uconn.edu/coastalaccess
Department of Energy & Environmental Protection, www.ct.gov/deep

Rhode Island:

Rhode Island Canoe/Kayak Association, www.ricka.org
Public Access to the Rhode Island Coast, www.crmc.state.ri.us/publicaccess/ri_access_guide.pdf
State of Rhode Island Division of Parks and Recreation, www.riparks.com
State of Rhode Island Department of Environmental Management, www.dem.ri.gov
Public Access, www.crmc.ri.gov/publicaccess/PublicAccess_Brochure.pdf

Instruction:

There are many top-notch kayak, kayak fishing, and SUP instructors in Connecticut and Rhode Island. The organizations below certify and provide contact information for several instructors, and the Internet can help with additional research.

American Canoe Association (ACA), www.americancanoe.org
Paddlesports North America, www.paddlesportsnorthamerica.org

Kayak Fishing Rhode Island:

Ocean State Kayak Fishing, www.oceanstatekayakfishing.com

Sea Kayak Level System for Group Paddles:

Referenced from the Rhode Island Canoe/Kayak Association (www.rickaseakayaking.org)

Level 1

No previous kayak experience is required.

Level 2

Participants should be able to:

Paddle 6 miles in a day.
Perform a wet exit.
Perform an assisted deep water rescue.

Maintain a heading for short distances without the use of a rudder.
Turn a kayak using forward and reverse sweep strokes.

Level 3

Participants should be able to:

Perform skills listed under Level 2.
Paddle 13 miles in a day.
Control a kayak in 15 knt to 20 knt winds.
Feel comfortable in 2–3 foot waves.
Handle surf and beach landings.

Level 4

Participants should be able to:

Perform the skills listed under Level 3.
Paddle 15 miles in a day.
Control a kayak in 20 knt winds.
Handle large ocean swells.

Level 5

Participants should be able to:

Perform the skills listed under Level 4.
Paddle 20+ miles in a day.
Control a kayak in 25 knt winds.

About the Author

David Fasulo has been sea kayaking throughout the East Coast since 2000, and sailing/racing in these waters, including offshore distance races to Bermuda and Nova Scotia, since 2003. Aside from sea kayak touring, David has envisioned and completed long-distance kayak circuits in the area such as the "Stonington Triangle" (Stonington, Connecticut; to Montauk, New York; to Block Island, Rhode Island; and back to Stonington in a day—54 miles in 14 hours) and the Connecticut section of the Connecticut River in a day (Massachusetts border to Old Saybrook Connecticut—70 miles in 13 hours). David was also part of the initial "rough water" explorations in the Fishers Island and Block Island Sound areas. He is a certified American Canoe Association (ACA) sea kayak instructor and participant in several Blackburn Challenge open ocean distance races. David is also the author of *How to Rock Climb: Self-Rescue* (1996, 2011) and *Rock Climbing Connecticut* (2002, 2015).

The author touring the Thimble Islands, Connecticut. **PHOTO RON GAUTREAU**